WITHDRAWN

# Events, Places and Societies

Edited by Nicholas Wise and John Harris

Routledge
Taylor & Francis Group

LONDON AND NEW YORK

First published 2019
by Routledge
2 Park Square, Milton Park, Abingdon, Oxon OX14 4RN

and by Routledge
52 Vanderbilt Avenue, New York, NY 10017

*Routledge is an imprint of the Taylor & Francis Group, an informa business*

*British Library Cataloguing-in-Publication Data*
A catalogue record for this book is available from the British Library

*Library of Congress Cataloging-in-Publication Data*
Names: Wise, Nicholas, 1983- editor. | Harris, John, 1972- editor.
Title: Events, places and societies / edited by Nicholas Wise and John Harris.
Description: Abingdon, Oxon ; New York, NY : Routledge, 2019. | Includes bibliographical references and index.
Identifiers: LCCN 2018054355| ISBN 9781138482470 (hbk : alk. paper) | ISBN 9781138482487 (ebk)
Subjects: LCSH: Special events–Social aspects–Case studies. | Special events–Management–Case studies.
Classification: LCC GT3405 .E97 2019 | DDC 394.2–dc23
LC record available at https://lccn.loc.gov/2018054355

ISBN: 978-1-138-48247-0 (hbk)
ISBN: 978-1-138-48248-7 (ebk)

Typeset in Times New Roman
by Integra Software Services Pvt. Ltd.

MIX
Paper from
responsible sources
FSC
www.fsc.org    FSC® C013056

Printed and bound in Great Britain by
TJ International Ltd, Padstow, Cornwall

# Contents

# Figures

# Tables

# Contributors

**Juan Miguel Alcántara-Pilar** is Associate Professor of Marketing at the University of Granada at the Faculty of Education, Economy and Technology of Ceuta. His areas of specialization and book and journal article publications are in marketing online, cross-cultural marketing, language effect on consumer behavior and behaviors in multi-racial communities.

**Lucia Aquilino** is a doctoral researcher at Glasgow Caledonian University. Her research focuses on events, tourism and community development. Her background is in tourism management/marketing, multicultural issues, linguistics and sociology. She earned her second MSc in International Hospitality and Tourism Management in 2014 from the University of Strathclyde.

**Tanja Armenski** is an Analyst at Tourism and the Centre for Education Statistics, Statistics Canada. She has a years-long experience in academia, particularly working at the University of Novi Sad (Serbia) as an Assistant Professor. She publishes broadly in the areas of destination competitiveness, event management and consumer satisfaction. She has been contracting as an external expert on numerous international tourism related projects.

**James Bowness** is a Lecturer in Sociology and Social Policy at Glasgow Caledonian University. His research interests include sporting communities, identities and nationalism. His PhD (2017) was titled *Physical Activity in Later Life: A Phenomenology of Ageing Men and Women in the Masters Highland Games.*

**Don Colley** is Assistant Professor and Undergraduate Coordinator at Oklahoma State University. His research interests include geographic education, sports geographies, radical activism, new media and youth culture. His most recent work is on young activists' perception and experience of the American Dream.

**José R. Díaz-Garayúa** is Assistant Professor at California State University, Stanislaus. He is a human geographer focusing on urban geography primarily in the fields of socio-economic inequalities and cultural politics of place. His current research examine art as a tool to represent Puerto Rico.

**Jelena Đurkin** is postdoctoral researcher at Faculty of Tourism and Hospitality Management, University of Rijeka, in Croatia. Her interests and current research focuses on social enterprises, cooperatives, community entrepreneurship and community-based tourism. She has authored and co-authored over 20 papers and book chapters.

**Lindsey Gaston** is a Senior Lecturer in the School of Education, Leisure and Sports Studies at Liverpool John Moores University. He received his PhD from Durham University in 2014. His research interests are diverse, from issues of gender and sexuality to operational behavior and historical perspectives of events.

**Alexandra Gillespie** is a graduate of the Department of Management, Marketing and Entrepreneurship at the University of Canterbury, Christchurch, New Zealand, and is currently engaged in extensive food tourism research.

**Bouke van Gorp** is a cultural geographer at the Faculty of Geosciences at Utrecht University. She has published on tourism representation, regional identity and marketing and the place of heritage in both fields.

**C. Michael Hall** is a Professor in the Department of Management, Marketing and Entrepreneurship, University of Canterbury, Christchurch, New Zealand; Docent, Department of Geography, University of Oulu, Finland and Visiting Professor in the School of Business and Economics, Linnaeus University, Kalmar, Sweden.

**John Harris** is Associate Dean of Research in the Glasgow School for Business and Society at Glasgow Caledonian University, Scotland. He is Leisure and Events Subject Editor for the *Journal of Hospitality, Leisure, Sport and Tourism Education* (JoHLSTE).

**Kari Jæger** is Associate Professor at the Department of Tourism and Northern Studies, UiT The Arctic University of Norway in Alta. Her research interests are in event and tourism studies, with an emphasis on festivals, identity and volunteering, and the connection between tourism and events.

**Natalie Koch** is Associate Professor of Geography and O'Hanley Faculty Scholar at Syracuse University's Maxwell School of Citizenship and Public Affairs. She is a political geographer focused on sport, geopolitics, nationalism and authoritarianism, and editor of *Critical Geographies of Sport: Space, Power, and Sport in Global Perspective* (Routledge, 2017).

**Trine Kvidal-Røvik** is Associate Professor at Department of Tourism and Northern Studies, UiT The Arctic University of Norway in Alta. Her research interests are linked to critical and cultural perspectives on identity, place and communication.

**Brij Maharaj** is an urban political geographer at the University of KwaZulu-Natal, Durban, South Africa, who has received widespread recognition for his research on mega-events and social impacts, segregation, local economic development, xenophobia and human rights, migration and diasporas, and has published over 150 scholarly papers on these themes.

**Velvet Nelson** is a Professor in the Department of Geography and Geology at Sam Houston State University in Huntsville, Texas, USA. She is a human geographer with a specialization in the geography of tourism, and author of *An Introduction to the Geography of Tourism* (Rowman and Littlefield, 2017, 2nd Edition).

**Brenda L. Ortiz-Loyola** is Lecturer at the Department of Modern Languages at California State University, Stanislaus. Her research has examined topics of race, nationalism, feminism and violence. Dr. Ortiz-Loyola's current research examines the representations of violence in nineteenth-century Hispanic Caribbean literature.

**Dorota Ostrowska** is Senior Lecturer in Film and Modern Media at Birkbeck College, University of London. She publishes in the areas of European film and television studies (Polish and French) and the history of film/media production, specifically concerning the cultural history of international film festivals with a special focus on questions of space.

**Vanja Pavluković** is Associate Professor, Faculty of Sciences, University of Novi Sad, Serbia. Her research areas are event management, destination competitiveness and travel agency management. She has been engaged in several European projects and has also published various peer-reviewed papers in international journals.

**Marko Perić** is Assistant Professor and Head of the Department of Management at the Faculty of Tourism and Hospitality Management, University of Rijeka. His fields of interest include strategic management, project management and sports management. He has co-authored four books and over 50 papers on management issues.

**Maurício Polidoro** is a geographer, has a PhD in geography and is currently an Associate Professor at the Federal Institute of Rio Grande do Sul and researcher at the Federal University of Rio Grande do Sul in the Post Graduate Program of Public Health in Porto Alegre, Brazil.

**Hans Renes** is a historical geographer at the Faculty of Geosciences at Utrecht University and Professor of Heritage Studies at the Faculty of Humanities at Vrije Universiteit Amsterdam, the Netherlands. He has published on landscape history in the Netherlands and Europe and on the relation between landscape heritage and planning.

**Nicholas Wise** is a Senior Lecturer in Events and Tourism Management in the Faculty of Education, Health and Community at Liverpool John Moores University. His research focuses on social regeneration, community and place image/competitiveness. His current research focuses on social regeneration linked to community change and local impacts in Southern and Eastern Europe.

**Xiaolin Zang** is a PhD candidate in the Faculty of Geosciences (Department of Human Geography and Spatial Planning) at Utrecht University, the Netherlands. She conducts research on dissonant heritage and public participation. Her current research focuses on how different stakeholders interpret and participate in heritage conservation.

# Events, places and societies
## Introducing cases, perspectives and research directions

*Nicholas Wise & John Harris*

There are events that are synonymous with a particular place, and there are events that help shape and promote places. There are also events that display critical meaning, challenging and contesting how we perceive events to impact on place and society. Given the rise of the global events industry, this book aims to critically frame how events impact upon places and societies, looking at a range of different events and how they impact different geographical scales. This collection will explore and discuss contemporary event cases from around the world to frame knowledge around the increased demands and pressures put on places and societies. The cases explored will help frame and position theoretical complexities by contextualizing what events mean in the very places where they are staged and performed. This involves recognizing histories and planning strategies, the purpose of bidding for an event or the local (organic) meanings that have emerged and changed in the place(s) where they are held. This helps us analyze how events have contributed to image transformations or have come to (re)define place identities as a result of wider social change. The cases explored in this book will help reflect on the interconnectedness of events, places and societies and how understandings differ across a range of international cases.

This work will build on the collections focusing on community to address geographical questions, issues and critical perspectives of events. There are some useful books and edited collections focusing on the social and cultural aspects of events (e.g. Dashper et al., 2014; Duffy & Mair, 2017; Jepson & Clark, 2015; Moufakkir & Pernecky, 2015; Richards et al., 2013; Smith, 2012). Our own edited collection on the wider area of sport, events, tourism and regeneration (Wise & Harris, 2017) showed the interconnectedness of sport, events and tourism in 12 international cases. While some research has looked at some geographical aspects of events (e.g. Cudny, 2014; Gammon & Elkington, 2015; Raitz, 1995; Waitt, 2008; Wise, 2015, 2017a, 2017b), little work has focused specifically on how places, people and societies are impacted by events. By looking at events of varying shapes and sizes, and focusing specifically on the subject of place, this work will present interdependent connections of events and place to articulate how societies are impacted.

It could be argued that events research is at a conceptual crossroads. Social scientists from a range of disciplines are interested in events. To date there has not been a collection that brings together and puts forward a geographically focused book, which both debates theoretical complexities while also contextualizing what events mean to particular places. Drawing upon a range of case studies from scholars in different parts of the world, this collection will critically assess some of the key factors showcasing how and why place is important. In developing this collection, we wanted to ensure that the cases were geographically diverse. This allows the collection to be truly international in scope. It is not the aim of this book to seek a solution to why the study of events is at a conceptual crossroads, but to show that the study of events is one that is truly interdisciplinary and that holistic geographical insight shows that there is more research needed in this emerging and bourgeoning area of study.

This book aims to critically frame perspectives and understandings of spaces, places, communities and identities. There are 16 chapters included in this book, and case studies focusing on events in: Brazil, China, Croatia, France, New Zealand, Puerto Rico, Qatar, Scotland, Serbia, South Africa, United States of America and Wales. The chapters build on a range of theoretical perspectives of space and place to critically evaluate the practice, impacts, legacies and management of events within specific contexts. Place is a holistic concept, and while this book argues for more (social) geographically informed research, the cases presented here may be relevant to scholars and students across the social sciences, development and management studies continuum. One of the main factors to consider when addressing events, places and societies is to not only recognize the needs of event managers and planners (who are often driven by financial constraints and agendas), but to understand local needs and social impacts facing people who reside in places, and/or those who travel to attend events.

This book begins with a chapter by **Velvet Nelson** that addresses the concept of place, to introduce how place is approached and to offer some conceptual directions further discussed in subsequent chapters. This introduction to place discusses how place is more than just a 'thing'; it is a way of seeing, knowing and understanding the world. This first chapter also addresses how conceptual notions of place offer a valuable framework for examining a range of issues associated with events by discussing the physical and symbolic creation and contestation of places, place names, sense of place, place attachment, place disruption, place identity, and place promotion, branding and reputation management.

Chapter 2 by **Natalie Koch** is the first case chapter looking at the politics of place surrounding the 2016 Union Cycliste Internationale (UCI) Road Cycling World Championships in Doha, Qatar. The primary venue for the event was 'the Pearl'– an artificial island community comprising mostly white, Western, middle- and upper-class residents. This was the finish line for each cycling race, as well as the associated temporary infrastructure for it, and all races passed through the Pearl, or in some cases were held entirely on the island. As one of the most elite areas of Doha, Pearl residents saw their space of privilege interrupted by the sudden influx of event staffers, who did not fit the white, non-Muslim and European norm of the Pearl. This chapter examines how residents and individuals involved in the cycling event experienced the transformation of the Pearl, vividly illustrating how places are never materially or experientially static. The chapter is based on the author's fieldwork at the event, where she argues that the intensity of the island's transformation reflects the general nature of the effects that sporting events have on places. She further highlights the perspective of Doha's wealthier residents to show how elites are not a homogenous, placeless group that uniformly support the agenda of sports-oriented urban boosterism. By taking seriously the privileged perspective of Pearl residents and their immense frustration over how their community was transformed for the 2016 Cycling Worlds, we can then begin to see how place is central to competing agendas and interests among elites.

The social impacts and implications of hosting festivals on a place and local community is the focus of Chapter 3 by **Vanja Pavluković, Tanja Armenski** and **Juan Miguel Alcántara-Pilar** looking at the EXIT Festival in Novi Sad, Serbia. Music festivals are often seen as a key motivator of the city's economy, but it is also important to consider that changes in social and cultural conditions that result from an activity, project or event hosted by the community became important aspects affecting the quality of life of its residents. This chapter explores the benefits and costs associated with music festivals, to contribute to a further understanding of social costs and explore the relationship between residents' levels of involvement and their perception of festivals' social impacts on host communities. Residents' involvement in this study was self-assessed as low, medium or high. The positive and negative social impacts of music festival were represented by six underlying factors: musical benefits, safety and security benefits, community benefits, economic and cultural benefits, social costs and environmental costs. A multivariate analysis was conducted to test the difference between residents' involvement and their perception of the social impacts of the EXIT music festival on the host community of Novi Sad. The results reveal that residents' involvement with the festival moderates their perception of festival social impacts on their host community. Residents with a higher levels of festival involvement have a better perception of positive social impacts and a lower perception of negative social costs. Only residents' perception of the 'musical benefits' showed not to be related to residents' involvement with the festival. This study has practical and theoretical implications, particularly in the domain of festival organization and local community involvement.

**Maurício Polidoro** in Chapter 4 aims to analyze the spaces, place, and landscapes of Brazil's Carnival from the perspective of a racialized geography.

The chapter focuses on multiscale perspectives of a central location (Rio de Janeiro) and the periphery (Porto Alegre). Racialized geographies consist of processes and dynamics that are inherent to the racial capitalist system. This, in turn, is supported by imperialist and colonialist forces which reproduce socio-spatial inequalities and body differentiation based on the racialization of individuals and groups. The Brazilian Carnival is known worldwide for its festivities and integration of different people, and therefore this chapter discusses how racialized geographies produce places and landscapes that are contested in Brazil.

Chapter 5 by **Nicholas Wise, Jelena Đurkin** and **Marko Perić** is concerned with managing placemaking, regeneration and community participation, focusing on Rijeka, Croatia, host of the 2020 European Capital of Culture (ECoC). ECoC promotes urban development (or redevelopment) as a driving force to promote new social legacies, job creation and civic re-positioning. The chapter argues that it is essential that ECoC host cities have long-term competitive strategies in place, aimed at strengthening the capacity of their city to deliver diverse cultural programmes and placemaking (locally) for its own citizens. It also addresses the idea that for researchers it is important to get a sense of how local planners and policy makers promote regeneration strategies for the benefit of the city, and discusses this around what placemaking initiatives are in place to benefit local residents and encourage the community to participate. Local residents, after all, will be the ones participating in, contributing to and therefore affected most by event-led regeneration. Local residents will also be most impacted by the outcome of social and economic policies, before, during and after the event. For Croatia, Rijeka was a strategic selection since Zagreb, Split and Dubrovnik (Croatia's well-known destinations), might not benefit as much as Rijeka will from the European funds. To understand the directions of regeneration and placemaking ahead of Rijeka 2020, this chapter is based on an analysis of content from official websites and the 2020 agenda is an attempt to better understand the city's strategy and approach ahead of the event. This chapter also considers insight from Glasgow, Scotland and Liverpool, England, hosts of the 1990 and 2008 ECoC respectively, to inform perspectives going forward based on what worked well for these previous hosts. This chapter's geographical focus engages with the notion of placemaking, and an emphasis on regeneration and community participation points to the impact on society going forward.

A cinematic sense of place focusing on embodied celluloid spectres on the red carpet in Cannes, France is the topic of Chapter 6 by **Dorota Ostrowska**. Established in the wake of the WW2 destruction of the 'old order', the Cannes International Film Festival has developed its own reputation on the world-renowned French Riviera. Nowadays, for the duration of the festival, and in the minds of the broader public throughout the year, the place signifies the event – the city of Cannes *is* the festival. The global media first arrived in Cannes following the celebrities; now they play a crucial role in establishing the dynamics between the location of the Cannes festival and the festival itself. Today it is the red carpet, the main visual trope associated with the festival and the focus of the media, which has led to this absorption of the city of Cannes and the wider Riviera region. At the same time, considering the media coverage, the red carpet, together with the actors and celebrities parading it, is more important than the films shown on screens at the festival. The films' invisibility only compares with the hypervisibility of the red-carpet participants. This chapter will examine the historical process that has led to the overwhelming importance of the red-carpet ceremony at the Cannes Film Festival. The reasons why this ceremony has become the most potent representation of the festival event and the wider region where the festival takes place, and the ways in which films screened at the festival are implicated in the 'attention economy' of the red carpet, are examined in this chapter.

Chapter 7 by **Xiaolin Zang, Bouke van Gorp** and **Hans Renes** focuses on the Qingdao International Beer Festival, by addressing place identity and colonial heritage. Recently, beer festivals have become popular events, popping up in many cities around the globe. The first edition of the beer festival in Qingdao was organized in 1991 by the Tsingtao Brewery to celebrate the town's hundredth anniversary. Since then, Qingdao International Beer Festival has grown to become the largest beer event in Asia. Tsingtao Brewery started in 1903 as the Germania Brauerei, part of the German colonial enterprise on the Chinese coast. In 1916, it was sold to a Japanese firm. Given this history of the brewery, it is interesting to see how the colonial origins are negotiated in the representations of the festival, for both tourists and local visitors. Drawing on textual analysis and fieldwork, this chapter analyzes narratives of the city carried forward by the beer festival.

Following the chapter on a popular beer festival in China, Chapter 8 by **Alexandra Gillespie** and **C. Michael Hall** looks at the Hokitika Wild Foods Festival in New Zealand, to explore a taste of place. The Hokitika Wild Foods Festival is one of New Zealand's most high-profile food tourism events. This has been a community-based event since it was first held in 1990, and the festival is grounded in the heritage and identity of the west coast of New Zealand's South Island. This chapter addresses how this food festival has faced a difficult balance between commercial and community imperatives, as well as critical responses to the availability of foods that are not part of standard New Zealand cuisine. The chapter also focuses on the culinary and community dimensions of the festival and the ways within which they weave issues of place identity and representation. This chapter includes a discussion of the difficulties the festival faces in the future as it responds to increased economic pressures.

Chapter 9 offers a different critical perspective to the impact of an event on a place and society, by addressing the forfeiture of the 2022 Commonwealth Games by Durban, South Africa – which was a bid won and lost by default. **Brij Maharaj** considers how Durban has attempted to market itself as a sporting mecca in South Africa's post-apartheid democratic era, using

an entrepreneurial approach to market the city and attract international investment. Moreover, Durban's Commonwealth Games 2022 bid was unique because
the other competitors withdrew from the race, suggesting that hosting such
large-scale events is not desirable given the costs associated with hosting. What
the chapter explores is how Durban subsequently lost the bid because of
a failure to meet critical deadlines, as well as reluctance by the South African
government to honor certain contractual responsibilities. In making the bid,
Durban was following a global trend whereby marketing the city as a mega-
event destination was a prominent neoliberal urban promotion strategy. However, no one comprehended the costs of hosting this in Durban. There was
clearly no understanding about why far wealthier cities like Edmonton withdrew
their bid, taking cognizance of public sentiment and economic realities. Critical
considerations address how the bid was flawed from the beginning, especially as
the central government support lacked enthusiasm. Durban was looking for
global glory, perhaps an escapist fantasy from its inability to address serious
social and economic problems. Clearly, lessons from the FIFA 2010 experience
were not being heeded.

Cultural sites of tension in the Iditarod of Alaska, the world's longest dog-
sledding race between Anchorage and Nome, are the focus of Chapter 10 by
**Trine Kvidal-Røvik** and **Kari Jæger**. The chapter uses this annual long-distance
sled dog race as a case study through which to discuss how events play a role
in how places are perceived, consumed and contested. Anchored in perspectives from event theories and critical cultural theories, the authors discuss how
an event like the Iditarod connects to Alaska as a place. Based on in-depth
interviews, the chapter explores issues surrounding cultural contestations and
power across Alaska along the Iditarod racecourse. Perspectives and discussions are intertwined and interconnected with global cultural trends, and this is
then aligned with understandings of Alaskan and event history. Place as understood in the context of Iditarod is investigated in this chapter. While such an
event covering a vast geographical area is staged, perceptions, meanings and
contestations based on what this staging entails depends on where one stand in
relation to history, place and the evolution of the event.

Chapter 11 by **Lucia Aquilino** and **John Harris** looks at the reinventing
and reimagining of rural Wales, focusing on the case of the World Alternative
Games. Rural communities often look at how event activities can reimagine
and reinvent places to increase tourism development and further develop
a sense of community. This chapter considers how small-scale events have
reshaped place and community within Britain's smallest town. The World
Alternative Games were first staged in Llanwrtyd Wells during the summer of
2012. It now takes place every two years and has attracted international
media attention for some of the wacky activities that contribute to the two
weeks of festivities. Based on qualitative research undertaken at the 2016
games, this chapter looks at how the engagement in event activities, from
organization to active participation, enacts a process of community development and of a new sense of rurality.

The next chapter by **James Bowness** moves to Scotland focusing on the Masters World Championship Highland Games. The role of place has taken on new importance in a globalized world where individuals can travel thousands of miles to participant in amateur sport. This chapter explores the importance of place and community in the Masters Highland Games, an event that brings athletes from various nations in a sporting event aimed at over 40-year olds. Observations and semi-structured interviews explored the experiences of these athletes and found that the community had moved away from the Scottish cultural associations that had previously been exclusionary to outsiders. The author concludes that a civic nationalism underpins this community who share the experience of being Masters athletes. These athletes find solidarity in their shared subjectivities, in a way that rejects the importance of genetic links to Scotland.

Chapter 13 by **Brenda L. Ortiz-Loyola** and **José R. Díaz-Garayúa** shifts the focus and direction of research to multi-site events. Their chapter addresses the display of identity politics in Puerto Rico, concerning cultural activism and placemaking surrounding the initiative *78 Pueblos y 1 Bandera* (78 villages and 1 flag). The one-star flag of Puerto Rico, 'la Monoestrellada', has been the most prominent piece of material culture in the island's landscape since its legalization in 1952 by the US government. It has been used in protests and revolts during both Spanish (to 1898) and American rule (after 1898). Similarly, the flag has been used by athletes and cultural ambassadors at international events. The flag is used as a tool in the political arena, and as an identity maker. Today, the flag is being used to express national pride across the island despite Puerto Rico's colonial status and economic crisis. The recent initiative of one person has grown into a more elaborate organization of volunteers to paint the Puerto Rican flag in every one of the 78 towns and cities of Puerto Rico. This practice has invigorated internal tourism and facilitated social interactions. This chapter shows how social interactions can be displays of informal events as well as contemporary demonstrations of cultural nationalism. It also constitutes a challenge to the colonial status and the practices of the Financial Oversight and Management Board appointed by the US government to remedy Puerto Rico's current economic crisis.

In Chapter 14, **Lindsey Gaston** highlights the importance of 'place-name' through the use of the Folsom Street Fair, an international leather fetish festival that attracts members from the gay leather and BDSM Communities from around the world. While this event originated on Folsom Street in San Francisco's SOMA (South of Market) district, the name 'Folsom' has become an important signifier for these communities, to the extent that satellite events have been established with the name of 'Folsom' to create authenticity and to replicate a 'Folsom' like community. The attempt to reproduce 'Folsom Street' aims to create an inclusive/exclusive safe and judgement free environment allowing participants to publicly explore and celebrate their sexual fetishes. This can be seen in the examples of Folsom Street East, which is hosted in New York City, Folsom Street North hosted in Toronto, Canada and Folsom Europe hosted in Berlin, Germany. This chapter illustrates how the shared symbolism of the name 'Folsom' creates a psychological sense of shared global place, a real sense of safe space and establishes boundedness and rootedness for the global fetish community.

Chapter 15 offers a different view of the representation of place. Here **Don Colley** and **John Harris** assess (re)presentations of Europe in a range of media coverage surrounding the 2008 Ryder Cup golf competition. The Ryder Cup has become one of the biggest events in international sport and represents one of the only sporting competitions where a team competes as Europe. Through textual and discourse analyses of internet articles, they highlight how a pan-European sports identity faces additional difficulties in being accepted externally because of the conflicting spatial imaginary presented through American media sources. It also shows the contested nature of a European identity and the particularly narrow imagining of Europe within dominant discourse.

Chapter 17 by **Nicholas Wise** links geographical and sociological interpretations of place and society by focusing on Diwali around the world. This event is internationally important and culturally significant, linking people around the world and suggesting how events reinforce imagined communities. The chapter reflects on a range of conceptual understandings of diaspora and imagined communities, staging and performing of culture and identity, sense of place and sense of community, landscape and aesthetic. A model is presented at the end to showcase the links between these areas to unite (some) understanding of how events impact place and society, and likewise how conceptual approaches of place and society help us understand events more holistically. A short conclusion then brings the collection together and identifies the main themes brought forward. The conclusion also looks at some possible future directions for research.

## References

Cudny, W. (2014). Festivals as a subject for geographical research. *Geografisk Tidsskrift-Danish Journal of Geography*, 114(2), 132–142.
Dashper, K., Fletcher, T. & Mccullough, N. (Eds) (2014). *Sports events, society and culture*. London: Routledge.
Duffy, M. & Mair, J. (2017). *Festival encounters: Theoretical perspectives on festival events*. London: Routledge.
Gammon, S. & Elkington, S. (Eds) (2015). *Landscapes of leisure: Space, place and identities*. Basingstoke: Palgrave Macmillan.
Jepson, A. & Clark, A. (Eds) (2015). *Exploring community events and festivals*. London: Routledge.
Moufakkir, O. & Pernecky, T. (Eds) (2015). *Ideological, social and cultural aspects of events*. Wallingford: CABI.
Raitz, K. (1995). *The theatre of sport*. Baltimore: Johns Hopkins University Press.
Richards, G., de Brito, M. & Wilks, L. (Eds) (2013). *Exploring the social impacts of events*. London: Routledge.

Smith, A. (2012). *Events and urban regeneration: The strategic use of events to revitalise cities.* London: Routledge.

Waitt, G. (2008). Urban festivals: Geographies of hype, helplessness and hope. *Geography Compass,* 2(2), 513–537.

Wise, N. (2015). Football on the weekend: Rural events and the Haitian imagined community in the Dominican Republic. In A. Jepson & A. Clarke (Eds). *Exploring community festivals and events.* London: Routledge (106–117).

Wise, N. (2017a). In the shadow of mega-events: The value of ethnography in sports geography. In N. Koch (Ed). *Critical geographies of sport: Space, power, and sport in global perspective.* London: Routledge (220–234).

Wise, N. (2017b). Rugby World Cup: New directions or more of the same? *Sport in Society: Cultures, Commerce, Media, Politics,* 20(3), 341–354.

Wise, N. & Harris, J. (Eds) (2017). *Sport, events, tourism and regeneration.* London: Routledge.

# 1   Introduction to place

*Velvet Nelson*

## Introduction

In a review article, Lewicka (2011) asks the question: How important are places for people today? She highlights the ways in which the world has changed since 'classical' studies such as those by Tuan (1975) and Relph (1976), citing factors such as increased mobility, globalization, and homogenization. Yet, concern about places is not new. In Relph's (1976) *Place and Placelessness*, he describes non-places as having few characteristics that situate them in their location, distinguish them from other places, or endow them with any significant meanings. In answer to her own question, though, Lewicka (2011, p. 209) writes, it is 'important to point to an intriguing paradox that despite the growing number of the so called non-places, not only have places not lost their meaning but their importance in the contemporary world actually may have grown'.

Geographers have long been interested in issues of place. In fact, place is considered fundamental to the discipline of geography. However, the study of place is very much an interdisciplinary endeavor. Place is more than just a 'thing'; it is a way of seeing, knowing, and understanding the world (Cresswell, 2015). As such, place provides an appropriate framework for this discussion of a range of topics associated with events. The subsequent chapters in this book engage with place in different ways, as it is assessed, contested, and consumed differently around the world and differs based on disciplinary perspective. In recent years, we have witnessed tremendous growth in events around the world, from community festivals to mega-events, with diverse themes and purposes (see Page & Connell, 2012; Wise & Harris, 2017). These events occur in places, transform them, and reflect them. Events are used to promote places, and the interactions that happen during events create new, and perhaps contested, meanings of place.

This chapter offers an introduction to the concept of place and considers some of the approaches to place that inform our understanding of events. Topics include the creation and contestation of places, place names, sense of place, place attachment, place disruption, and place identity from social science perspectives, as well as place promotion, branding, and reputation management.

This brief discussion is by no means comprehensive and could include many other concepts and perspectives, but offers some conceptual guidance to provide a base for the range of cases included in this book.

## Making and experiencing place

Place is an undeniably powerful concept. It is such a widely used term that we often rely on a common-sense understanding of it. However, as a topic of academic inquiry, scholars from a variety of disciplines using diverse approaches have often presented competing ideas about place (Vuolteenaho & Berg, 2009). In addition, there has been overlap between concepts (Jorgensen & Stedman, 2001) and confusion over terminology. These issues led one author to describe the literature on place as incoherent (Devine-Wright, 2009). Thus, before considering the relationship between place and events, it is worth taking a closer look at the concept.

Places have a location and a physical setting. Indeed, the meanings of places may be tied to the physical features of a location (Campelo, 2015), and some authors argue that place attachment is often based on physical features (Stedman, 2003). However, the concept of place goes well beyond these components (Relph, 1976). Places are socially constructed. Simply stated by Campelo (2015, p. 58), 'places are brought alive by people'. People transform spaces into places. They create places, name them, and give them meaning. They contest them, experience them, and represent them to others. According to Pine and Gilmore's 4E model (1998), people attend events to experience places and performances for the purpose of entertainment, education, escapism or aesthetics. This conceptualization and framework on the experience economy has been adopted in a number of studies in the sport and events literature (e.g. Perić et al., 2017; Westwood et al., 2018; Ziakas & Boukas, 2014).

The place-making processes occurring around the world are never ending (Cresswell, 2015). Places are produced both physically and symbolically. This production is a contested and ideological process (Cohen, 1995). As such, a place can be examined in terms of its physical setting or its setting for social activity as well as its ideological construction. For example, Anderson (1991) examines the construction of Chinatown in the case of Vancouver, Canada. Such a place is characterized by specific physical structures (e.g. stores, pagodas), which create a setting for certain social interactions, but it is also ideologically constructed as a place of difference (Cresswell, 2015). Cohen (1995) finds that attention is typically given to such physical structures or visual representations but argues for further integration of sensory processes in the production of places.

More specifically for our purposes, places are also 'made' for the purposes of tourism and events. Tourism stakeholders produce places physically to enable tourism and tourist functions (Bærenholdt & Haldrup, 2006). For example, mega-events require the creation of new fixed infrastructure including stadia or event centres as well as supporting accommodation and leisure facilities. In addition, places are physically transformed from everyday spaces to the places of events through temporary infrastructure as well as the often-significant influx of people (Hall & Page, 2012). Stakeholders also produce places symbolically to convey certain ideas that are of interest to potential visitors (Bærenholdt & Haldrup, 2006). Alderman et al. (2012) emphasize that the material and discursive processes of production are interrelated. Tourists also have a part to play in the place-making process as both producers and consumers (Everett, 2012). Bærenholdt and Haldrup (2006) argue that research should pay greater attention to the complex and heterogeneous networks that produce tourist places in the modern world.

Even the process of naming places is part of place making (Vuolteenaho & Berg, 2009). Tuan (1991, p. 688) writes, 'Naming is power – the creative power to call something into being, to render the invisible visible, to impart a certain character to things'. He argues that names have the ability to distinguish places (Tuan, 1991). Although place names are often 'taken for granted', they can be politically charged (Vuolteenaho & Berg, 2009). Place names act as symbols that hold historical or cultural meanings and play a role in shaping the place identities (Hakala et al., 2015). The meanings associated with place names may also be deliberately intended to shape ideas about that place (Anholt, 2010a).

Much attention has been given to street names. These names have practical functions in designating locations and facilitating navigation; they can also be cultural signifiers that convey certain ideas (Azaryahu, 2009). For instance, Alderman (2009) considers the commemoration of Martin Luther King Jr. through street names throughout the United States to be a part of a larger movement to address the exclusion of African Americans from the national historical consciousness. In another case, Shoval (2013) notes the use of street names to enhance tourist development and destination attractiveness in the case of the Old City of Acre, Israel. He discusses the conflict that exists between these names and the unofficial oral names used by residents. Some streets that have a particular sentimental value are used for formal and informal events, as we see in Chapter 14 on Folsom Street.

Sense of place has long played a role in understandings of place. This refers to the association with and emotional attachment to places based on the meanings given to those places (Cresswell, 2015). It is one of the ways we are connected to the world and therefore an integral part of the human experience (Relph, 1997). Scholars have long argued that sense of place develops with sensory, cognitive, and affective experiences over time (Campelo, 2015), and has been explored in the event studies literature (see Derrett, 2003). Thus, it has typically been associated with the places in which we live and with which we have a significant relationship. Tuan (1975, p. 164) writes that 'sense of place is rarely acquired in passing. To know a place well requires long residence and deep involvement'. Residents' sense of place may be conveyed to visitors as a means of promoting distinctiveness or as an expression of pride. In a study of community cultural festivals, Derrett (2003) finds that these events reflect both the community's sense of itself and its sense of place.

Even more informal sporting events can offer useful context on place, identity, and community. For example, Wise (2015) found that weekend football matches organized by Haitians were a way to create a sense of place despite feelings of being out of place in the Dominican Republic.

Researchers have also recognized that we may acquire a sense of place through other means as well (Cresswell, 2015). In particular, we can develop a sense of place for the places that we visit, although perhaps in different ways (Nelson, 2017). Some studies find that visited places can indeed be deeply meaningful for tourists, while others consider differences in sense of place for residents and visitors (Kianicka et al., 2006). Additionally, the concept has been adapted for tourism in various contexts. For instance, sense of place has been used to represent the ways in which visitors can gain insight into the characteristics of destinations, such as a meal that is 'true to place' (Scarpato & Daniele, 2003), or is perceived as getting an authentic experience. While numerous studies in the field of tourism look at sense of place and experiences whilst being mobile, more work is needed in the area of event studies taking similar approaches.

Place attachment is viewed as a part of a larger sense of place (Amsden et al., 2011). Both personal and social interactions can contribute to an emotional connection, typically positive, to a place (Jorgensen & Stedman, 2001; Stedman, 2003). It is a feeling of rootedness or belonging in that place. Again, familiarity is a part of this attachment both in terms of detailed knowledge of and care for a place (Relph, 1976). Despite longstanding concerns about the role of place in the modern world, studies continue to show peoples' strong attachment to places (Lewicka, 2011). Gu & Ryan (2008) discuss the impact of tourism on place attachment. Depending on the nature of tourism in a place, this may be positive or negative. For example, in the study of a Chinese hutong, tourism was recognized as providing an impetus for the preservation of architectural heritage in the face of urban change. This architectural heritage featured prominently in residents' place attachment (Gu & Ryan, 2008).

Although the focus has often been on the attachment to the places in which people live, Lew (1989) notes that visitors to a place may wish to feel the sense of belonging experienced by residents. Recent scholarship has given further attention to attachment to places other than permanent residences (Brown et al., 2016; Lewicka, 2011). Derrett (2003) contends that events create opportunities for visitors to experience and connect to a place. Kaplanidou et al. (2012) consider the potential for destinations that host recurring sport events to generate place attachment among tourists. In particular, the authors argue that active sport tourists (i.e. those who participate in the event) directly engage with the place in terms of both its physical and social environments. Thus, such visitors may be more likely to develop an attachment to that place. A positive experience can help create attachment, and this has the potential to translate into greater loyalty to both the event and the destination. Likewise, studies by Lee, Kyle, and Scott (2012) and Brown et al. (2016) consider the relationship between place attachment, satisfaction, and destination loyalty in the case of events ranging from community-based agricultural festivals in the former to the Olympic Games in the latter.

Place disruption refers to the processes of change in a place that affect place attachment. These changes, physical or social, can lead to a sense of displacement as well as emotions such as anxiety or loss (Devine-Wright, 2009). Place disruption can be a product of tourism. For example, in Gu and Ryan's (2008) study, some respondents indicated an eroded place attachment. This was attributed to the disruption to typical community social interactions caused by the influx of outsiders. The negative emotions that result can lead to 'place-protective action' (Stedman, 2002), or various efforts to prevent changes that people believe will affect place attachment (Devine-Wright, 2009).

Because of the direct correlation between attachment and change, place disruption is more commonly considered to occur among residents than tourists. However, past and potential visitors can also experience a sense of disruption when a place is threatened. Nelson (2010) examines the social media responses to news reports about a proposed oil refinery project on the Caribbean island of Dominica. This was viewed as a threat to Dominica's 'nature island' identity. She found that even those who had no previous first-hand experience with the destination expressed a sense of loss about something that might happen.

In the environmental psychology literature, the term 'place identity' is used to refer to the ways in which components of a place contributes to an individual's sense of self or identity (Devine-Wright, 2009). However, in the tourism literature, place identity is used to refer to the meanings attached to places for internal or external audiences (Kneafsey, 2000). Such place identities are constructed through various historical, cultural, and political discourses (Govers & Go, 2009). In addition, tourism has a part to play in the construction and reproduction of place identities, particularly the ideas of place that are presented to external audiences (Light, 2001). De Bres & Davis (2001) find that community festivals can celebrate and enhance place identity. Examples of this are further outlined in Boissevain's (2013) book looking at community gatherings across the Mediterranean, where communities organize events to celebrate their history, identity, and place.

## Promoting and managing place

While the above section outlined insight on place from a social science perspective (in line with most of the chapters in this book), the events industry is often management focused. Thus, it is also important to recognize how place is promoted to help understand how places are managed. Place promotion refers to the application of marketing tools to communicate ideas and images about a place to a target audience. It is a selective representation of place with the intention of shaping perceptions of that place as well as decisions to visit (Nelson, 2017). Place promotion is part of the place-making processes discussed above (Morgan, 2004). Although attention is typically focused on the symbolic production of places through the creation and communication of place meanings, Schöllmann et al. (2000) note that place promotion may also lead to a physical reshaping of places.

More broadly, place branding has been used as a metaphor for the ways places compete with each other for a variety of purposes, including the needs of businesses, residents, and visitors (Anholt, 2010b). A place brand is intended to create a sense of uniqueness or differentiation from other places to gain a competitive advantage (Ashworth, 2009). While many scholars have found place branding to be a powerful tool, especially in the highly competitive tourism industry (Hudson & Ritchie, 2009), critics have argued that places are complex and significantly more difficult to 'brand' than products. Places have a past, and place brands must typically follow historical ideas (Hall & Page, 2012). More-over, the process of producing, promoting, and supporting a place brand must involve a multitude of stakeholders in that place and encompass a diverse set of products and services (Konecnik & Go, 2008). In recognition of this, Campelo (2015) argues for a community-centred approach to place branding. The result-ing place brand should reflect the meanings residents attach to their place. As with place promotion, places may be physically (re)developed in the branding process or subsequently to support the brand (Hall & Page, 2012).

Although Anholt is credited with proposing the term 'place brand', he argues that places have 'brands' in the sense that they have reputations (Anholt, 2010a). Place reputations are the composite of ideas and impressions held by external audiences (Cleave & Arku, 2015). Destination-marketing organizations may attempt to create a brand that identifies and communicates the core characteristics of the place, but place reputations cannot be entirely controlled by local stakeholders. It is a cultural phenomenon shaped by vari-ous factors (Nelson, 2017). Place reputations are considered important in a place's development and success in the modern world (Anholt, 2010a). Thus, people around the world attempt to improve or manage the reputation of their place as they compete to attract businesses, residents, and tourists (Anholt, 2011). Place reputation management involves efforts to modify the reputation so that it is closer to how stakeholders would like the place to be perceived (Morgan et al., 2011).

Events have been an integral part of various promotion, branding, and/or reputation-management strategies for places (see Wise & Harris, 2017). Events have been viewed as a means of creating a sense of distinctiveness for raising awareness about and increasing the competitiveness of a place (Ashworth, 2009). This widespread perception may be seen as places around the world bid for and host mega-events despite significant criticisms about the viability of such events. However, countries and cities continue to bid because politicians believe high-profile events showcase the power and influence of a place in the world (see Henderson, 2017; Koch, 2017; Rojek, 2013). There are concerns about the net economic benefits of hosting mega-events in light of the costs associated with building or upgrading facilities. This is certainly the case when we consider large-scale events, as short-term gains are more commonly found than longer-term sustained impacts. For instance, once one event ends (e.g. the FIFA World Cup or Olympic Games), preparations in the next place have already started. This has led scholars to critically question the long-term value of events in achieving place competitiveness (Hall & Page, 2012). The increased attention that comes with events may be short lived or may highlight deficiencies in the place (Ashworth, 2009). More broadly, stakeholders need to go beyond creating new slogans or logos in their efforts to (re)create ideas of place. They need to find real ways of supporting the idea of the place, and various events can be part of this process (Herstein & Berger, 2013).

## Conclusion

As stated by Cresswell (2015, p. 6), 'Place … is both simple (and that is part of its appeal) and complicated'. This chapter has only skimmed the surface of what place is, what it means to people, and how we can use it to understand the world. Nonetheless, this brief discussion provides an important foundation for the remaining chapters as they consider a diverse set of events ranging from Brazil's well-known Carnival or the Hokitika Wildfood Festival held in a small town in New Zealand, to the celebration of beer in Qingdao, China or how the European Capital of Culture has the potential to recreate Rijeka, Croatia. Place constitutes a key theme throughout these case studies. Moreover, the concepts associated with place discussed in this chapter offer a framework for examining the issues associated with the events that will be presented in subsequent chapters, including the ways in which places are transformed, contested, promoted, and understood through events.

## References

Alderman, D.H. (2009). 'Street names as memorial arenas: The reputational politics of commemorating Martin Luther King Jr in a Georgia County'. In L.D. Berg and J. Vuolteenaho (eds.) *Critical toponymies: The contested politics of place naming* (179–198). London: Routledge.

Alderman, D.H., Benjamin, S.K. and Schneider, P.P. (2012). 'Transforming Mount Airy into Mayberry: Film-induced tourism as place-making'. *Southeastern Geographer*, 52 (2), 212–239.

Amsden, B.L., Stedman, R.C., and Kruger, L.E. (2011). 'The creation and maintenance of sense of place in a tourism-dependent community'. *Leisure Sciences*, 33, 32–51.

Anderson, K. (1991). *Vancouver's Chinatown: Racial discourse in Canada, 1875–1980*. Montreal: McGill-Queen's University Press.

Anholt, S. (2010a). 'Definitions of place branding – Working towards a resolution'. *Place Branding and Public Diplomacy*, 6 (1), 1–10.

Anholt, S. (2010b). *Places: Identity, image and reputation*. Houndmills: Palgrave Macmillan.

Anholt, S. (2011). 'Competitive identity'. In N. Morgan, A. Pritchard, and R. Pride (eds.) *Destination brands: Managing place reputation*, 3rd ed. (21–31). Florence, KY: Routledge.

Ashworth, G.J. (2009). 'The instruments of place branding: How is it done?' *European Spatial Research and Policy*, 16 (1), 9–22.

Azaryahu, M. (2009). 'Naming the past: The significance of commemorative street names'. In L.D. Berg and J. Vuolteenaho (eds.) *Critical toponymies: The contested politics of place naming* (53–70). London: Routledge.

Bærenholdt, J.O. and Haldrup, M. (2006). 'Mobile networks and place making in cultural tourism: Staging Viking ships and rock music in Roskilde'. *European Urban and Regional Studies*, 13 (3), 209–224.

Boissevain, J. (2013). *Factions, friends and feasts: Anthropological perspectives on the Mediterranean*. Oxford: Berghahn Books.

Brown, G., Smith, A., and Assaker, G. (2016). 'Revisiting the host city: An empirical examination of sport involvement, place attachment, event satisfaction and spectator intentions at the London Olympics'. *Tourism Management*, 55, 160–172.

Campelo, A. (2015). 'Rethinking sense of place: Sense of one and sense of many'. In M. Havaratzis, G. Warnaby, and G.J. Ashworth (eds.) *Rethinking place branding: Comprehensive brand development for cities and regions* (51–60). Cham: Springer.

Cleave, E. and Arku, G. (2015). 'Place branding and economic development at the local level in Ontario, Canada'. *GeoJournal*, 80 (3), 323–338.

Cohen, S. (1995). 'Sounding out the city: Music and the sensuous production of place'. *Transactions of the Institute of British Geographers*, 20 (4), 434–446.

Cresswell, T. (2015). *Place: An introduction*, 2nd ed. Chichester: John Wiley & Sons.

De Bres, K. and Davis, J. (2001). 'Celebrating group and place identity: A case study of a new regional festival'. *Tourism Geographies*, 3 (3), 326–337.

Derrett, R. (2003). 'Making sense of how festivals demonstrate a community's sense of place'. *Event Management*, 8, 49–58.

Devine-Wright, P. (2009). 'Rethinking NIMBYism: The role of place attachment and place identity in explaining place-protective action'. *Journal of Community & Applied Social Psychology*, 19, 426–441.

Everett, S. (2012). 'Production places or consumption spaces? The place-making agency of food tourism in Ireland and Scotland'. *Tourism Geographies*, 14 (4), 535–554.

Govers, R. and Go, F. (2009). *Place branding: Glocal, virtual and physical identities, constructed, imagined and experienced*. Houndmills: Palgrave Macmillan.

Gu, H. and Ryan, C. (2008). 'Place attachment, identity and community impacts of tourism – The case of a Beijing Hutong'. *Tourism Management*, 29, 637–647.

Hakala, U., Sjöblom, P., and Kantola, S.P. (2015). 'Toponyms as carriers of heritage: Implications for place branding'. *Journal of Product & Brand Management*, 24 (3), 263–275.

Hall, C.M. and Page, S.J. (2012). 'Geography and the study of events'. In S.J. Page and J. Connell (eds.) *The Routledge handbook of events* (148–164). London: Routledge.

Henderson, J. (2017). 'Sports events, tourism, development and regeneration: A perspective from Gulf States of Abu Dhabi, Dubai and Qatar'. In N. Wise and J. Harris (eds.) *Sport, events, tourism and regeneration* (9–23). London: Routledge.

Herstein, R. and Berger, R. (2013). 'Much more than sports: Sports events as stimuli for city re-branding'. *Journal of Business Strategy*, 34 (2), 38–44.

Hudson, S. and Ritchie, J.R.B. (2009). 'Branding a memorable destination experience. The case of 'Brand Canada''. *International Journal of Tourism Research*, 11, 217–228.

Jorgensen, B.S. and Stedman, R.C. (2001). 'Sense of place as an attitude: Lakeshore owners attitudes toward their properties'. *Journal of Environmental Psychology*, 21, 233–248.

Kaplanidou, K., Jordan, J.S., Funk, D., and Rindinger, L.L. (2012). 'Recurring sport events and destination image perceptions: Impact on active sport tourist behavioral intentions and place attachment'. *Journal of Sport Management*, 26, 237–248.

Kianicka, S., Buchecker, M., Hunziker, M., and Müller-Böker, U. (2006). 'Locals' and tourists' sense of place: A case study of a Swiss Alpine village'. *Mountain Research and Development*, 26 (1), 55–63.

Kneafsey, M. (2000). 'Tourism, place identities and social relations in the European rural periphery'. *European Urban and Regional Studies*, 7 (1), 35–50.

Koch, N. (2017). *Critical geographies of sport: Space, power and sport in global perspective.* London: Routledge.

Konecnik, M. and Go, F. (2008). 'Tourism destination brand identity: The case of Slovenia'. *Brand Management*, 15 (3), 177–189.

Lee, J.J., Kyle, G., and Scott, D. (2012). The mediating effect of place attachment on the relationship between festival satisfaction and loyalty to the festival hosting destination. *Journal of Travel Research*, 51 (6), 754–767.

Lew, A.A. (1989). 'Authenticity and sense of place in the tourism development experience of older retail districts'. *Journal of Travel Research*, 27 (4), 15–22.

Lewicka, M. (2011). 'Place attachment: How far have we come in the last 40 years?' *Journal of Environmental Psychology*, 31, 207–230.

Light, D. (2001). '"Facing the future": Tourism and identity-building in post-socialist Romania'. *Political Geography*, 20, 1053–1075.

Morgan, N. (2004). 'Problematizing place promotion'. In A.A. Lew, C.M. Hall, and A.M. Williams (eds.) *A companion to tourism* (173–183). Malden, MA: Blackwell.

Morgan, N., Pritchard, A., and Pride, R. (2011). 'Tourism places, brands, and reputation management'. In N. Morgan, A. Pritchard, and R. Pride (eds.) *Destination brands: Managing place reputation*, 3rd ed. (3–20). Florence, KY: Routledge.

Nelson, V. (2010). '"R.I.P. Nature Island": The threat of a proposed oil refinery on Dominica's identity'. *Social & Cultural Geography*, 11 (8), 903–919.

Nelson, V. (2017). *An introduction to the geography of tourism*, 2nd ed. Lanham, MD: Rowman & Littlefield.

Page, S.J. and Connell, J. (2012). 'Introduction'. In S.J. Page and J. Connell (eds.) *The Routledge handbook of events* (1–24). London: Routledge.

Perić, M., Wise, N., and Dragičević, D. (2017). 'Suggesting a service research agenda in sport tourism: Working experience(s) into business models'. *Sport, Business and Management: An International Journal*, 7 (1), 58–76.

Pine, B.J. and Gilmore, J.H. (1998). 'Welcome to the experience economy'. *Harvard Business Review*, 76 (4), 97–105.

Relph, E. (1976). *Place and placelessness.* London: Pion Limited.

Relph, E. (1997). 'Sense of place'. In S. Hanson (ed.) *Ten geographic ideas that changed the world* (205–226). New Brunswick, NJ: Rutgers University Press.

Rojek, C. (2013). *Event power: [How global events manage and manipulate].* London: Sage.

Scarpato, R. and Daniele, R. (2003). 'New global cuisine: Tourism, authenticity and sense of place in postmodern gastronomy'. In C.M. Hall, L. Sharples, R. Mitchell, N. Macionis,, and B. Cambourne (eds.) *Food tourism around the world: Development, management and markets* (296–313). Amsterdam: Butterworth Heinemann.

Schöllmann, A., Perkins, H.C. and Moore, K. (2000). 'Intersecting global and local influences in urban place promotion: The case of Christchurch, New Zealand'. *Environment and Planning A*, 32, 55–76.

Shoval, N. (2013). 'Street-naming, tourism development and cultural conflict: The case of the old city of Acre/Akko/Akka'. *Transactions of the Institute of British Geographers*, 38 (4), 612–626.

Stedman, R.C. (2002). 'Toward a social psychology of place: Predicting behavior from place based cognitions, attitude, and identity'. *Environment and Behavior*, 34 (5), 561–581.

Stedman, R.C. (2003). 'Is it really just a social construction? The contribution of the physical environment to sense of place'. *Society and Natural Resources*, 16, 671–685.

Tuan, Y.-F. (1975). 'Place: An experiential perspective'. *Geographical Review*, 65, 151–165.

Tuan, Y.-F. (1991). 'Language and the making of place: A narrative descriptive approach'. *Annals of the Association of American Geographers*, 81 (4), 684–696.

Vuolteenaho, J. and Berg, L.D. (2009). 'Towards critical toponymies'. In L.D. Berg and J. Vuolteenaho (eds.) *Critical toponymies: The contested politics of place naming* (1–18). London: Routledge.

Westwood, C., Schofield, P., and Berridge, G. (2018). 'Agricultural shows: Visitor motivation, experience and behavioural intention'. *International Journal of Event and Festival Management*, 9 (2), 147–165.

Wise, N. (2015). 'Football on the weekend: Rural events and the Haitian imagined community in the Dominican Republic'. In A. Jepson and A. Clarke (eds.) *Exploring community festivals and events* (106–117). London: Routledge.

Wise, N. and Harris, J. (2017). *Sport, events, tourism and regeneration*. London: Routledge.

Ziakas, V. and Boukas, N. (2014). 'Contextualizing phenomenology in event management research: Deciphering the meaning of event experiences'. *International Journal of Event and Festival Management*, 5 (1), 56–73.

# 2 Privilege on the Pearl

## The politics of place and the 2016 UCI Road Cycling World Championships in Doha, Qatar

*Natalie Koch*

"The Pearl" is an affluent community situated on an artificial island on the northern end of Doha, Qatar. A primarily residential development of over 12,000 residents, it is one of the only areas in Qatar where foreigners may own real estate (Koch, 2014). As a result, it has become an elite enclave for Doha's most affluent, white, Western residents. This affluence is on full display through its carefully coordinated aesthetics, stunning cleanliness and sense of order (see Figure 2.1). The Pearl was designed to be Doha's most exclusive community for foreign residents, who could not only enjoy its luxurious environs but also would be assured a comfortable sense of insulation from the grit and grime that might be found elsewhere in the city.

When Qatar was selected to host the 2016 Union Cycliste Internationale (UCI) Road Cycling World Championships, the Pearl was chosen as the centre of action for the one-week event. Qatar's leaders have been actively developing the capital, Doha, as a way to showcase the country's modernity and prosperity (Koch, 2014; Koch, 2018; Rizzo, 2013; Salama & Wiedmann, 2013). Much of the city's recently transformed urban landscape is impressive, but only in the Pearl is such a coherent image of affluence and Western-style modernity so compactly visible. Local organizers thus considered the Pearl to be the best venue for putting this image of modernity on display for foreign visitors and television audiences of the Cycling World Championships (hereafter "Worlds"). This meant the finish line for each cycling race, and all associated temporary infrastructure for it, was located on the Pearl, so all races either passed through, or were held entirely on, the island. Constantly referenced by officials and in race-related publications as being "iconic" and "luxurious," the Pearl seemed to fit well with the organizers' imaging intentions.

In practice, however, certain logistical issues intruded to challenge this agenda and upset local residents. One particular issue was that there is only one road-bridge to access the Pearl (Figure 2.2). Since most of the races crossed over the bridge, it had to be shut down to traffic for much of the day during the week of Worlds. This created significant issues for Pearl residents seeking to get to and from their homes, as well as limiting spectators' access to the event. Disruptions elsewhere in Doha were minimal, since the races did not move through many other parts of the city. A second

*Figure 2.1* View from the Pearl.
Source: Natalie Koch (2016).

point of contention for Pearl residents was the influx of visitors to the island. The visitors of concern were not the athletes or spectators, however, but the event staffers, who did not fit the white, non-Muslim, and European norm of the Pearl. Since the experience of living on the Pearl was true to its marketing as a *Western* enclave in Doha, many residents were uncomfortable with having their space of privilege suddenly opened to event staff, race marshals, and security guards, who hailed primarily from South and Southeast Asia and Africa. Through an "event ethnography" of the 2016 Worlds in Doha, this chapter examines the politics of place through the lens of privilege on the Pearl and how this was articulated and experienced by the island's residents.

## Place and the politics of identity

Place has been a core concern in geographic theory for decades, historically being theorized as contingent, socially constructed, and inherently relative to any individual's personal experiences (Agnew, 1987; Agnew & Duncan, 1989; Cresswell, 2015; Hoelscher, 2011; Keith & Pile, 1993; Paasi, 2003; Pred, 1984, 1986; Tuan, 1977). This constructivist or relational approach positions place

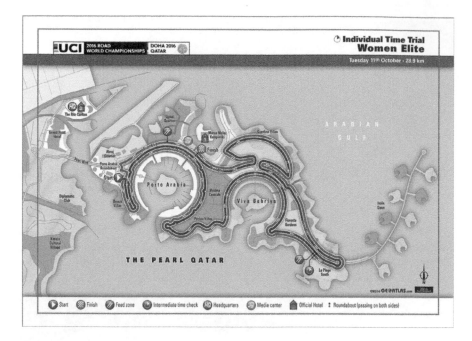

*Figure 2.2*  Race map showing one of the course routes on the Pearl.
Source: Doha Cycling (2016).

not as a static category, but one that is always in the process of becoming. Viewed relationally, place is thus intimately connected with the politics of identity: "How one identifies oneself – and how one is identified by others – may vary greatly from context to context; self- and other-identification are fundamentally situational and contextual" (Brubaker, 2004, p. 41).

Because place and the processes of identification are both inherently subjective, they are necessarily about power relations among people. In this chapter, I move away from an ever-present impulse to locate an objective essence of "place" by instead asking how particular individuals imagine one particular place: "the Pearl" in Doha. I also limit my case study to a short window of time: during the one-week period in October 2016, when the community was the primary site for the Worlds. Through my ethnographic research, a brief snapshot of the cycling event's transformation of the Pearl illustrates how place is never experientially or materially static. I show how the social and spatial demands of hosting sporting events have a special ability to transform particular places.

While the politics of identity is an important theme in the literature on sports, *place* has received comparatively little attention (but see Bale, 1982; Vertinsky & Bale, 2004). Where it has been addressed in sports studies, this work is limited in two ways. First, although all events are necessarily limited in their temporal scope, much of the writing on the place-based impacts of sporting events does not give sufficient attention to time. As Yeoh & Kong (1996, p. 55) emphasize, the making of a place is closely intertwined with the passage of time, as well as "being 'in', moving 'through' and experiencing changing places". Time must be central to any analysis of place – and especially if we are to understand the different temporal scales at which events touch the places and people they do. To investigate the impact of the 2016 Worlds on the Pearl, scholars might expose different issues by analyzing on a shorter or a longer time horizon. In this chapter, I adopt a short-term approach to highlight the intensity of the transformations that took place on the island over the one-week period of the championship. Short-lived as they were, the dynamics I address reflect a general pattern of how sporting events affect places: some-times the changes they bring are fleeting and at other times they are lasting.

Second, research on sporting events tends to focus on the negative impacts they have for the general population or the poor (e.g. Boykoff, 2014; Gaffney, 2010; Orttung & Zhemukhov, 2017; Ren, 2009). This is the logical result of critical social scientists' concern with broader issues of social justice. But the flip side of the effort to raise awareness about the potential harms of hosting sporting events is that many scholars do not ask many questions about who stands to profit. In much of this writing, the benefits are imagined to accrue to a city or country's political and economic elites, who are largely characterized as a homogeneous group with financial rewards at stake. This works in direct opposition to ordinary citizens or marginal communities, who are cast as being essentially connected to par-ticular places (usually urban neighborhoods), which are threatened by sport-ing event hosting plans. In this chapter's case study of the Pearl, which is one of the most elite communities in the Arabian Peninsula, I challenge this characterization as a caricature. Interrogating identity politics in this privil-eged community opens new perspectives on fissures within the often black-boxed grouping of social, cultural, and economic "elites". As this chapter demonstrates, and as recent scholarship on collapsed sporting event bids has shown (e.g. Lauermann & Vogelpohl, 2017), elites themselves are often at odds when it comes to the impact on communities.

In examining the case of the Pearl, we see that many more "elite" actors are caught up by events than planners alone. Viewed through the perspective of privileged actors, this study sheds light on how place is central to competing agendas and interests *among* elites. Crucially, this also *places* elite actors by seeing them as situated actors rooted to and involved in making particular places, rather than as part of an abstract group simply presiding over any par-ticular sporting event. By taking seriously the narratives of privileged residents on the Pearl, and their immense frustration over how their community was transformed for the 2016 Cycling Worlds, we can begin to trace how sporting events might expand or simply cast new light on political fissures among elites.

In the context of Qatar, understanding the politics of privilege requires special attention to "expatriate" cultural identity politics. Through a critical approach to place, this chapter thus extends the small but important body of scholarship on privilege and whiteness in the Gulf region (e.g. Coles & Walsh, 2010; Kanna, 2014; Vora, 2014; Walsh, 2007, 2014). It also puts this work in conversation with interdisciplinary scholarship on what Croucher (2009) terms "migrants of privilege" (see also Beaverstock, 2011; Kunz, 2016; Leonard, 2008), who have stressed the importance of elite migrants or expatriate communities in shaping urban landscapes of privilege. In theorizing such "landscapes of privilege," it is important to examine "privileged groups with resources and power to build landscapes, to protect themselves with invisible walls of zoning, and to shape their own identities through these landscapes" (Duncan & Duncan, 2004, p. 27). This case study takes this injunction seriously to demonstrate how the transformations brought to the Pearl for 2016 Cycling Worlds led to new contestations over place, identity, and privilege on the Pearl, and speaks to broader dynamics unfolding around sporting events, places, and societies across the globe.

## Connections undone: mobility and privilege

The Pearl's lone bridge, which was entirely closed to traffic for much of the day during the week of the Worlds, created significant mobility challenges for Pearl residents, who had to plan ahead to get on and off the island for their daily activities. Race planners knew this would be a problem, so in an effort to minimize the disruption caused by the event, they developed several responses. The first was simply to suggest to residents that they stay elsewhere in Doha for the week and they worked to secure discounts at a handful of hotels for those that chose to do so. These discounts were nominal and the hotels chosen were some of the most expensive in the city (such as the ultra-luxury St. Regis Hotel), so pursuing this option would have required that residents were willing to part with a substantial amount of money. Indeed, when one Pearl resident posted to a community Facebook page an advertisement for the St. Regis's "stay action package" for the event, it sparked a number of angry replies:

RG: Seen this? The St.Regis have put together a stay action package for Pearl residents!

SP: Bargain 😂

LM: Can we offset it against our rent???

CJ: Why would you pay qr6,000 to stay in qatar hotel for 7 nights when you live in qatar?? Lol. I'd rather spend the money and book a flight somewhere!

LM: Exactly!!!

CJ: LM, do they think we fell of the special bus!

LM: CJ, obviously – and we lick the Windows all the way there!!! It's just a joke that they think we should check in somewhere rather than stay in our homes!!

NA: Cashing in on other peoples misfortune

CB: That's exactly what I thought. (October 2)

While this thread clearly demonstrates the residents' anger, it also evinces a strong sense of entitlement and no small amount of ableist intolerance (which inflect many expressions of privilege the world over). Yet some residents were presumably less appalled by the prospect of booking rooms at the St. Regis during the Worlds, and instead exercised their privilege by paying for a hotel. I did not have access to any numbers, but I encountered a number of individuals in Doha who had chosen to do so, though a more popular (and cheaper) option was to stay with friends or family elsewhere in the city.

Residents who chose to remain at home during the Worlds had two options for getting on and off the island when the bridge was closed on race days: they could either leave or enter the Pearl by car when the roads were still open, or they could take a "water taxi" ride on a *dhow* boat across the bay at any point in the day. Since the roads were closed at odd and inconvenient times for most people, the former was often not the best option. The alternative was thus to take the water taxi. Many did so – albeit grudgingly because the trip was complicated and took an inordinate amount of time to travel a short distance. The 20-minute boat-ride shuttled travellers between one dock on the Pearl and Katara Cultural Village – a posh retail and cultural venue across the harbor. Getting to and from these pick-up points could take quite a long time, however. This was because, if one was in the Doha city centre and wishing to get to the Pearl, the water taxi option included a number of steps: a car ride to the Katara Cultural Village, a 10-minute walk to the docks from the taxi drop-off or parking lot, between 5–30 minutes of waiting for a boat, a 20-minute boat trip, and after disembarking on the Pearl, a series of golf cart trips and transfers across the island to finally arrive at one's neighborhood block (broken up because of the series of canals and bridges that the carts could not pass). I made the trip approximately four times and it took about 90–120 minutes each way. An additional layer of complication was added when going into Doha, if one did not have a car waiting in the parking lot (though most Pearl residents did): when disembarking at Katara, there were no buses or other special accommodations to transfer people to the city centre and hailing a taxi was nearly impossible. This posed a major challenge for race spectators, but for Pearl residents accustomed to easily jumping in the car and going wherever they wanted, whenever they wanted, the sudden imposition of these restrictions felt like a particularly egregious violation of their mobility.

In observing the discussions of a Pearl Facebook group in the weeks leading up to Worlds, the community was abuzz with anxieties about the event and many Pearl residents were angry about not being consulted about having their island effectively put on lock-down for nearly a week and a half. Several representative comments from the discussion board were:

AH: It's unbelievable that "the powers that be" thought it would be perfectly acceptable to organize this insane circus without any consultation with residents. There is simply no reason why these races couldn't be spread out a lot more over the city and country instead of heaping massive inconvenience on one group of residents in particular. So far, there has been no word as to what people are expected to do with regards to school kids, getting to the airport, etc, how emergency vehicles will get to where they may be needed etc. (September 25)

NT: It's a shame that the event has brought a lot of anguish, stress and inconvenience to those who keep the place alive. (October 2)

AV: I have a friend who is working with the event who is trying to alleviate the situation for residents talking to the stupid committee (the one who needs a place to stay here during the event from my other post. Apparently these twats planning it have been in Doha for less than 1 month – so they don't know how Doha "works", they don't even know how their own catering will come in and are asking employees to be on site when they well know they're not local to The Pearl (they don't even know how their own people will come in or out!). Completely stupid, she's pulling her hairs too. (October 2)

Most posts centred on more practical inquiries, such as advice about how to get to or from the island, or whether roads were open. Many of these posts demonstrate the community's exasperation about having their mobility limited, as well as the poor race organization and failure to keep to schedules or notify residents of changes:

RC: All roads in the Pearl closed this morning for one hour. Unnotified.

TR: Are we really surprised? We are preparing for Carmaggedon over here.

FA: This is really messed up .. I guess we cannot count on the road closure schedule that was shared as roads can be closed sporadically without notice. (October 6)

MV: I guess everyone has noticed the great organization skills of the Pearl management this morning. Another big mess in the roads on no notice!!! Any info on the plans forward will be highly appreciated ... (October 5)

EC: It would appear that while they are unable to supply marshalls or traffic police for the road closures this morning they are monitoring their twitter feed and removing anything about traffic disruption on the Pearl !!!! (October 5)

LS: Hi ladies, what is everyone doing ref school run when we are in prison on the pearl???? (September 28)

MG: Does anyone know if dogs can go on the water taxis next week? Mine has a vet appointment. (October 5)

RS: I've seen this: [Twitter feed image from UCI RWC Doha 2016: We wish to inform residents that pets are not permitted aboard our public transportation vessels. We regret any inconvenience. #QATraffic] 😊

MG: So he needs to swim to his appointment 😊 (October 5)

Such content suggests consistent tones of anger and frustration running through most posts. But there is certainly a self-selection bias among those posting. Based on my meetings with residents during my time in Doha the dialogue across the city was so negative that several residents took it upon themselves to write blog posts showing how they were "making the most of a bad situation" by documenting all the wonderful amenities and activities available when they could not easily leave the Pearl (e.g. Bagley, 2016; Rizvi, 2016). But when one woman posted such an entry from her personal blog (clumsychic.com), in which she documented all the enjoyable activities and services that the event organizers put together for residents, she was roundly chastised by another woman. Their exchange again suggests how the transformation of the Pearl for the UCI event cast new light on the community's fissures, here along the lines of working and non-working residents:

ND: All well and good to play tourist but what about the people who live there and have to go to work. At the end of the day all I want to do is go home and chill for a bit. This I can't do because the road is blocked until 5/5.30 and then if you attempt to go home at this time you have to deal with the traffic. For me it means having to be out of my home from 6/630am until 6/30pm at night. I don't want to play tourist, I want to go home! This is so NOT helpful.

KN: Yeah I would feel the same way. It was the weekend yesterday so we thought we'd utilize the facilities being offered and share our experience on the blog since I myself didn't know what was going on or how to get to places especially for a stay at home mom like myself. I apologize that you don't find this helpful.

In discussing these optimistic blog posts and related newspaper stories, one visitor I spoke with suspected that they were paid for by a public relations firm. Based on my own interactions with the white, Euro-American expat community in Doha and having previously worked with such media stories in Qatar (see Koch, 2016), my sense was they actually arose unprompted. To be sure, they strictly conformed to the norms of congratulatory speech that is typically printed in Qatar, but they should also be understood as a genuine response to the overarching negative atmosphere among residents.

The authors of the optimistic commentaries sought to directly challenge the negative spirit of critics, whom they largely dismissed as privileged and exceedingly imperial in their outlook. But as in so many other contexts around the world, this anti-imperial attitude is often itself quite imperial. For instance, one post reacted to a flurry of complaints:

Come on people it's 8 days, enjoy the buzz and there is one. We walked to MC this morning, people are out walking and speaking to you, the marshals and Police are being helpful and friendly, we bought 24 bottles of water in Spinneys and distributed them to the Police and Marshals on the way back, we have had a ball this morning. (October 8)

This "benevolent" expat subject position resonates strongly with the various identity performances of expat women in post-colonial Hong Kong discussed by Leonard, (2008). As she and other scholars of privileged expat migrants consistently emphasize, these communities are often quite fractured. Some individuals bristled at what they saw as another's sense of entitlement or imperialism, while often overlooking their very own outlook.

The interesting question here is how certain narratives come to be stigmatized as problematic expressions of privilege and imperial mind-sets when they had gone completely unremarked upon or unnoticed previously (Foucault, 1991). In this case, the cycling event became a turning point for certain members of this community. Its transformation of the *island as a place*, even if brief, created an opportunity for these competing narratives about *one's place as an expat* in Doha to arise. Whatever their motives, and wherever individual residents fell on the optimistic/pessimistic spectrum about the event, the very fact that many in the elite expat community viewed the positive accounts as "alternative" (or staged) illustrates the degree of Pearl residents' indignation at having their space of privilege disrupted. But going well beyond airing their frustration online, residents were active in lodging complaints with the organizers and others they perceived as authority figures. For example, one woman shared with the Facebook group the letter she sent to United Development Company, the developer in charge of the Pearl:

> I'm sure you must have been made aware by now the anger and frustration that most Pearl residents are feeling now regarding the upcoming road closures, both because of the lack of consultation, the utter lack of respect shown to the residents and the unprecedented disruption that we will have to endure. This will most definite have a further negative effect on how many people view The pearl, not to mention all this is to host a sport that is riddled with drug cheats and corruption, now under the spotlight yet again.

Of course not all Pearl residents were so active in lobbying for more consideration of their logistical needs. The above example illustrates how community members were quite accustomed to and comfortable with certain forms of civic engagement, largely due to their elite and Western backgrounds. Indeed, the outcry did lead to action. Although they could not halt the event, residents did receive extensive concessions and accommodations from the organizers as a result (or in anticipation) of their agitating, including a special "Residents' Hub" tent with various amenities and children's activities, special medical services and emergency helicopter service, extended water taxi service beyond that available to the general public, and "resident cards" for discounts at restaurants, shops, and even hotels if they chose to stay elsewhere for the duration of the Worlds.

So even where democratic input might have been shut down, some residents' refusal to remain complacent forced open certain spaces of connectivity and concessions. Nonetheless, these concessions did not satisfy certain Pearl residents, who allowed their criticisms to be printed in local newspapers. In doing so, they again exercised their privilege to critique local decision-making – a notable practice in a context where more marginalized expats would fear reprisal for speaking out against official policies (most commonly taking the form of losing one's job and residency permit). Residents were well aware of the significance of speaking critically "on the record". This became clear when a *Doha News* reporter (see Walker, 2016) solicited comments from the Facebook group and various respondents explicitly stated their willingness to be quoted:

NQ: I am very annoyed as my son has just started school after 6 months being at home. He's just settling in. Keeping him out is not an option. He uses the bus and pick up times will be ok as it's early in the morning. But school comes out at around lunch time with him being dropped at around 2pm. I have a baby at home and can't exactly stay away from home the whole day or even half a day as baby doesn't sleep or feed if not at home. You can quote me. (September 25)

ES: I have two children, they finish school at 1pm and 2pm, my options are to leave my home at 6:30 am for the entire day and arrive back with the children just in time to transfer them straight into bed, or keep them off school for an entire week. The only information we have been given so far is the road closure map, if there is any sort of plan for residents access during those hours they haven't shared it with us. With children only just settling into school after the late start this year it's going to be very disruptive. For working parents it's going to be a logistical nightmare.

LW: Are you happy to be quoted saying this?

ES: Yes that's np (September 25)

It is important to note that the criticisms aired concerned family issues. Given the oft-repeated stereotype that Qataris are extremely family-friendly, residents clearly perceived this issue as the safest realm for criticism: the comments here all work to pull at heartstrings, rather than critiquing the government in any overtly "political" manner. Overall, these commentaries and far more diffuse conversations in the expat community demonstrate how the temporally limited but spatially discrete undoing of connections for the Worlds completely altered the Pearl as a place of privilege. Places are never closed in on themselves and, especially for elites, they are often defined by the mobility that they afford. A relational understanding of place thus helps us to see how the cycling event both challenged residents' ability to claim their privilege through uninhibited movement, but also how it led to new dialogues among residents as they negotiated appropriate responses to the event – and their own subject positions in the process.

## Bodies out of place: policing social exclusivity on the Pearl

The restrictions on residents' mobility over the course of the event was the main focus of these critiques, but their space of privilege was also interrupted by the sudden influx of event staffers, who did not fit the white, non-Muslim, and European norm of the Pearl. Janitorial crews, security guards, and course marshals (who were stationed all over the island to ensure that no one walked into the roads) were primarily poorly paid South Asian or African expat men (see images in Figure 2.3). Residents regularly interact with this demographic, but far less frequently on the Pearl, where they dress less modestly than they would elsewhere in Doha. The Pearl thus serves (and indeed has been marketed) as a Western enclave, where they are freer to engage in culturally familiar practices, just as Coles & Walsh (2010, p. 1323) note of expat social spaces in Dubai, which allow them "to maintain familiar practices that were culturally inappropriate in Dubai, for instance drinking alcohol or walking around in swimming costumes."

As former British protectorates, the Gulf Arab states share this history and clubs were an important aspect of expat life in the region, coming to be seen as a "haven" where Western expats "could, in the absence of old friends and relatives, relax with 'their own kind'" (Coles & Walsh, 2010, p. 1322). For some of Doha's elite expats, this kind of spatial enclave is particularly valuable – not just as a physical space of comfort in a foreign country, but also for the social dimension that makes it a *place* of comfort. The narrative of mingling with one's "own kind" is often framed along national lines, though racial categories are often deeply embedded in this imaginary, even if implicit. As an island, the Pearl is spatially more extensive than expat clubs found elsewhere in the world, but the community's social milieu similarly reinforces the "routine production of Self/Other boundaries" (Coles & Walsh, 2010, p. 1322). So too does its aesthetic ordering result in landscapes of privilege, which are "a subtle but highly effective mechanism of exclusion" (Duncan & Duncan, 2004, p. 7).

Aestheticized landscapes are highly effective at obscuring class- and race-based forms of social exclusion, as well as "the exploitation that produces them" (Duncan & Duncan, 2004, p. 26). As an enclave space organized around a particularly Western and elitist aesthetic, the Pearl allows residents to experience what scholars describe as "painless privilege", allowing them to "spatially and visually insulate themselves from uncomfortable questions of race and poverty", which makes that privilege possible (Duncan & Duncan, 2004, p. 9), and is much more apparent in other parts of Doha. For this reason, many Pearl residents were uncomfortable with the perceived influx of a new demographic on the island during the Worlds, as it challenged their ability to keep those visual cues of social inequality out of sign and out of mind. Though this discomfort became apparent to me throughout my experience of moving about the island during the event, it was not a major focus of discussion on the residents' Facebook group. On October 10, 2016, a woman

*Figure 2.3* (a) Top image: Spectators departing after a race, while East Asian cart-drivers negotiate excessive demand to move them along to the next pick-up point; (b) Bottom image: View from the race finish line, with primarily white European spectators and a South Asian janitor looking on (far left).

Source: Natalie Koch (2016).

posted about an incident of allegedly being ogled by an event security guard, as described and discussed among other female Pearl residents in the following thread:

KM: Ladies out alone with dogs during these races … .the UCI security were just filming me on their personal mobile phone while I was out with my dog and not for anything official if you get what I mean!!! He was trying to be sneaky about it but he did a dreadful job, caught him red-handed! There was a Lekhiwya [Qatari internal security force] officer I've told him and he was less than impressed and went over to talk to them too … Sorry to rant but this sort of thing just sickens me so if this sort of thing bothers you just be aware that it's happening.

ES: Do you think he was maybe filming your dog rather than you?

KM: No! I'm sure the dog was on the video too of course, but the way he was doing it he was trying to be a perv! ☹

SP: ☹

KF: These dudes are from different countries and are very flirtatious, one spoke to me yesterday. Typical. Don't feel bad, it's something they believe is appropriate ….

ND: Because we are westerners, they wouldn't do it with their own womenfolk.

KF: ND, indeed…..

CL: Thanks for posting. Glad you reported it.

MG: Disgusting, everyday I get stared at or approached when I'm with my dog – not just during the cycling but it's much worse with these "helpers"

MP: I have to deal with disgusting attention on daily basis when we walk with my dog, wish I could report it all the time!

AR: Disgusting.

CL: What's most important is that we stick together and look out for one another. If you SEE something, SAY something.

KM: I can hold my own with it … but my concern I guess is if people are letting their daughters out to walk their dogs alone … just to have your wits about you a little more!

LT: Sheesh … sorry to hear that KM!! Did you wall ball that shizzle out of your system?! on a serious note though they need educating, it's total ignorance

KM: I need to wall ball him in his face!!

MM: I have never seen police man to even look at any woman here . So probably he was just checking smth on his phone and not taking video for shure:)

The racist and Orientalist contours of this discussion are not unfamiliar to anyone who has circulated in white, Western expat crowds in the Gulf states. On the Pearl, as elsewhere in Doha, the low-paid guards and workers are never Euro-American or white. The act of denigrating them here is not framed through explicitly racial language, but through cultural otherness and differences based on national origin. For instance, one woman writes that "these dudes are from different countries" and that their behaviour is somehow "typical". She also explains it as being a social or cultural norm: "Don't feel bad, it's something they believe is appropriate". Though framed more as a defense of this behavior, such ascriptions of cultural backwardness here and in wider conversations among privileged Western expats are both more and less explicit, with comments such as "they need educating, it's total ignorance" representing one end of the spectrum and tropes such as "their own *womenfolk*" and "*these* 'helpers'" marking them off in a more casual manner.

This conversation also sets the commentators apart from the security guards and other lower-class workers in Doha, both by emphasizing that this dynamic unfolds because "we are westerners," as well as through several calls for them to "stick together and look out for one another". The event here serves as a platform for these residents to articulate the very category of "westerners" in specific, more cohesive ways. The sense of community that these women seek to conjure in this exchange is here inflected by a sense of benevolence and caring, but emphatically for *one another* and in the face of apparent threats from *others*. Here again, the act of denigrating these men and questioning their motives (or rather, attributing pernicious motives to them) is clearly positioned not as a form of xenophobia, but instead framed as one of self-defense and concern for the group's integrity and the safety and well-being of "their daughters". The boundaries between these privileged women and their ostensible cultural Others are also policed through frequent references to "disgust". This began with the first post author's comment that the incident "sickens me", subsequently widening to a series of comments about how disgusted these women feel in being watched as they move through urban space in Doha on a regular basis. Yet many feel frustrated about their inability to do anything about this unwelcome attention, as seen when one the resident notes: "wish I could report it all the time!"

The transformation of the Pearl for the Worlds is important here because it facilitated KM's sense of and actual agency in doing something concrete. Not only did she report the incident to an official (an act that could easily lead to an employee's dismissal), but she also clearly felt that it was important to teach others in her community about being on guard and to "report bad behavior!!" Furthermore, since residents and event staffers substantially outnumbered the spectators and athletes on the Pearl, the event illustrates how diffuse encounters related to the production of such a sporting event go well beyond the athlete/spectator binary that is often the focus in writing about sports. The Pearl residents were exceptional in their ability to push back because they had at their disposal time, resources, connections, and previous experience with civic involvement from having lived in democratic states in the West. Similar to their efforts to lobby for additional accommodations, when they learned about how the event would restrict their mobility, the event opened up certain opportunities to (re)assert their privilege and a claim a right to move about their community around a particularly Western conception of public space, dress, and gender relations – while ultimately reinforcing the Pearl as a place that excludes, or at least stigmatizes, certain (lower) classed and (non-white) racialized bodies that disrupted unspoken norms in their social enclave.

## Conclusion

As I suggested at the outset of this chapter, "place" can often appear to defy definition. If, however, we move beyond a search for its essence and toward a relational understanding, we can begin to see how *place-making* involves a deeply political set of practices. Identity politics are inherently bound up with these practices and, in the unique case of one elite enclave in Doha, wealthy, predominantly white, and Euro-American expats are deeply committed to policing the boundaries of privilege through the social and material construction of the Pearl as a place. Yet in approaching place relationally, it is essential to understand how it fluctuates temporally – and this is the power of examining place through the lens of sporting events. Events such as the 2016 UCI Road Cycling World Championships in Doha, which demanded a complete, if brief, alteration of parts of the city's urban fabric, forms of mobility, and flows of individuals, shed light on how place is never experientially or materially static. In highlighting the role of time, this chapter has sought to augment the literature on sporting events and place, which has done little to take this into account. Furthermore, in focusing on the privileged communities affected by Worlds, I have sought to push beyond the typical focus of research on sporting events on the negative impacts they have for the general population or the poor. If scholars are to explain the persistence and appeal of hosting large (and small) sporting events, it is essential to understand the full spectrum of attitudes, affinities, and concerns of groups at different points in the social hierarchy. It is also essential not to assume too great a degree of coherence among "elites" involved in and impacted by events in their locales. As this chapter has illustrated through the lens of place, we can see how events open new fissures among certain groups, as well as the need for scholars to see these identity politics play out in real time.

## References

Agnew, J. (1987). *Place and politics: The geographical mediation of state and society.* Boston: Allen & Unwin.

Agnew, J. & Duncan, J. (Eds.) (1989). *The power of place: Bringing together geographical and sociological imaginations.* Boston: Unwin Hyman.

Bagley, P. (2016). 24 hours at home on the Pearl Qatar. *Follow Your Sunshine*, 8 October. www.followyoursunshine.me/2016/10/24-hoursat-home-on-pearl-qatar.html (last accessed 25 March 2017).

Bale, J. (1982). *Sport and place: A geography of sport in England, Scotland and Wales.* London: C. Hurst.

Beaverstock, J. (2011). Servicing British expatriate 'talent' in Singapore: Exploring ordinary transnationalism and the role of the 'expatriate' club. *Journal of Ethnic and Migration Studies*, 37(5), 709–728.

Boykoff, J. (2014). *Activism and the Olympics: Dissent at the games in Vancouver and London.* New Brunswick: Rutgers University Press.

Brubaker, R. (2004). *Ethnicity without groups.* Cambridge: Harvard University Press.

Coles, A. & Walsh, K. (2010). From 'Trucial state' to 'postcolonial' city? The imaginative geographies of British expatriates in Dubai. *Journal of Ethnic and Migration Studies*, 36(8), 1317–1333.

Cresswell, T. (2015). *Place: An introduction.* Malden: Blackwell.

Croucher, S. (2009). Migrants of privilege: The political transnationalism of Americans in Mexico. *Identities*, 16(4), 463–491.

Duncan, J. & Duncan, N. (2004). *Landscapes of privilege: The politics of the aesthetic in an American suburb.* New York: Routledge.

Foucault, M. (1991). Questions of method. In G. Burchell, C. Gordon, & P. Miller (Eds.). *The Foucault effect: Studies in governmentality* (73–86). Chicago: University of Chicago Press.

Gaffney, C. (2010). Mega-events and socio-spatial dynamics in Rio De Janeiro, 1919–2016. *Journal of Latin American Geography*, 9(1), 7–29.

Hoelscher, S. (2011). Place – Part II. In J. Agnew & J. Duncan (Eds.). *The Wiley-Blackwell companion to human geography* (245–259). Malden: Wiley-Blackwell.

Kanna, A. (2014). 'A group of like-minded lads in heaven': Everydayness and the production of Dubai space. *Journal of Urban Affairs*, 36(s2), 605–620.

Keith, M. & Pile, S. (Eds.) (1993). *Place and the politics of identity.* New York: Routledge.

Koch, N. (2014). 'Building glass refrigerators in the desert': Discourses of urban sustainability and nation building in Qatar. *Urban Geography*, 35(8), 1118–1139.

Koch, N. (2016). Is nationalism just for nationals? Civic nationalism for noncitizens and celebrating National Day in Qatar and the UAE. *Political Geography*, 54, 43–53.

Koch, N. (2018). The geopolitics of sport beyond soft power: Event ethnography and the 2016 Cycling World Championships in Qatar. *Sport in Society*, 21 (12), 2010–2031.

Kunz, S. (2016). Privileged mobilities: Locating the expatriate in migration scholarship. *Geography Compass*, 10(3), 89–101.

Lauermann, J. & Vogelpohl, A. (2017). Fragile growth coalitions or powerful contestations? Cancelled Olympic bids in Boston and Hamburg. *Environment and Planning A*, 49(8), 1887–1904.

Leonard, P. (2008). Migrating identities: Gender, whiteness and Britishness in post-colonial Hong Kong. *Gender, Place & Culture*, 15(1), 45–60.

Orttung, R. & Zhemukhov, S. (2017). *Putin's Olympics: The Sochi games and the evolution of twenty-first century Russia.* New York: Routledge.

Paasi, A. (2003). Region and place: Regional identity in question. *Progress in Human Geography*, 27(4), 475–485.

Pred, A. (1984). Place as historically contingent process: Structuration and the time-geography of becoming places. *Annals of the Association of American Geographers*, 74(2), 279–297.

Pred, A. (1986). *Place, practice, and structure: Social and spatial transformation in southern Sweden, 1750–1850.* Totowa: Barnes & Noble.

Ren, X. (2009). Olympic Beijing: Reflections on urban space and global connectivity. *The International Journal of the History of Sport*, 26(8), 1011–1039.

Rizvi, S. (2016). UCI Doha 2016. *Whats Up Doha*, 12 October. www.wud.qa/blog-post /uci-doha-2016/ (last accessed 26 March 2017).

Rizzo, A. (2013). Metro Doha. *Cities*, 31, 533–543.

Salama, A. & Wiedmann, F. (2013). *Demystifying Doha: On architecture and urbanism in an emerging city.* Burlington, VT: Ashgate.

Tuan, Y.-F. (1977). *Space and place: The perspective of experience.* Minneapolis: University of Minnesota Press.

Vertinsky, P. & Bale, J. (Eds.) (2004). *Sites of sport: Space, place and experience.* New York: Routledge.

Vora, N. (2014). Expat/expert camps: Redefining labor within Gulf migration. In A. Khalaf, O. AlShehabi & A. Hanieh (Eds.). *Transit states: Labour, migration and citizenship in the Gulf* (170–197). London: Pluto Press.

Walker, L. (2016). Access to the Pearl-Qatar to be restricted during cycling event. *Doha News*, 26 September. https://dohanews.co/access-to-the-pearl-qatar-to-be-restricted-during-cycling-event/ (last accessed 26 March 2017).

Walsh, K. (2007). "It got very debauched, very Dubai!" Heterosexual intimacy amongst single British expatriates. *Social & Cultural Geography*, 8(4), 507–533.

Walsh, K. (2014). Placing transnational migrants through comparative research: British migrant belonging in five GCC Cities. *Population, Space and Place*, 20(1), 1–17.

Yeoh, B. & Kong, L. (1996). The notion of place in the construction of history, nostalgia and heritage in Singapore. *Singapore Journal of Tropical Geography*, 17(1), 52–65.

# 3 Social impacts and implications of hosting festivals on the place and local community

## The EXIT Festival in Novi Sad, Serbia

*Vanja Pavluković, Tanja Armenski, & Juan Miguel Alcántara-Pilar*

### Introduction

Festivals are one of the most frequently organized events, happening at destinations across the world, with numbers increasing year-on-year (Kim et al., 2015). Getz and Page (2016) pointed out that music festivals are becoming a cultural and touristic 'must-visit' phenomena. As such, it becomes crucial for the success of travel destinations to offer such events. There is a wide range of festival-related research including that on the festival experience (e.g. Lee et al., 2017), audience motivation (e.g. Chang & Yuan, 2011; Yolal et al., 2012), satisfaction (e.g. Lee & Kyle, 2014), intention to re-visit (e.g. Savinovic et al., 2012) place marketing (e.g. Lee et al., 2012) and festival impacts (e.g. Pavluković et al., 2017). Getz and Page (2016) highlighted that events and festivals are primarily driven by economic benefits. Consequently, much research has been devoted to assessing economic impacts, while other outcomes, particularly social ones, have been neglected for many years due to the difficulty of collecting tangible data and evidence. Nowadays researchers have devised ways to assess and understand social and cultural outcomes, with a new range of indicators and measurement scales available (Aquilino et al., 2018; Bimonte & Punzo, 2016; Deery et al., 2012; Wise & Perić, 2017). However, in many destinations, especially in emerging ones such as Serbia, the social impacts of events remain under-researched.

This chapter explores the relationship between resident involvement with the festival and their perception of social benefits and costs that the festival brings to the host community and the place of Novi Sad. The analysis is conducted on the EXIT Festival held in Novi Sad, Serbia, using a modified version of the Festival Social Impact Attitude Scale (FSIAS). Multivariate analysis was used to test for the relationship between residents' involvement in the festival and their perception of its social impacts on host communities. To a discussion of the literature concerning events and social impacts on place and community is where this chapter now turns.

**Social impacts**

There have been many definitions of social impact. Conceptually, many of those definitions recognize social impact to be the positive or negative changes in social and cultural conditions, which directly or indirectly result from an activity, project, or programme (Carneiro et al., 2018; Duffy & Mair, 2018; Eusébio et al., 2016) and issues and concerns that affect the quality of life for residents of a place (Fredline et al., 2003; Wise et al., 2017). Similarly, the impact of festivals refers to both positive and negative influences on the local community that can be tangible (such as additional income, jobs, tax revenues for locals) or intangible (such as community pride, enhanced image of the place) and which generally has been categorized into economic, environmental, socio-cultural, and political impacts (Arcodia & Whitford, 2007; Delamere et al., 2001; Fredline et al., 2003; Kim & Petrick, 2005; Reid, 2007; Small et al., 2005).

As noted, researchers have predominantly focused on the economic impacts of the festivals on host destinations. But increasingly, scholars are focusing more attention on social impacts assessments to determine the 'quality' of the festival and attest to the true 'value' the festival adds to society (Carneiro et al., 2018; Wood, 2017). Therefore, the research interests have begun to move away from the assessment of solely economic impacts towards the social impacts festivals exert on host communities.

In the existing body of literature, there was a significant attempt to systematize the socio-cultural impacts of festivals. Robertson et al. (2009) identified six thematic sections that represent festivals: (1) policy; (2) stakeholders and contested meaning; (3) social impacts and social impact measurement scales; (4) community and networks; (5) community and social capital; and (6) festival directors. Deery and Jago (2010) marked off three thematically related categories: (1) studies that deal with measurement scales development to assess the social impacts of festival and events; (2) studies that examine how residents' perceptions of the event influence community support for that same event (see also Gursoy & Kendall, 2006); and (3) papers that focus on local authorities and policy recommendations for enhancing the social impacts of events (see Wood, 2005). Some of the studies used the (Festival Social Impact Attitude Scale FSIAS), as in the present study, developed by Delamere (2001) and Delamere et al. (2001), and the Social Impact Perception (SIP) scale developed by Small and Edwards (2003).

Each of the previous studies referenced above addressed different understandings of how events can create social impacts and/or have an impact on host communities. Deery and Jago (2010), in their work of social impacts of events and the role of anti-social behavior, grouped the positive impacts of events on communities into two categories: (1) the social and economic impacts such as increased employment and standard of living, economic, and entertainment benefits of events; and (2) the longer-term impacts such as enhanced community image and pride, preservation of local culture, an increased skill base, and new facilities.

Both of these have significant benefits for place and society. The most successful long-term events, according to the same authors, are seen to promote the host destination and enhance community pride. Similarly, Dwyer et al. (2000, p.185) also discuss 'psychic income', referring to civic pride, as an important positive impact of events which entails opportunities for home hosting and socio-cultural interaction. Social impacts also benefit managers and planners who make future decisions on how to include and enable locals (see Aquilino et al., 2018).

On a positive note, a festival can generate increased revenues and job opportunities for locals (Dwyer et al., 2000), add life to the city, and give residents renewed pride (Richards & Wilson, 2004; van den Berg, 2012), helping to shape and create a sense of place and community (Wise & Harris, 2016). Thus, Gursoy et al. (2004) argue that festivals may reinforce social and cultural identity and help to build social cohesion by strengthening ties within a community. Such insight builds on Arcodia & Whitford's (2007) discussion suggesting that festivals raise awareness and can encourage a more effective use of community resources and expertise, and contribute to the development of social networks that can be maintained even a long time after the festival ends. Community festivals offer researchers an opportunity to evaluate sense of community and sense of place as social implications of festivals, based on the interactions of people, place, and culture (Duffy & Mair, 2018).

There are also several negative impacts of festivals, such as changes in community values, environmental costs, noise, crowds, risky sexual behaviors, abuse of alcohol and drugs, conflicts with festival visitors, xenophobia, and commodification and exploitation of culture and traditional ways of life (Arcodia & Whitford, 2007; Deery & Jago, 2010; Dwyer et al., 2000; Getz & Page, 2016). Community collaboration and organizational involvement before, during, and after the festival is a must to enhance community well-being and support for the festival in the longer term (Bagiran & Kurgun, 2016). Similarly, Gursoy and Kendall (2006) argue that community support for a festival is affected directly and/or indirectly by the level of community concern, ecocentric values, community attachment, perceived benefits, and perceived costs of the festival. Derrett (2003) claims that festivals contribute to a sense of community because they allow community members to work towards and share a purpose. Moreover, they provide opportunities for support, empowerment, participation, and safety, each relating to helping people achieve a sense of belonging. Van Winkle and Woosnam (2014) examined the relation between sense of community and residents' attitudes towards the social impacts of a festival. According to them, sense of community appears to contribute to residents' ability to see the implications of hosting events. Festival managers must listen to the concerns of residents, to understand whether people's sense of community is high or low, as this will bear relation to the long-term success of an event. The greater the positive impacts or perceived benefits of an event, the more positive and supportive the host community will be.

# Research methodology

## *About EXIT*

EXIT is a summer music festival held annually (the first weekend of July) at the Petrovaradin Fortress on the Danube River in Novi Sad, Serbia since 2000 (see Wise & Mulec, 2015). It originated from a student movement during the struggle for democracy in Serbia and the Balkan region, and now promotes social and political messages (Wise et al., 2015). More than 2.5 million people from over 60 countries around the world have visited the festival so far. The festival contributes significantly to the national economy by about €15 million (on average) annually, and the total contribution to the national tourist industry since 2000 has exceeded 100 million euros (Pavluković et al., 2017).

## *Research instrument*

The research used the Festival Social Impact Attitude Scale (FSIAS) (see Delamere, 2001; Delamere et al., 2001). The FSIAS originally comprised 21 social-benefits-related items and 26 social-costs-related items. The scale was initially used to measure the social impacts of Edmonton Folk Music Festival on the local community of Edmonton, Alberta, and later it was validated in several different settings with different geographies and types of music (pop, rock, country) (see Bagiran & Kurgun, 2016; Dragićević et al., 2015; Pavluković et al., 2017; Rollins & Delamere, 2007; Woosnam et al., 2013).

The present study used the FSIAS modified specifically for the case of the EXIT festival. The scale was modified based on the results of an expert panel discussion with academics and event managers from Serbia. Experts were invited to discuss FSIAS and suggest scale adjustments; 20 original items from the FSIAS (Delamere, 2001) were kept and 11 new items were proposed. The final measurement scale consists of 31 items with good internal consistency ($\alpha=0.88$). Five-point Likert scaling was used for ranking respondents' agreement/disagreement on the festival's impacts on the local community. In addition, the questionnaire comprises a section on the socio-demographic characteristics of respondents (gender, age, education, occupation, work experience) and their experience of attending EXIT.

## *Sampling, data collection and data analyzes*

The questionnaire was translated into the Serbian language as the target research population were residents of Novi Sad, the festival's host community. The research was conducted in the period between June and September 2014. The timing of the research coincided with the summer months when the EXIT festival takes place. The questionnaires were distributed electronically among residents using social media. Three hundred and one members of the community responded to the survey, and after data screening 24 responses were dropped because they were not complete. A total of 277 were retained for the analysis.

## Research results

### Respondents' profile

A descriptive summary of respondent characteristics is presented in Table 3.1. Respondents were mostly under the age of 31 years, as this age cohort is most familiar with the event and the younger population is represented because they are more responsive to electronic surveying through social media. Most respondents are employed in the private sector (40.1%) while the high share of unemployed respondents (40.1%) represents students and youth who are loyal visitors to the EXIT festival. Experienced respondents who visited the festival more than three times dominated the sample and around half of the respondents have lived in Novi Sad for more than 20 years.

### Exploratory factor analysis of modified FSIAS

The exploratory factor analysis is conducted to extract a lower number of unobserved factors that represent the social benefits and costs of the EXIT festival. Underlying factors were extracted by principal components analysis with Promax rotation and the optimal number of factors was determined by a range of cut-off criteria such as eigenvalue near to one, a percentage of variance, item communalities, factor loadings, and parallel analysis (Blunch, 2010). Based on the criteria mentioned above, 28 items were retained in the analysis representing the six-factors solution that explained 61.17% of the variance. The six factors were labelled based on the core variables that constituted them.

Factor one, 'Musical Life Benefits' (F1) describes locals' opinion of the festival and their involvement in the organization of the festival. Factor two comprises three items related to the security of both locals and visitors during the festival; hence it is named 'Safety and Security Benefits' (F2). Factor three, 'Community Benefits' involves items mostly related to the destination's image and promotion of the city hosting the festival as well as improving the sense of national pride and identity of the local community (F3). Factor four, 'Economic and Cultural Benefits' consists of items related to the festival impact on locals' well-being and quality of life, such as an opportunity for additional income and new places of employment, the opportunity to learn new things, meet different cultures, and experience a multicultural environment during the festival (F4). The fifth factor describes 'Social Costs' of the festivals, such as crowds, divergence from normal routine, and privacy of everyday life for the local community (F5). Factor six, 'Environmental Costs' is related to noise, littering, and increased crime in host location during the festival (F6).

*Table 3.1* Respondent characteristics for the survey conducted for this study.

| Characteristics | Absolute frequencies | (%) |
|---|---|---|
| **Gender** | | |
| Female | 183 | 66.1 |
| Male | 94 | 33.9 |
| **Age** | | |
| Less than 31 | 160 | 57.8 |
| Between 31–41 | 86 | 31.0 |
| More than 41 | 31 | 11.2 |
| **Years of residence in Novi Sad** | | |
| Less than 10 years | 71 | 25.6 |
| Between 10 and 20 years | 72 | 26.0 |
| More than 20 years | 134 | 48.4 |
| **Occupation** | | |
| Public sector and NGO | 55 | 19.9 |
| Private sector | 111 | 40.1 |
| Unemployed | 111 | 40.1 |
| **Level of education** | | |
| High school | 61 | 22.0 |
| 2-years higher education | 27 | 9.7 |
| Graduate studies | 123 | 44.4 |
| Post-graduate studies | 66 | 23.8 |
| **Work related to tourism sector?** | | |
| Yes | 47 | 17.0 |
| No | 230 | 83.0 |
| **Festival attendance experience** | | |
| Yes | 204 | 73.6 |
| No | 73 | 26.4 |
| **Frequency of visits to the festival** | | |
| Never | 73 | 26.4 |
| Ones | 31 | 11.2 |
| Two times | 24 | 8.7 |
| Three times | 23 | 8.3 |
| More than three times | 126 | 45.5 |
| **Total** | **277** | **100.0** |

## First and second order confirmatory factor analysis of FSIAS

To confirm the six-factorial substructure of the FSIAS, representing two main positive and negative dimensions of the EXIT festival as perceived by residents, first and second order confirmatory factor analysis (CFA) was conducted across the 28-item scale. The initial CFA model of the first order was specified so that each observable item represents only one of six latent dimensions. Measurement errors were uncorrelated, and the fit of the model was poor. Inspection of the residuals matrix and the modification indices suggested dropping items with low factor loadings (> 0.60) to achieve a significant improvement of the models. A final first order CFA model comprises 20 items loading on the six-factorial structure: SB- χ2 (d.f.)=397.72 (162); GFI=0.90; RMSEA=0.06; SRMR= 0.06; CFI=0.97; IFI=0.97; NFI=0.94.

After completing the first order CFA, a second order CFA was built to test the soundness of the substructure of the six latent factors empirically representing the positive and negative dimension of festival impacts. The second order model shows a good fit: SB- χ2 (d.f.)=435.99 (170); GFI=0.89; RMSEA=0.06; SRMR=0.07; CFI=0.97; IFI=0.97; NFI=0.94 (see Figure 3.1).

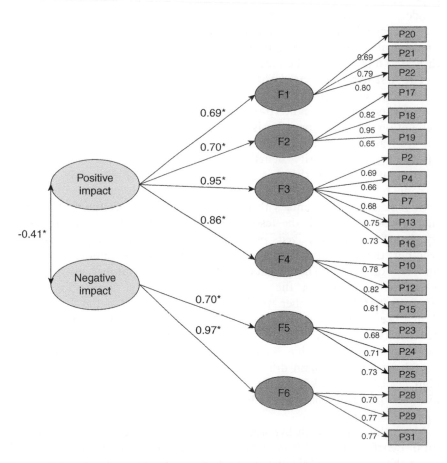

*Figure 3.1* Results of second order confirmatory factor analysis.

*Testing reliability*

To test the reliability of the second order CFA measurement, model average variance extracted (AVE) and construct reliability (CR) were computed for the six latent factors. The AVE and CR of six constructs surpassed the threshold values of 0.50 and 0.70, respectively (see Table 3.2). Therefore, it can be concluded that the indicators for all six factors were enough in terms of how the measurement model was specified. The summary of the second order CFA model is presented in Table 3.2.

*Hypothesis formulation: moderation effect of involvement/number of visits*

To test the moderation effect of levels of involvement on residents' perception of the EXIT festival's impacts on the local community, various covariance analyzes (ANOVA) were carried out. The FSIAS factors were treated as the dependent variables and resident involvement with the festival was an independent variable. The resident involvement variable was derived from a frequency of festival visits ranging from low involvement (have never visited the festival), medium (visited ones or two times) or high involvement (visited three and more times). The summary of results is shown in Table 3.3.

The first hypothesis assumed that the factor 'Musical Life Benefits' has a positive relationship with resident involvement. The ANOVA on this factor was not significant ($p > 0.10$), therefore it was concluded that the perception of music benefits is not moderated by the number of times the festival was visited (Figure 3.2). The second hypothesis proposed that the 'Safety and Security Benefits' would have a positive relation to the number of visits, and this was confirmed ($p < 0.01$) (Figure 3.3). The Bonferroni test shows the main difference between residents with high involvement and residents with medium and low involvement. The higher their involvement with the festival, the more positively safety and security benefits are perceived by residents. The third hypothesis tested whether the perception of community benefits was moderated by the number of visits. The results show that the number of visits has a significant effect on the visitors' perception of community benefits ($F = 9.45$; $p < 0.00$). In other words, residents who visited the festival more than once formed a more positive perception of the festival community benefits (Community Benefits = 20.53) than those who had never visited the festival (Community Benefits = 18.33) (Figure 3.4). The Bonferroni test shows that the main difference exists between residents with low and high levels of festival involvement. Residents with a medium involvement did not perceive community benefits any differently from those with a low involvement.

Meanwhile, the fourth hypothesis proposed that the 'Economic and Cultural Benefits' would be moderated by resident involvement. The results show the significant difference between the medium and high involvement

Table 3.2 The first and second order CFA of modified FSIAS items.

| 2nd order CFA | 1st order CFA | β (t Value) | Code | and Variables labels | B (t Value) | AVE | CR | AVE (2ND order) | CR (2ND order) |
|---|---|---|---|---|---|---|---|---|---|
| | | | P20 | Festival programme is always rich and diverse | 0.69 * | | | | |
| | F1 | 0.69 (7.85) | P21 | The local community is involved in the organization of the festival | 0.79 (10.21) | 0.58 | 0.81 | | |
| | | | P22 | Local community attitudes towards organization of the festival are acknowledged | 0.80 (9.70) | | | | |
| | | | P17 | A high security level for visitors during the festival | 0.82 * | | | | |
| | F2 | 0.70 (9.58) | P18 | A high security level for local residents during the festival | 0.91 (12.34) | 0.66 | 0.85 | | |
| Positive impact | | | P19 | The visitors of festival behave properly | 0.65 (8.86) | | | 0.65 | 0.88 |
| | | | P2 | Hosting the festival improves the identity of the local community | 0.69* | | | | |
| | | | P4 | The festival enables the local community to present itself to others (visitors) as special and unique | 0.66 (9.28) | | | | |
| | F3 | 0.95 (10.63) | P7 | The local community has a sense of national pride when hosting the festival | 0.68 (10.35) | 0.50 | 0.83 | | |
| | | | P13 | The local community gains positive recognition for hosting the festival | 0.75 (11.43) | | | | |
| | | | P16 | The festival is of great importance as it allows visitors to learn about local culture | 0.73 (9.79) | | | | |

(Continued)

Table 3.2 (Cont.)

| 2nd order CFA | 1st order CFA | β (t Value) | Code and Variables labels | β (t Value) | AVE | CR | AVE (2ND order) | CR (2ND order) |
|---|---|---|---|---|---|---|---|---|
| | F4 | 0.86 (12.24) | P10 | Hosting the festival gives an opportunity to local residents to learn new things | 0.78* | | | | |
| | | | P12 | The local community can meet different cultures and have multicultural experiences during the festival | 0.82 (14.05) | 0.55 | 0.78 | | |
| | | | P15 | Due to the organization of the festival, the local population has the opportunity to make additional income | 0.61 (9.26) | | | | |
| | F5 | 0.70 (6.39) | P23 | The organization of the festival disrupts normal routine and everyday life of the local community | 0.68* | | | | |
| | | | P24 | Public spaces and facilities for entertainment and recreation are overused during the festival | 0.71 (9.47) | 0.50 | 0.75 | | |
| Negative Impact | | | P25 | The influx of festival goers reduces privacy within the local community | 0.73 (9.42) | | | 0.72 | 0.83 |
| | | | P28 | Noise levels in the city increase during the festival | 0.70* | | | | |
| | F6 | 0.97 (7.32) | P29 | Litter increases to unacceptable levels during the festival | 0.77 (12.02) | 0.56 | 0.79 | | |
| | | | P31 | Crime in the community increases during the festival | 0.77 (10.67) | | | | |

Note (*): Value not calculated since the parameter was established at 1 to set the scale for the latent variable; β: Standardized Factor Loading

*Table 3.3* FSIAS factor differences by levels of involvement.

| | FSIAS Factor | Means (Std. Err.) | | | ANOVA Results | |
|---|---|---|---|---|---|---|
| | | Low | Medium | High | F | P |
| H1 | Musical Life Benefits | 9.98 (0.30) | 10.07 (0.34) | 9.87 (0.23) | 0.12 | 0.88 |
| H2 | Safety and Security Benefits | 9.55 (0.30) | 10.20 (0.33) | 11.17 (0.21) | 10.95 | 0.00 |
| H3 | Community Benefits | 18.33 (0.52) | 18.82 (0.55) | 20.53 (0.28) | 9.45 | 0.00 |
| H4 | Economic and Cultural Benefits | 10.37 (0.31) | 12.00 (0.35) | 12.45 (0.20) | 12.04 | 0.00 |
| H5 | Social Costs | 10.01 (0.36) | 12.71 (0.41) | 9.01 (0.23) | 2.78 | 0.06 |
| H6 | Environmental Costs | 10.78 (0.34) | 9.96 (0.37) | 9.16 (0.23) | 7.93 | 0.00 |

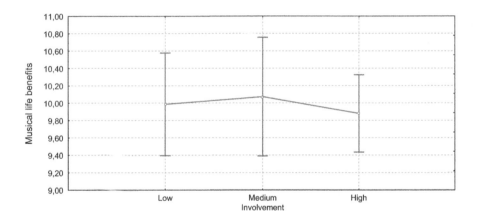

*Figure 3.2* Musical life benefits.

groups and the low involvement group (F: 10.37; p<0.00) (Figure 3.5). In view of these results, the fourth hypothesis can be confirmed. The fifth hypothesis tested the difference between involvement and the perception of 'Social Costs'. The results showed that residents with a high level of involvement perceived the social costs of the festival to be lower than those of medium and low involvement (F: 2.78; p<0.10). The Bonferroni test shows no difference between low and medium festival involvement, while difference does exist between residents with low and high involvement (see Figure 3.6). Finally, the results show the significant differences between the level of involvement and the perception of environmental costs (F: 9.16; p<0.00).

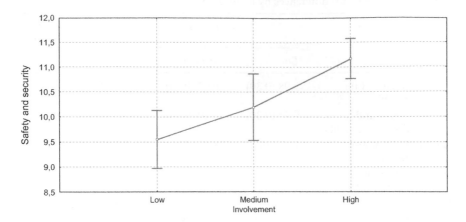

*Figure 3.3* Safety and security benefits.

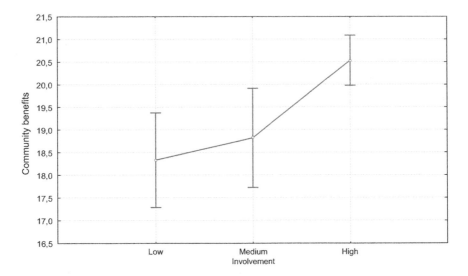

*Figure 3.4* Community benefits.

The latter was significantly higher for residents with a low involvement (Environmental Costs: 10.78) than for those with a high involvement (Environmental Costs: 9.16). The sixth hypothesis can, therefore, be confirmed. The Bonferroni test shows that, as before, the main difference exists between residents with low and medium involvement and those with a high involvement (Figure 3.7).

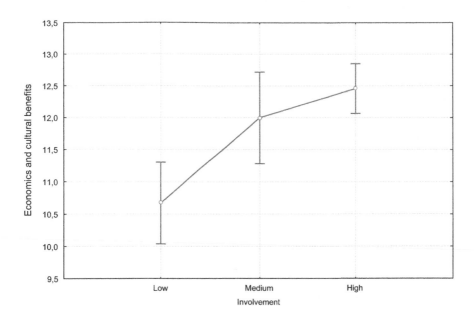

*Figure 3.5* Economic and cultural benefits.

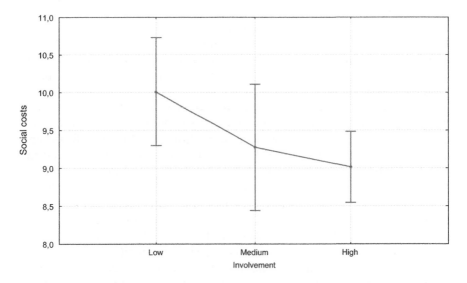

*Figure 3.6* Social costs.

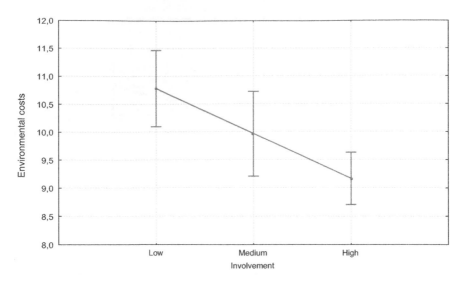

*Figure 3.7* Environmental costs.

## EXIT'S impact on residents of Novi Sad

This study explored the relationship between residents' involvement with the EXIT festival and their perception of the social benefits and costs that the festival has had on the host community. The explorative and confirmatory factor analyzes were used to reveal the underlying structure of the festival's social impacts. Multivariate analysis was then used to test the difference between resident involvement and their perception of the festival's impacts on the host community of Novi Sad.

The moderation effect of resident involvement was confirmed in five of the six factors that represented social benefits and costs of the EXIT festival on the hosting community. Resident perception of 'Musical Life Benefits', describing locals' attitudes towards the organization of the festival and their opinion of the festival's musical offerings, was the only factor to show no difference across the three involvement groups. This may imply that the regional festival organizers acknowledged the community values and the importance of using honesty, responsibility, and cooperation when making choices for the conduct of their event, in line with Derrett's (2003) findings. Festival organizers can also increase local community involvement by extending the programme of the festival. Offerings such as exhibitions, street celebrations and special interest events create an opportunity for everyone in the local community. Traditional engagement with the cultural and natural heritage and business community are significant elements of the

EXIT festival that provide the ground for diverse cultural events, celebrations, and exhibition offerings.

The aspect of resident safety and security during the festival was perceived differently by those who attended the festival and those who did not. Particularly, the 'Safety and Security' benefits were perceived more positively by residents with a high involvement than those with a medium or low involvement. Gursoy and Kendall (2006) argue that community support for a festival is affected directly and/or indirectly by the level of community safety concern. Derrett (2003, p.55) suggests that organization of a community safety committee, involving resident volunteers to seek solutions of a 'local nature through strategic partnerships, rebranding the town, and generating street entertainment', can provide residents with an overall view of their community. They can then be more willing to contribute to the solution of community problems.

Residents' perception of 'Community Benefits', representing positive recognition for hosting the festival, national pride, and the enhanced identity of the local community, differs significantly between residents with a low and high festival involvement. Duffy and Mair (2018) argue that a community's sense of image, pride, relationships, and networking, stems from a shared vision of a healthy community. The healthy community involves working together on community issues and problem-solving. Festivals can provide an opportunity for community benefits offerings such as workshops, skills development workshops, dreaming places, graffiti walls, and similar (Derrett, 2003).

Economic and cultural benefits, representing an opportunity for residents to learn new things and cultures, to have multicultural experiences during the festival, and to earn additional income, is moderated by locals' involvement with the festival. Particularly, residents with high and medium involvement tend to perceive more opportunities to prosper economically from the festival than those with a low involvement. Similarly, residents who are involved in the festival value the opportunity to meet people from other countries, and to learn about other cultures and languages more than those who are not involved. In line with this result, Gursoy and Kendall (2006) show that community support is impacted by the level of perceived opportunity for community prosperity, but also community attachment and identity. Ulrich (1998) also adds that festivals help create communities of values, the values residents recognize in the feelings of ownership and belonging, by strengthening distinct identities of their own.

Duffy and Mair (2018) argue that festivals, through their embodied participants, can facilitate feelings of inclusion in a community. The findings from their study demonstrate that local community events can indeed tell stories that describe the community, referring to who they are and what they are about. Sound, vision, and the festival ambience emerged as elements of key importance. This involves enhancing national pride and community belonging, especially when there is music by local musicians—someone that a community can identify with. Festival ambience, on the other hand, represents the communities' cultural and natural heritage—referring to, in the case of EXIT, the fortress, rivers, and surrounding mountains that the community also takes pride in (these are also subsequent tourism features).

The results showed that residents with high involvement, perceived 'Social Costs' of the festival to be lower than those with medium and low involvement. Similarly, Shanka and Taylor (2004) found that repeat festival attendees had more positive attitudes towards the festival and its impact than did first-time attendees. The literature indicates that like any other type of (tourism) development, festivals generate crowds in streets and public places which affects the privacy and normal (everyday) routines of residents (see Tosun, 2002).

Practical implications suggest that festival organizers dedicated to minimizing the costs of the event and maximizing the place and community benefits should strive to engage with residents with lower and medium involvement to understand the ways in which the festival is negatively impacting upon community life. Woosnam et al. (2016) suggest this could be done through broad community consultation (in the form of town hall meetings or resident surveys), or through other means of communication (such as requesting feedback via social media to start a discussion online). Involving residents (including first-time visitors and repeat visitors, as well as those residents who are not involved in the festival) is important to ensure that a balanced understanding of impacts is achieved. Consulting these different groups of individuals may provide a better insight into the costs associated with the festival.

The results show significant difference between the level of involvement and the perception of environmental costs. The latter was significantly higher for residents with a low involvement (Environmental Costs: 10.78) than for those with high involvement. According to Deery and Jago (2010) residents are willing to accept short-term irritation (such as traffic, parking problems, noise, littering) as they are aware of the numerous benefits which festivals generate. However, increased crime during the festival over the long term can significantly decrease resident support for the festival and can result in a wider negative image of the destination (Deery & Jago, 2010), as well as impacting upon community wellbeing and quality of life.

To enhance the future sustainability of the festival and community support, festival management and local authorities need to acknowledge residents' opinions of environmental costs. Specifically, residents who have never visited the festival should be targeted by administrators through broad community consultation before, during, and after the festival, as they perceived environmental costs to be higher. In this context, festival management can follow the practice of the best environmentally friendly festivals around the globe (Business Destination, 2018), but also implement their own projects/strategies developed in collaboration with community representatives (e.g. renewable energy projects, waste management, noise management, tree planting, supporting educational programmes, school and playground adaptations). Residents with high levels of involvement can be useful in directly managing the environmental costs of the festival and in promoting the environmentally friendly activities of the festival organizers. In this context, they can be involved on many levels, including volunteering in the implementation of the festival's eco-friendly projects in the community, or by organizing workshops with festival administrators on the topic of festival impacts.

## Concluding remarks

As addressed in the previous section, if the benefits and costs of the festival are identified, then actions can be taken by festival managers and local authorities to enhance the positive and reduce the negative aspects of hosting the festival. Festival managers must acknowledge the opinions of host community members with both low and high involvement to be sure that all perspectives are considered.

Small (2007) and Woosnam et al. (2013) note that within any given community, residents will perceive the same festival impact in different ways based on their socio-demographic classification and previous festival attendance. Therefore, future research would need to examine whether differences exist between different groups of residents according to their socio-demographic variables, so to maximize understanding of the impact of the EXIT festival on the place (Novi Sad) and society (local community residents). Moreover, perceptions of impacts as well as the festival itself change over time. Hence, this and similar studies on festival impacts should be conducted on a regular basis, as community attitudes as well as consumer demands change.

## References

Aquilino, L., Armenski, T., & Wise, N. (2018). Assessing the competitiveness of Matera and the Basilicata Region (Italy) ahead of the 2019 European capital of culture. *Tourism and Hospitality Research*. doi:10.1177/1467358418787360.

Arcodia, C., & Whitford, M. (2007). Festival attendance and the development of social capital. *Journal of Convention and Event Tourism, 8* (2), 1–18.

Bagiran, D., & Kurgun, H. (2016). A research on social impacts of the Foça Rock Festival: The validity of the Festival Social Impact Attitude Scale. *Current Issues in Tourism, 19* (9), 930–948.

Bimonte, S., & Punzo, L.F. (2016). Tourist development and host-guest interaction: An economic exchange theory. *Annals of Tourism Research, 58*, 128–139.

Blunch, J.N. (2010). *Introduction to structural modelling using SPSS and AMOS*. London: SAGE.

Business Destination (2018). Available at: www.businessdestinations.com/destinations/the-10-best-environmentally-friendly-festivals/. Accessed on August 20, 2018.

Carneiro, M.J., Eusébio, C., & Caldeira, A. (2018). The influence of social contact in residents' perceptions of the tourism impact on their quality of life: A structural equation model. *Journal of Quality Assurance in Hospitality & Tourism, 19* (1), 1–30.

Chang, W., & Yuan, J. (2011). A taste of tourism: Visitors' motivations to attend a food festival. *Event Management, 15* (1), 13–23.

Deery, M., Jago, L., & Fredline, L. (2012). Rethinking social impacts of tourism research: A new research agenda. *Tourism Management, 33* (1), 64–73.

Deery, M., & Jago, L. (2010). Social impacts of events and the role of anti-social behaviour. *International Journal of Event and Festival Management, 1* (1), 8–28.

Delamere, T.A., Wankel, L.M., & Hinch, T.D. (2001). Development of a scale to measure resident attitudes toward the social impacts of community festivals, Part I: Item generation and purification of the measure. *Event Management, 7* (1), 11–24.

Delamere, T.A. (2001). Development of a scale to measure resident attitudes toward the social impacts of community festivals, Part II: Verification of the scale. *Event Management, 7* (1), 25–38.

Derrett, R. (2003). Making sense of how festivals demonstrate a community's sense of place. *Event Management, 8* (1), 49–58.

Dragićević, V., Bole, D., Bučić, A., & Prodanović, A. (2015). European capital of culture: Residents perception of social benefits and costs-Maribor 2012 case study. *Acta GeographicaSlovenica, 55* (2), 283–302.

Duffy, M., & Mair, J. (2018). Engaging the senses to explore community events. *Event Management, 22* (1), 49–63.

Dwyer, L., Mellor, R., Mistilis, N., & Mules, T. (2000). A framework for assessing 'tangible' and 'intangible' impacts of events and conventions. *Event Management, 6* (3), 175–189.

Eusébio, C., Carneiro, M.J., & Caldeira, A. (2016). A structural equation model of tourism activities, social interaction and the impact of tourism on youth tourists' QOL. *International Journal of Tourism Policy, 6* (2), 85–108.

Fredline, L., Jago, L., & Deery, M. (2003). The development of a generic scale to measure the social impacts of events. *Event Management, 8* (1), 23–37.

Getz, D., & Page, S.J. (2016). Progress and prospects for event tourism research. *Tourism Management, 52*, 593–631.

Gursoy, D., & Kendall, K.W. (2006). Hosting mega events: Modeling locals' support. *Annals of Tourism Research, 33* (3), 603–623.

Gursoy, D., Kim, K., & Uysal, M. (2004). Perceived impacts of festivals and special events by organizers: An extension and validation. *Tourism Management, 25*, 171–182.

Kim, S.S., & Petrick, J.F. (2005). Residents' perceptions on impacts of the FIFA 2002 World Cup: The case of Seoul as a host city. *Tourism Management, 26* (1), 25–38.

Kim, Y.H., Duncan, J., & Chung, B.W. (2015). Involvement, satisfaction, perceived value, and revisit intention: A case study of a food festival. *Journal of Culinary Science & Technology, 13* (2), 133–158.

Lee, H., Hwang, H., & Shim, C. (2017). Experiential festival attributes, perceived value, satisfaction, and behavioral intention for Korean festivalgoers. *Tourism and Hospitality Research.* doi:10.1177/1467358417738308.

Lee, J., & Kyle, G. (2014). Segmenting festival visitors using psychological commitment. *Journal of Travel Research, 53* (5), 656–669.

Lee, J., Kyle, G., & Scott, D. (2012). The mediating effect of place attachment on the relationship between festival satisfaction and loyalty to the festival hosting destination. *Journal of Travel Research, 51* (6), 754–767.

Pavluković, V., Armenski, T., & Alcantara-Pilar, J.M. (2017). Social impacts of music festivals: Does culture impact locals' attitude toward events in Serbia and Hungary?. *Tourism Management, 63*, 42–53.

Reid, S. (2007). Identifying social consequences of rural events. *Event Management, 11*, 89–98.

Richards, G., & Wilson, J. (2004). The Impact of cultural events on city image: Rotterdam, Cultural 762 Capital of Europe 2001. *Urban Studies, 41* (10), 1931–1951.

Robertson, M., Rogers, P., & Leask, A. (2009). Progressing socio-cultural impact evaluation for festivals. *Journal of Policy Research in Tourism, Leisure and Events, 1* (2), 156–169.

Rollins, R., & Delamere, T. (2007). Measuring the social impact of festivals. *Annals of Tourism Research, 34* (3), 805–808.

Savinovic, A., Kim, S., & Long, P. (2012). Audience members' motivation, satisfaction, and intention to re-visit an ethnic minority cultural festival. *Journal of Travel & Tourism Marketing, 29* (7), 682–694.

Shanka, T., & Taylor, R. (2004). Discriminating factors of first-time and repeat visitors to wine festivals. *Current Issues in Tourism, 7* (2), 134–145.

Small, K. (2007). Social dimensions of community festivals: An application of factor analysis in the development of the Social Impact Perception (SIP) scale. *Event Management, 11*, 45–55.

Small, K., & Edwards, D. (2003). Evaluating the sociocultural impacts of a festival on a host community: A case study of the Australian festival of the book. In T. Griffin & R. Harris (Eds.), *Proceedings of the 9th annual conference of the Asia Pacific Tourism Association* (580–593). Sydney, Australia.

Small, K., Edwards, D., & Sheridan, L. (2005). A flexible framework for evaluating the socio-cultural impacts of a (small) festival. *International Journal of Event Management Research, 1* (1), 66–77.

Tosun, C. (2002). Host perceptions of impacts: A comparative tourism study. *Annals of Tourism Research, 29* (1), 231–253.

Ulrich, D. (1998). Six practices for creating communities of value, not proximity. In F. Hesselbein, M. Goldsmith, R. Beckhard, & R.F. Schubert (Eds.), *The community of the future* (155–166). San Francisco, CA: Jossey-Bass Publishers.

van den Berg, M. (2012). Femininity as a city marketing strategy: Gender bending Rotterdam. *Urban Studies, 49* (1), 153–168.

Van Winkle, M.C., & Woosnam, M.K. (2014). Sense of community and perceptions of festival social impacts. *International Journal of Event and Festival Management, 5* (1), 22–38.

Wise, N., Flinn, J., & Mulec, I. (2015). Exit Festival: Contesting political pasts, impacts on youth culture and regenerating the image of Serbia and Novi Sad. In T. Pernecky & O. Moufakkir (Eds.), *Ideological, social and cultural aspects of events* (60–73). Wallingford, UK: CABI.

Wise, N., & Harris, J. (2016). Community, identity and contested notions of place: A study of Haitian recreational soccer players in the Dominican Republic. *Soccer & Society, 17* (4), 610–627.

Wise, N., & Mulec, I. (2015). Aesthetic awareness and spectacle: Communicated images of Novi Sad, the Exit Festival and the event venue Petrovaradin Fortress. *Tourism Review International, 19* (4), 193–205.

Wise, N., Mulec, I., & Armenski, T. (2017). Towards a new local tourism economy: Understanding sense of community, social impacts and potential enterprise opportunities in Podgrađe Bač, Vojvodina, Serbia. *Local Economy, 32* (7), 656–677.

Wise, N., & Perić, M. (2017). Sports tourism, regeneration and social impacts: New opportunities and directions for research, the case of Medulin, Croatia. In N. Bellini & C. Pasquinelli (Eds.), *Tourism in the city: Towards and integrative agenda on urban tourism* (311–320). Berlin: Springer Vieweg.

Wood, E.H. (2017). The value of events and festivals in the age of austerity. In E. Lundberg, J. Armbrecht, T.D. Andersson, & D. Getz (Eds.), *The value of events* (10–35). London: Routledge.

Wood, E.H. (2005). Measuring the economic and social impacts of local authority events. *International Journal of Public Sector Management, 18* (1), 37–53.

Woosnam, K., Van Winkle, C., & An, S. (2013). Confirming the festival social impact attitude scale in the context of a rural Texas cultural festival. *Event Management, 17*, 257–270.

Woosnam, K.M., Jiang, J., Van Winkle, C.M., Kim, H., & Maruyama, N. (2016). Explaining festival impacts on a hosting community through motivations to attend. *Event Management, 20* (1), 11–25.

Yolal, M., Woo, E., Cetinel, F., & Uysal, M. (2012). Comparative research of motivations across different festival products. *International Journal of Event and Festival Management, 3* (1), 66–80.

# 4 The spaces, places, and landscapes of Brazil's Carnival

## Racialized geographies and multiscale perspectives of Rio de Janeiro and Porto Alegre

*Maurício Polidoro*

### Introduction

In February 1932, Rio de Janeiro, then the capital of Brazil, threw a masquerade ball to impose the new post-colonial cultural reality. Using the catchphrase *Masquerade Ball*, as held in Europe during Carnival, the event was an attempt to establish new relations with the metropolis, which sought to distance itself from the typical colonial carnival celebrations named *Entrudo*, following the new airs of modernity that spread across the northern hemisphere during the time. The *Entrudo* was an annual event held during Easter among slaves and the poorer urban classes, in a country whose colonization was based on Jesuit Christianization. The event included using bowls to throw lemon-scented water and sand on other participants. Despite attempts at prohibiting this practice in Rio de Janeiro in 1604 due to its inherently violent nature, it lasted until 1854, when police repression finally put an end to the practice in response to water being swapped for a mixture of urine and faeces. The elite had the custom of performing this in a domestic environment, as depicted in the English painter Augustus Earle's *Carnival Scene* in 1822. The more affluent watched the event from a higher level, with their homes rising above the street, where water balloons were thrown at those passing below.

The end of the *Entrudo* enabled a new regime of social events to emerge. The Masquerade Ball thus introduces another way of living in the city, a kind of urbanity foretold by European culture, whose architectural and urban implications reached their climax at the turn of the century with a hygienist urban plan. The end of slavery and the lack of public policies for racial integration called for private places to celebrate Carnival, so Rio de Janeiro's City Theatre (Teatro Municipal) was the chosen place. The absence of black people in the events did not seem to bother the oligarchy, who appropriated some African-Brazilian cultural symbols (such as Samba and the *umbanda* beat) and who were constantly alerted by perplexed authors such as Lima Barreto, Jean-Paul Sartre, and Simone de Beauvoir about the absence of former slaves and their descendants. In 1960 de Beauvoir famously questioned: where are the blacks? (which echoes hauntingly to this day).

After the end of the slave-trade economy in 1888, Brazil removed blacks from certain spaces. Despite the abolition of slavery, the cultural heritage of the Big House (the land owner's residence) and Slave Quarters, which defined housing structures at the time, were gradually adapted to post-colonial architecture. The Slave Quarters, attached to the Big House, became the quarters of a recurring character among Brazilian middle and high classes—the housemaid—and, by extension, tenements (*cortiços*) and *favelas* as family units for blacks and the poor. Degrading work relations became the only moment of contact between whites and blacks in a so-called "racial democracy" (i.e. a regime of harmonious coexistence between the races, where black submission to white supremacy was deemed *normal*).

This normalization of blacks as subordinates is supposedly lessened during Carnival. Despite Brazil never having enacted racist laws such as Jim Crow in the United States and Apartheid in South Africa, the subtlety of racial relations have achieved a resounding perversity in the national socio-spatial configuration (Nascimento, 2017; Skidmore, 2012). One of the numerous events that depict this situation occurred 16 years after the Masquerade Ball, in the same theatre. The *Anjo Negro* play, by novelist Nelson Rodrigues, included a white actor playing the part of the black protagonist after a request by the theatre's cultural commission. Despite the prevalence of non-whites in the Brazilian capital (over 40% of its inhabitants were slaves at the end of the 19th century) and theatre companies formed by blacks, the lack of black actors with enough talent to take the stage in the emerging national theatre culture was used as justification for the choice of a white actor with a blackened face.

In 2017, in the north-eastern state of Pernambuco (where 62% of the population are black) a costume contest by an advertising agency awarded trip tickets to two white men for their simulation of blackface and large genitalia as a reference to the well-endowed black man stereotype (Ribeiro, 2017). In the same year, a morning TV programme from a major media outlet (TV Globo) started a culinary segment in which a white man dressed as a black woman in reference to the *Negra Maluca* (a crazy black woman) character. On the same channel, one of their most important news anchors was fired after appearing on tape making racist remarks (Folha de São Paulo, 2017). At the Medicine University of São Paulo, students wore blackface as proof of "racial integration" at the institution. These typical Brazilian events are masked by supposed racial democracy and are a way of legitimizing racism and white supremacy as essential and basic parts of social relations (Santos, 2015).

Given the context presented, this chapter seeks to debate Carnival, the main Brazilian event, from a racial perspective. In addition, it names a reality in which there is an intersection of the racial perspective with discussions on gender identity, sexuality and social class, as discussed in the literature (see Bairros, 1995; Crenshaw, 2002; Davis, 2016; Ribeiro, 2017). In this chapter, it is argued that *place* and *landscape* cannot be conceived as "natural" (i.e.

divorced from their racial content). As stated by Kobayashi & Peake (2000) seeing racism as an active process in contemporary society implies observing how *whiteness* and *color-blind racism* act as a dominant, normative, and ordinary power that controls bodies, values, and institutions, and particularly space as a segregated social landscape. Normalizing the racial democracy discourse is a powerful way of supporting the minimization of current racial, gender, and sexual differences. It is therefore essential to better comprehend *place* and *landscape* as parts of a racialized spatial whole.

Traditional divisions between public and private, rich and poor, natural and anthropized, hide realities that can only be unveiled by close observation of their multiscale complexities. No trustworthy analysis is possible in countries colonized by white supremacy without acknowledging racialized socio-spatial development. This must necessarily point to a rediscovery of traditional geographic concepts: space, place, and landscape. It is from within this theoretical framework that this chapter aims to debate how Carnival, Brazil's hallmark event, interacts with spaces, places, and landscapes that establish atypical socio-racial relations which are nevertheless widely supported by the development of racial capitalism.

## Capitalism and racial geographies in Brazil

Harvey (2003) advocates the idea that primitive accumulation is a continuous process which is inherent to the development of the capitalist system. In turn, Lencioni (2012) sees primitive accumulation (production of capital) as a first step and accumulation by dispossession as a second step. Dispossession is defined as the act of using fraud or violence to deprive someone of something they own or to which they have the right. Thus, racial capitalism can be conceived as a system whose principles are based on violence, racism, colonialism, and imperialism. According to Clarno (2017), the violence of racial capitalism is related to the exploitation of labor via slavery, servitude, peonage, or exploitation via low wages, which are not considered aberrations, but integrative resources that are inherent to the capitalist mode of production. Bonds (2018) notes that the uneven development of places is simultaneously a racialized process of (de)valorization and (dis)accumulation that relies upon legal and extra-legal racialized violence. Interpreting colonial Brazil is only possible when done historically, by observing the limits of imperialism and the global definitions of labor divisions, in which race and gender play important roles (see Lewis, 2018).

Racial thinking, based on positivist and Darwinian theories, was introduced in Brazil starting in 1870 (18 years before the end of slavery). At that moment, due to the influence of European theories, the idea of a supposed hierarchy of species, in which the physical inferiority of the continent and the frailty of its population were irrefutable, was predominant. For geographers, the theory of environmental determinism by German geographer Friedrich Rätzel collaborated with racist imperialist projects. Maps such as the world map of human races and the actions of geographic determinism (Haeckel, 1884) turned geography into a definitive tool for legitimizing, persuading, and maintaining the rhetoric behind colonial practices. In Brazil, at the end of the 19th century, national museums were created as part of a movement to encompass the so-called social evolutionists and scientists (Schwarcz, 1993). By turning the "typical Brazilian man" into an object of study, concepts and examples of aspects of human inferiority started to be formulated, and whitening was seen as a form of racial cleansing.

The abolition of slavery strengthened the idea of black degeneration and of the misfortune caused by racial miscegenation in Brazil. Popular thinking thus saw the possibility of national development as even more distant, since the country would be destined to failure due to its racial miscegenation. Eugenics had an important role in this process and, through phrenology techniques and police repression, enabled the creation of legal institutions which criminalized non-whites. Blacks were doomed to be imprisoned. In the 20th century, post-colonialism can be seen in Brazil in the form of land expropriation or financial and institutional limitations of access forged by a racialized state. This dynamic of landscape change through the highly exclusionary and segregated process of urbanization or the division of rural lands by white hegemonic groups, is associated in racial capitalism to settler colonialism (Clarno, 2017). Slaves were frequent victims of sexual violence by landowners and formed complex family scenarios in the Big House, which is reflected mainly by the figures of the *mulato* and *mulata* (a man or woman of mixed white and black origin). In contrast to Australia and Canada, the post-colonization period of Brazil was already composed by a mixed and black landscape. According to Schwarcz (1993), in the 1930s, Bahia, Rio de Janeiro, and São Paulo enacted campaigns for "racial maintenance" and attempts at sterilizing "sick groups" (i.e. black and mixed people).

Racial debates were therefore ignored due to the impossibility of whitening and homogenizing the country, and approaching the topic in Brazil is still highly controversial (Schwarcz, 1993). Despite being partially refuted today, racial democracy as a harmonious social relation in Brazil hides the violence, socio-spatial segregation, and exploitation of labor in a context of imperialism and reigning colonialism in diverse areas of academia and media (Schwarcz, 1993). It is necessary to uncover the historically built racial geographies of the country and discover how they articulate in understanding space, places, landscapes, and events in Brazil to proceed with a more attentive and reliable reading of reality to build a less racist society.

Historical racial segregation is incorporated today just as before. According to Santos (2002), cities that follow the modern standard superpose, juxtapose, and oppose bright spaces (occupied by the rich) and opaque spaces (occupied by the poor). Security plays a fundamental role in maintaining these boundaries, normalizing and moulding places and landscapes. For instance, the *landscape* is a part of the territorial configuration which is visible (Santos, 2002) and reflects the arrangement of objects in a transtemporal manner (i.e. from past and present). For Wise (2018), *place* is a part of space in which the complementary notions of community and identity converge, where social interactions occur and where daily experiences happen (see also Wise, 2015; Wise & Harris, 2016). Tuan (1977) explains how place in modern society is relatively stable and relates to the routines of certain social groups. For Tuan (1977), *place* is a static world of organized meanings. In the context of a racialized society, where white supremacy permeates spatial and geo-institutional configurations, it is possible to understand *place* and *landscape* as reflections of this process. In the context of a racialized geography, how does racial integration happen *within* places? As an important event which shapes and provides content to places and landscapes, would Brazil's Carnival be a possible way of achieving racial integration?

During part of the 19th century, slaves dominated street trade. In a certain way, this enabled them to exert some kind of hegemony over those spaces. While their owners rested during the hottest hours of the day, slaves worked and led social lives on the streets, to the point of foreigners believing they had arrived in Africa instead of Brazil. Instead of passive victims of the slavery process, slaves actively participated in the formation of their own culture. The manifestations of this culture mark black contribution to Carnival in Rio de Janeiro (Ferreira, 2005).

## Places and landscapes of the Brazilian Carnival

The Brazilian Carnival has a myriad of meanings and definitions, particularly intensity and importance, to the point of being internationally defined as a synonym of its own country and nationally renowned as its most important festivity (Martone, 2016). Despite analyzes about its touristic and economic impact, the event has consolidated international interest surrounding the city of Rio de Janeiro and, consequently, other destinations in the country for the first few months in the year. Transportation and national integration issues are still noted when referring to surrounding events in Brazil (see Wise, 2018), and there is still a need to consider and evaluate the social impact of events in Brazil (see Coakley & Souza, 2013; Curi et al., 2011; Darnell, 2012; Wise & Hall, 2017) and local cultural meanings.

Considering the significance of Samba in Brazil to place and staged cultural landscapes, there is no silence able to resist Samba, particularly during the days of Carnival. It is currently considered a national icon but finds its origins in folk roots. Indeed, cultural heritages are hybrid and complex processes which rebuild and rearrange various signs of identification (Canclini, 2002). But it is undeniable that the cultural richness of Samba is a result of African-Brazilian expression and heritage, bestowed by blacks and *mulatos* from *favelas* in Rio de Janeiro (Bark et al., 2001). Since the populist dictatorship of Getúlio Vargas (1930–1945), Samba has become the mouthpiece both of governmental auspices of the time, and of criticisms and sarcastic remarks regarding the national reality.

After the prohibition of the *Entrudo* in Rio de Janeiro, Carnival became a turning point event for the arrival of modernity. Executing master plans and large reforms on urban areas managed by important foreign city planners such as Le Corbusier, gave these cities a *nearly industrialized* urban aspect marked by the colonial-tropical ambiguity and a strong European influence. In Rio de Janeiro, the occupation of central areas and side lanes of main avenues by the least affluent provided a favorable scenario for Afro-Brazilian cultural manifestations by people with a lower income, giving rise to Carnival blocks. The same happened in Porto Alegre where Carnival was organized by former slaves and free blacks in areas that underwent an intense social cleansing process (also including spaces for cross-dressers). Meanwhile, the wealthier classes paraded with the few convertibles that shared the main streets of Brazilian state capitals with trams and animal-powered transportation methods at the start of the 20th century.

In Rio de Janeiro, the Masquerade Ball at the city theatre can be used as a geographic reference to analyze what was happening only 900m away, at Largo do Rossio (now Praça Tiradentes). As a place for illegal homosexual encounters, Carnival provided the possibility of interacting with the street festivities on the nearby avenue to homosexuals whose gender performativity did not comply with the standards of the time. In 1934, Dictator Getúlio Vargas created the Tourism Commission (the same year the Union of Samba Schools was established). The federal district government then started to direct public resources specifically to Samba school competitions, in the larger context of the coup's increasing populism, and Carnival songs (*marchas*) sought to paint Brazil as desired by the current political regime. This scenario also demonstrates a typically Brazilian ambiguity: although Vargas had Nazi-fascist tendencies, as shown by historical records of his approximation with Adolf Hitler as well as the constant practices of torture and persecution of minorities for over a decade (De Oliveira, 2008), Carnival consisted of three days in which gender subversion and inter-racial coexistence were allowed.

Historically, Carnival has forged the image of Brazil as a paradise for sexual outcasts and transgressors of traditional gender roles (Green, 2000). Homosexuality and the racial tone of Carnival songs directly explore these themes and reinforce Brazilian racial ambiguity. In the 1950s, a song composed by João Roberto Kelly, "Maria Sapatão" (referring to a homosexual woman), is still sung to this day in Carnival events:

> Mary the dyke, dyke, dyke
> During the day she is Mary, at night she is John
> Being a dyke is in fashion
> The world applauds

> It's amazing, a success
> In Brazil and abroad.

The same composer wrote another Carnival hit, "Mulata Bossa Nova", which ambiguously associates the *mulata bossa nova* to a *"doll"* (a term which can be used to refer to cross-dressers) who *"snubs blonds and brunettes in Brasil"*.

Another well-known Brazilian Carnival song titled "Mulata" refers to the expression attributed to enslaved women of the colonial period who mothered children from systematic rapes by landowners and also refers, in its etymology, to the crossing of species of animals: donkeys with mares or horses with donkeys (Ribeiro, 2017). The lyrics of this Carnival song are as follows:

> Your hair does not deny it, mulata
> Because your colour is mulata
> But since I can't have your colour, mulata
> Mulata, I want your love
> You have a Brazilian taste
> Your soul is indigo
> Mulata, little mulata, my love
> I was named your intervening lieutenant
> When you came to the Land, my dear
> Portugal declared war
> Competition was colossal
> Vasco da Gama against the naval brigade.

The song states that the *mulata*, does not carry a disease (related to her phenotype) and, in this sense, is the source of attraction for an army of men and is apt for intervention.

Carnival is an important event in Brazil, as this annual event redefines places and landscapes throughout the country following a trend of hyper-sexualisation and racialization, spreading a liberal tone which is supported by discrimination against gender, race, and sexual orientation. A notorious example is the *Globeleza*, a character from the main TV channel in the country, TV Globo (Goldenberg, 2010). Since the end of the 1980s, every February this channel airs a naked black woman covered in glitter dancing Samba as a vignette for the Carnival TV coverage. The black *mulata* woman is a recurring target of racist Carnival songs. In 1985, Luiz Caldas released "Negra de Cabelo Duro" with these lyrics:

> Black woman with the rough hair
> Who does not like to comb it
> When she goes down Baixa do Tubo
> The black man starts to yell

> Look, black woman with the rough hair
> Who does not like to comb it
> The black man starts to yell
> Grab her, grab her
> Black woman with the rough hair
> Which comb is the one that combs you
> Your curly hair
> Will not straighten even with sand
> Take a shower and set it on fire
> Which comb is the one that combs you.

The lyrics refer to a common practice by black women, that of combing their hair with hot combs in order to reduce curls (Gilliam & Gilliam, 1995).

Despite sounding seemingly absurd in the current context, the structural nature of racism has been recognized to the point that the United Nations (2013) put forth a declaration on the matter. The aforementioned examples reverberate the racial capitalism that permeated the national culture and used stereotypes and racist and sexist practices to perpetuate inequality. An advertisement for a beer company that sponsored the 2016 Carnival suggested women should "*Leave your No at home,*" indicating how, to this day, Carnival is a moment in which the negotiation of subjectivities such as race, gender, and sexual orientation falls under the heteronormative model, where white supremacy rules the game.

In this sense, Carnival has become Brazil's hallmark event, with a multiscale repercussion that boosts the economy while also redefining social and racial segregation as a part of social and spatial relations. Even though street Carnival (as it has been historically produced) reached its peak in the latest decade, socioeconomic markers and their intersection with race and sexuality aspects contribute to the largest festivity in Brazil. The next section discusses how Carnival operates inside a panorama of racialized geographies in the southernmost capital of the country, Porto Alegre. In this scale, despite being a part of the national industrial axis, Porto Alegre is moved to the periphery of events held in São Paulo and Rio de Janeiro due to its strictly regional breadth.

## From the centre to the periphery: Carnival in Porto Alegre

During the 20th century, the popular Carnival in Porto Alegre was developed almost exclusively by popular groups and blacks, promoting a long-lasting association of these groups to Samba, its institutions, and their Carnival parades (Duarte, 2013). The events were held every February in area known as African Colony, which nowadays comprises the Cidade Baixa, Azenha, Bom Fim and Rio Branco neighborhoods (see Figure 4.1). It must be noted that, at least until the 1950s (when street Carnival became popular in Porto Alegre), Samba and its festivities were attached to groups of "hoodlums" by the population in general, in a clearly racist allusion to events promoted by the poor.

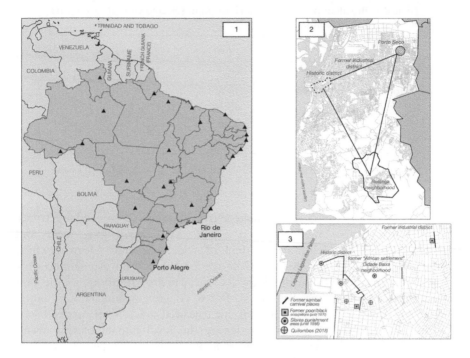

*Figure 4.1* Location of Rio de Janeiro and Porto Alegre (1), Location of Porto Seco, Restinga Neighborhood (former African Settlement) (2) and the African Settlement (3).

Under the strong influence of Rio de Janeiro, the Carnival festivities in Porto Alegre were more reserved and held in segmented clubs, where whites and blacks did not mix. It is important to highlight that Grêmio, the main football team in Porto Alegre, did not allow black players into the team until 1952. The relatively low percentage of non-whites, when compared to the national average and to the main capitals of Brazilian states (see Table 4.1), caused the state of Rio Grande do Sul and its capital to be regarded as the "Brazilian Europe" in the popular imaginary. This assertion is further reinforced by the characteristics that are inherent to a humid subtropical climate, which can only be found in the southern region of the country. On the other hand, the data shown in Table 4.1 reveals that the black population is more spread out on a national scale. Salvador, the first capital of Brazil, in the state of Bahia (northeast) consists of 79.6% blacks, whereas Porto Alegre, the southernmost capital, consists of 79.2% whites. In Porto Alegre, the European-influenced urban reform from the first half of the 20th century, inspired and proposed by Alfred Agache, kick-started the dislodgement of the poor and blacks from central areas.

*Table 4.1* Brazilian population distribution in selected capitals according to race/color, 2010.

| Spatiality | White | Black | Indigenous | Asian |
|---|---|---|---|---|
| Brazil | 47.7 | 50.7 | 0.4 | 1.2 |
| Porto Alegre | 79.2 | 20.4 | 0.2 | 0.2 |
| Rio de Janeiro | 51.1 | 48.1 | 0.1 | 0.7 |
| Salvador | 18.9 | 79.6 | 0.2 | 1.3 |
| São Paulo | 60.6 | 37.2 | 0.1 | 2.1 |

Source: Data Recovery System of the Brazilian Institute of Geography and Statistics (SIDRA/IBGE, 2010).

Until the 1970s, Porto Alegre held Carnival events organized by tribes. Five Carnival tribes used Carnival as a way of criticizing local and national politics. This and the context of widely eugenic reforms (which completely wiped out the African Colony) led the city government to promote a Carnival model inspired by Rio de Janeiro, resulting in the creation of the first Samba School of Porto Alegre: Academia de Samba Praiana in 1960. This Samba School spearheaded a Carnival model based on thematic and allegoric floats, widening the local impact of this event. The first parade following this new Carnival model happened in 1961, reported by the local ZeroHora newspaper. With the financial support of Pepsi-Cola, Academia de Samba Praiana paraded on the main avenues of the city since they were widened as a result of the city's population growth. In the same period, the industry in the capital of Rio Grande do Sul was significantly developed, widening its magnitude and constituting a metropolitan region in 1977.

From 1968–2003, four main avenues were used as the main stage of Carnival in Porto Alegre, but in 2003 the city government installed a Cultural Complex 22km away from the region where the event was previously held. Associations of residents from developing middle-class neighborhoods (Menino Deus, Cidade Baixa, Bom Fim, and Rio Branco) mobilized themselves to pressure Public Power into removing the event from the region. The removal of the mostly black population was accompanied by a broad movement to eliminate spaces historically known for the cultural exchanges which took place inside them. Besides Carnival, bars, clubs, and other public meeting spaces were gradually reduced with the development of real estate speculation and the active colonial police, responsible for ensuring the standardization of privileged places. The distance of the Carnival site in Porto Alegre (which, unlike Rio de Janeiro, was historically promoted and organized by blacks until at least the 1990s) is a good example of how white supremacy articulates capital accumulation strategies and space segregation to shape places and landscapes in the metropolis.

Another striking difference between Carnival in Porto Alegre and in other Brazilian cities is that while "Rio de Janeiro and São Paulo use Carnival to develop tourism and build the image of the city's 'culture', Carnival in Porto Alegre is regarded with little interest by public agencies" (Duarte, 2011). According to a study by Duarte (2011), until 2011, Carnival in Porto Alegre seems to have dedicated efforts to modernize itself in the new location. In other words, the event has been aiming to simulate the Rio de Janeiro model, once again transforming the event into a spectacle through a discourse of professionalization and commercialization. The ranking of Samba Schools (which now total 25 in Porto Alegre) is based on the availability of financial resources (i.e. sponsors who undoubtedly co-participate in the Carnival parades). Thus, Samba Schools with less financial support (reduced marketing resources) depend on building support networks to fulfil their community aspirations. However, aligned to a racist society, the black roots of the event in Porto Alegre are reflected in the "modern" Carnival, following the Rio de Janeiro model, therefore the middle and upper classes are reluctant to participate in this manifestation. This is confirmed by the first ever cancellation of Carnival in Porto Seco, in 2018, justified by a supposed lack of public resources and maintenance of the infrastructure of the venue.

However, the once-banned street Carnival blocks have seen a significant resurgence in several Brazilian cities, as well as in Porto Alegre. In 2018, street Carnival blocks were active for 18 days between January and March in Porto Alegre, funded by the state government of Rio Grande do Sul and by the city government. These neighborhood events, which had been initially dislodged to Porto Seco, were further sponsored by communication companies, large breweries, and private transportation apps. Pharmaceutical and tobacco companies feature on advertisements, especially in private leisure spaces. The new characteristic relies mainly on the distance from the initial ideals behind the city's street Carnival and Samba Schools themselves, eliminating the critical side of Samba and giving way to a myriad of rhythms, from unpretentious Samba to Rio de Janeiro funk. Although beats typical of the Afro-Brazilian *umbanda* religion are still present, strictly Afro-Brazilian blocks dedicated to a political and counter-hegemonic movement in this era of body and event commodification are a minority.

Restinga, a neighborhood 30km from the area formerly known as African Colony, is home to a population dislodged by major housing projects of the 1970s. Here there are two Samba schools dedicated to mobilizing residents of the blackest neighborhood in the capital of Rio Grande do Sul. With a 40% black population (the average for Porto Alegre is 20% and for the state of Rio Grande do Sul is 15%), Estado Maior da Restinga (founded in 1977) and União da Tinga (founded in 1989) mobilize the community in search of financial support and materials to create costumes and floats every year.

Since 1979, Estado Maior da Restinga has paraded 49 times, with six Sambas dedicated to black themes, ranging from Africa to criticism of invading colonists. The same happens at União da Tinga, where, out of 26 parades since 1991, six were dedicated to exploring issues of race, thus proving the Afro-Brazilian tradition of Carnival in Samba schools of Porto Alegre. The fact that the first Samba school was created at the beginning of the process of construction of the neighborhood is an indication that the issue of race permeated that population in a conscious and political way since its beginnings. Carnival, although outside the commercial circuit, constituted itself as a relevant event for the cultural and political manifestation of the periphery of the metropolis and as a challenge to the status quo supported by white supremacy.

## Carnival of ambiguities: contestation and commodification

This chapter presented how the development of racial capitalism produced racialized geographies with direct impacts on the conformation of landscapes, places, and events in Brazil. As an annual hallmark event in Brazil, Carnival was used to exemplify the argument. The spread of the centre–periphery model manifests itself in different scales in Brazil. Rio de Janeiro, the driving force behind national culture, was a proponent of the rules of a commoditized Carnival (i.e. Samba schools and funding provided mainly by private capital). However, this model finds obstacles in Porto Alegre because of the resistance from middle and upper classes towards the "Samba school". The inevitable criticism towards a racialized event such as the Carnival of Porto Alegre found its historic resistance in 2018, where the city government, ruled by a coalition of far-right political parties, cancelled the event, and gave priority to a Carnival organized in street blocks, once prohibited due to their critical and political content. However, the current spatial configuration of social and racial segregation does not seem to bother local politicians like it did before.

Although in 2018 the mayor of Rio de Janeiro, who was elected by a coalition of far-right parties and is a representative of the Neo-Charismatic Universal Church of the Kingdom of God, suggested that Carnival would not be funded, he quickly took back his words and stated that "a person who does not like Samba cannot be a good mayor" (O Globo, 2018) Although the content of Sambas of Rio de Janeiro has changed, now promoting political criticism and moving away from the racist content of decades ago (be it by hypersexualizing black women or discriminating sexual orientation and gender identity minorities), it is difficult to confirm that Carnival is an event of racial integration. The Brazilian trend of *camarotização* (creating separate spaces according to social class, in both public or private places) is at its highest during Carnival when tickets for the Samba schools parade in Rio de Janeiro and São Paulo cost from US$50 to

$7,000. Different national and multinational companies have priority places in the stands that are occupied by the local elites and celebrity guests.

This centre–periphery model is reproduced in different cities. In the case of Porto Alegre, nine Carnival songs in 2018 on the 18 street Carnival blocks focused on criticizing conservative candidates, ministers of the Supreme Court, and racial and sexual intolerance. Funding from city and state governments, as well as the contribution of local entrepreneurs, mildly comforts the population living in the neighborhoods where street Carnival blocks are located (with mostly white residents) and those who live farther away and have the financial conditions to use various private urban mobility options via apps that promote special travel packages during the three days of February. In the periphery, the event is made possible by networks of solidarity and self-funding, where racial criticism is persistent. The unwillingness to allocate a place for Samba school Carnival indicates to some extent that the local government is less concerned with protests from the central region and more with those that echo in the semi-paved and unpaved streets of the territories located behind the remaining mountains in a geology destroyed by accelerated urbanization.

Carnival, although an important moment of counteraction and resistance of minorities, perpetuates the image of Brazil as a country where black skin is stigmatized due to it being directly connected to body and sex. Its historical development still holds important symbols that perpetuate the commodification of bodies and establishes the image of the black woman as the main protagonist. In contrast to the overtly racist, sexist, and sexually intolerant songs of older times, recent political manifestations in Carnival songs still need a longer period of realization, considering that in various capitals throughout Brazil the days dedicated to street Carnival blocks increase significantly every year, in parallel with the disapproval of fiscal austerity policies. However, it is worth remembering that the most distant neighborhoods still lack public support for consolidating their annual leisure moment. Retaking the reading of space, landscapes, and places requires a perspective of racialized geography in which intersectionalities impose themselves in the construction and envisaging of a new space-time, although social class is an important variable.

## References

Bairros, L. (1995). Nossos feminismos revisitados. *Revista Estudos Feministas*, 3(3), 458–463.

Bark, M., T. Escasany, and G. O'Hare. (2001). Samba: A Metaphor for Rio's Favelas? *Cities*, 18(4), 259–270.

Bonds, A. (2018). Race and Ethnicity I: Property, Race, and the Carceral State. *Progress in Human Geography*. DOI: 10.1177/0309132517751297.

Canclini, N.G. (2002). *Consumers and Citizens: Globalization and Multicultural Studies*. Minneapolis: University of Minnesota Press.

Clarno, A. (2017). *Neoliberal Apartheid: Palestine/Israel and South Africa after 1994*. Chicago: University of Chicago Press.

Coakley, J. and D.L. Souza. (2013). Sport Mega-Events: Can Legacies and Development Be Equitable and Sustainable? *Motriz: Revista De Educação Física*, 19, 580–589.

Crenshaw, K. (2002). Documento para o encontro de especialistas em aspectos da discriminação racial relativos ao gênero. *Revista Estudos Feministas*, 10(1), 171–188.

Curi, M., J. Knijnik, and G. Mascarenhas. (2011). The Pan American Games in Rio de Janeiro 2007: Consequences of a Sport Mega-Event on a BRIC Country. *International Review for the Sociology of Sport*, 46, 140–156.

Darnell, S.C. (2012). Olympism in Action, Olympic Hosting and the Politics of 'Sport for Development and Peace': Investigating the Development Discourses of Rio 2016. *Sport in Society*, 15, 869–887.

Davis, A. (2016). *Women, Race and Class*. São Paulo: Boitempo.

De Oliveira, D. (2008). *Os soldados alemães de Vargas*. Curitiba, Paraná: Jurssuá Editora.

Duarte, U.C. (2011). *O carnaval espetáculo no Sul do Brasil: Uma etnografia da cultura carnavalesca nas construções das identidades e nas transformações da festa em Porto Alegre e Uruguaiana*. Porto Alegre: Universidade Federal do Rio Grande do Sul (UFRGS).

Duarte, U.C. (2013). A cultura carnavalesca em Porto Alegre: O espetáculo, a retória e a organização da festa. *O&S – Salvador*, 20(64), 165–182.

Ferreira, F. (2005). *Inventando Carnavais: O surgimento do carnaval carioca no século XIX e outras questões carnavalescas*. Rio de Janeiro: Editora UFRJ.

Folha de São Paulo. (2017). Globo TV Channel Dismisses William Waack after Racism Accusation. September 11, 2017.

Gilliam, A. and O. Gilliam. (1995). Negociando a subjetividade de mulata no Brasil. *Revista De Estudos Feministas*, 2(95), 525–543.

Goldenberg, M. (2010). The Body as Capital. Understanding Brazilian Culture. *VIBRANT – Vibrant Virtual Brazilian Anthropology*, 7(1), 220–238.

Green, D. (2000). *Beyond Carnival*. São Paulo: Editora da UNESP.

Haeckel, E. (1884). *Historie de la création des êtres organisés d'aprés de lois naturelles*. Paris: C. Reiwald Editeurs.

Harvey, D. (2003). *New Imperialism*. Oxford: Oxford University Press.

Kobayashi, A. and L. Peake. (2000). Racism out of Place: Thoughts on Whiteness and an Antiracist Geography in the New Millennium. *Annals of the Association of American Geographer*, 90(2), 392–403.

Lencioni, S. (2012). Acumulação primitiva: Um processo atuante na sociedade contemporânea. Confins (Paris). *Número* 14. Available from: https://journals.openedition.org/confins/7424?lang=pt.

Lewis, J.S. (2018). The Land Question. In: Global Territories, transnational histories. Institute on Inequality and Democracy. UCLA Luskin. Available from: https://challengeinequality.luskin.ucla.edu/wp-content/uploads/sites/4/2018/04/Race-and-Capitalism-digital.pdf [Accessed April 19, 2018].

Martone, D. (2016). The Carnival 2016. *Streetnotes*, 25(1), 64–85.

Nascimento, A. (2017). *O genocídio do negro brasileiro: Processo de um racismo mascarado*. São Paulo: Perspectiva.

O Globo. (2018). Crivella canta: "Quem não gosta de samba, bom prefeito não é". Available from: https://oglobo.globo.com/rio/crivella-canta-quem-nao-gosta-de-samba-bom-prefeito-nao-veja-video-1-22277489 [Accessed April 20, 2018].

Ribeiro, D. (2017). *O que é lugar de fala?* Belo Horizonte: Letramento.

Santos, J.R. (2015). *Saber do negro*. Rio de Janeiro: Pallas.

Santos, M. (2002). *A natureza do espaço. Técnica e tempo. Razão e emoção*. São Paulo: Editora da Universidade de São Paulo.

Schwarcz, L.M. (1993). *O Espetáculo das Raças – Cientistas, instituições e a questão racial no Brasil 1870–1930*. São Paulo: Companhia das Letras.

SIDRA/IBGE. (2010). Sistema de Recuperação de Dados do Instituto Brasileiro de Geografia e Estatística – Tabela 3145. Available from: https://sidra.ibge.gov.br/tabela/3145 [Accessed April 24, 2018].

Skidmore, T.E. (2012). *Black into White: Race and Nationality in Brazilian Thought*. São Paulo: Companhia das Letras.

Tuan, Y.-F. (1977). *Space and Place: The Perspective of Experience*. Minneapolis: University of Minnesota Press.

United Nations. (2013). Grupo de Trabalho da ONU sobre Afrodescendentes divulga comunicado final sobre visita ao Brasil. Available from: https://nacoesunidas.org/grupo-de-trabalho-da-onu-sobre-afrodescendentes-divulga-comunicado-final [Accessed April 21, 2018].

Wise, N. (2015). Placing Sense of Community. *Journal of Community Psychology*, 43(7), 920–929.

Wise, N. (2018). Towards a More Enabling Representation: Framing an Emergent Conceptual Approach to Measure Social Conditions Following Mega-Event Transformation in Manaus, Brazil. *Bulletin of Latin American Research*. Available from: https://onlinelibrary.wiley.com/doi/10.1111/blar.12775.

Wise, N. and G. Hall. (2017). Transforming Brazil: Sporting Mega-Events, Tourism, Geography and the Need for Sustainable Regeneration in Host Cities. In *Sport, Events, Tourism and Regeneration*, edited by N. Wise and J. Harris, 24–39. London: Routledge.

Wise, N. and J. Harris. (2016). Community, Identity and Contested Notions of Place: A Study of Haitian Recreational Soccer Players in the Dominican Republic. *Soccer & Society*, 17(4), 610–627.

# 5 Renewing Rijeka for 2020

## Managing placemaking, regeneration, and community participation

*Nicholas Wise, Jelena Đurkin, & Marko Perić*

### Introduction

Events are playing an increasingly important role in renewing places by catalysing local, regional, and national culture (Richards & Palmer, 2010; Smith, 2012; Wise & Harris, 2017). The European Capital of Culture (ECoC) promotes urban development (or redevelopment) as a driving force to promote new social legacies, job creation, and civic re-positioning (Richards et al., 2013; Richards & Wilson, 2007; Spirou, 2011). It is essential that ECoC host cities have long-term competitive strategies in place, aimed at strengthening the capacity of their city to deliver diverse cultural programmes and placemaking (locally) for its own citizens. For researchers it is important to get a sense of how local planners and policy-makers promote regeneration strategies for the benefit of the city and discuss this around what placemaking initiatives are in place to benefit local residents and encourage the community to participate. Local residents, after all, will be the ones participating in, contributing to, and therefore affected most by event-led regeneration (see Wise, 2016). Local residents will also be most impacted by the outcome of social and economic policies, before, during, and after the event. Crouch (2011) notes that it is important to consider competitiveness alongside the growth of emerging niche industries – such as events in this case – to understand wider impacts. Hosting the ECoC will come to define a destination for years to come, as observed in research focusing on previous hosts such as Glasgow 1990 (García, 2005; Mooney, 2004), Rotterdam 2001 (Richards & Wilson, 2007), Cork 2005 (O'Callaghan & Linehan, 2007), Liverpool 2008 (Spirou, 2011) and Guimarães 2012 (Keofoed, 2013). From the sample of ECoC research, what needs more attention is expanded discussions of ECoC strategy and regeneration initiatives to include more insight on placemaking and community participation. This social emphasis will help explore new insight beyond wider economic agendas and prospective tourism growth. Going further, scholars also critically evaluate projected (or intended) legacies of future events (see Evans & Van Huer, 2013) and how prospective planning can help create social impacts (Hixson, 2013; Wise et al., 2017). As Clark and Wise (2018) argue, and Wise (2018) frames from an events perspective, more research on social regeneration impacts and opportunities is needed so that researchers can further explore social conditions, such as community participation and placemaking.

In 2020 Rijeka, Croatia, will host the ECoC. Rijeka was nominated because it was an opportunity to regenerate the city by investing in and upgrading infrastructure to attract people to the destination. Rijeka is a strategic selection since Zagreb, Split, and Dubrovnik, Croatia's well-known destinations, might not benefit as much as Rijeka can from the European funds. What is significant about Rijeka 2020 is it will mark 30 years since Glasgow 1990, which was arguably one of the most successful ECoC programmes given the extensive regeneration and significant image transition (Spirou, 2011). Like Glasgow, Rijeka is a second-tier city in its county. While Glasgow and Rijeka may seem vastly different based on culture, identity, language, and positioning in Europe, both cities do share a similar industrial shipbuilding past. Likewise, Liverpool was also an ECoC host in 2008 and much of the regeneration initiatives did help recreate a new image of Liverpool, but it also transformed Liverpool through placemaking and reviving the city's heritage – to improve the city's image. While legacies are intended and impacts are strategic, earlier points noted by Evans (2001) still challenge researchers to consider if cultural-led regeneration is aimed at recreating a greater sense of community cohesion, so to result in (or at least promote) placemaking. Or, is culture embedded in the contemporary regeneration process as a means to increase consumption amidst the decline of other industries and thus be solely aligned with new investment opportunities and image recovery? Glasgow and Liverpool each benefitted from the ECoC when their local economies needed recovery from stagnation. Grodach (2017) argues that culture is increasingly a driver of economic development, suggesting that a strong cultural planning agenda is needed to ensure that the community is engaged so that place-based expressions can enhance local capacity building and attributes of placemaking such as community cohesion.

To understand the directions of regeneration and placemaking ahead of Rijeka 2020, analyzing content from official websites and the 2020 agenda is an attempt to better understand the city's strategy and approach ahead of the event. This chapter will address placemaking, regeneration, and community participation, and when necessary will look to insight and successes from Glasgow and Liverpool to inform points and perspectives going forward. The chapter will address what worked well for both of these cities in subsequent sections based on findings from ECoC related research. This chapter's geographical focus engages with the notion of placemaking, and an emphasis on regeneration and community participation points to the impact on society going forward. A review of some key conceptual understandings is where this chapter now turns.

## Placemaking, regeneration, and community participation

Tuan's (1974, p. 4) notion of *topophilia* literally refers to an 'effective bond between people and place'. There is an emphasis here on cultural and social meanings portrayed in events at all scales and across different impacts, in particular how events impact the residents of a place. To put Tuan's (1974) perspective into practice, the notion of placemaking refers to an intangible social impact that results from hosting events (Richards, 2017; Richards et al., 2013). Geographers have noted three accepted categories for conceptualizing place: 'place as location', 'place a locale', and 'sense of place' (Agnew, 1987). Placemaking arguably merges each of these conceptualizations, because it happens in a physical place, through interactions of people, and surfaces meanings embedded in everyday life and experiences (Cresswell, 2014; Rose, 1995). As outlined in the introduction chapter of this book, events may become synonymous with a place. But just because we recognize an event and a place, this is a macro understanding that is reinforced by place imaginaries or geographical imaginations. Placemaking is rooted locally and helps people associate based on a shared identity, which also helps reinforce a sense of place among residents (Liu, 2016). Also, community involvement, including support for an event, is an important factor in predicting the strength of a person's attachment to a community or place (Derrett, 2003; Liu, 2014). Improving access to cultural projects and programmes for the local population, and using different methods to encourage participation, is essential, if a place wants to achieve desired socio-cultural impacts from the event (see Palmer, 2004). Using public spaces, initiatives can assist people to attend or participate in the main programme, participate in 'free' events, or receive discounted tickets or dedicated transport (Liu, 2014). Involving local stakeholders and managing their expectations can be analyzed through the perspective of an event's poetics and politics, where 'poetics' include the presentation of ECoC in an attractive manner to win local support and attract outside attention, and 'politics' is about actually seeking legitimacy, mobilizing community support, and managing local dissatisfaction (Ooi et al., 2014).

Rijeka hosts Croatia's oldest carnival, which is also considered the world's third oldest (Rijecki Karneval, 2018). While many events are also rooted in a place's history, it is the continual making of such events that have an impact on local society. In a city such as Rijeka, where they have a strong foundation for hosting events locally, regionally, and nationally, the ECoC is an opportunity for the city to enhance their presence in Europe and internationally through place and image regeneration. Pride in place is another social impact associated with hosting events, and this can help reinforce placemaking at both the micro- and the macro-scales. Richards (2017, p. 9) mentions that cities are moving 'towards a more proactive use of events in order to drive a wide range of different policy agendas'. Part of more contemporary urban agendas is to move away from solely physical aspects of placemaking to more 'purposeful event staging' (Richards, 2017, p. 9) founded on local social and cultural programmes that aim to involve community residents (see Connolly, 2013; García, 2004, 2005; Hixson, 2013). Such arguments position placemaking as central to contemporary regeneration practices, especially when we consider social regeneration and how change both directly and indirectly impacts local residents (see Ginsburg, 1999; Wise & Perić, 2017). Later sections in this chapter will present and reflect on content outlining regeneration activities in Rijeka ahead of 2020. Research focusing on intangible benefits resulting (or not resulting) from new urban development cannot be generalized. Social leveraging is evident in the need to consider social outcomes, but it is important to acknowledge that desired outcomes are often merely proposed and are easily overshadowed by the influence of economic impacts and the demand for more tangible evidence (Chalip, 2014; Smith, 2012). These 'softer' impacts aligned with placemaking can range from collective reinforcements of sense of community and civic pride, to renewed attitudes and behaviors (Smith, 2012).

When we interpret placemaking and regeneration from past examples, we are reminded of Glasgow 1990 and Liverpool 2008. Both cities underwent extensive urban regeneration to prepare the city for the ECoC, and reclaiming urban spaces by reinventing them was not only aimed at tangible outcomes, but also at creating semblances of civic pride, new employment/enterprise opportunities, and a platform from which to create eventful legacies to grow newly founded service industries from the shadow of past industry. The intangible social impacts of regeneration help shape the future of the destination and lasting legacies are aimed at leveraging events to enable and influence locals to get involved in future activities (Agha et al., 2012; Liu, 2016; Smith, 2012). Rijeka shares a very similar story and history with Glasgow and Liverpool. As a post-industrial city along Croatia's Adriatic coast, local shipbuilding industries suffered as manufacturing struggled to compete in globalized markets and stagnation was evident as industrial bases and new divisions of labor shifted to the global south. The ECoC 2020 represents a renewed opportunity for Rijeka, and the city has much to learn and gain from previous successful cases.

## Managing placemaking, regeneration, and community participation ahead of Rijeka 2020

Discussions offered in this chapter aim to understand and evaluate how the strategies explain the event (ECoC 2020), place (Rijeka), and society (local community). By assessing and addressing content on the 2020 vision through placemaking, regeneration initiatives, and how planners intend to motivate and involve the community, this chapter offers both a review and critique of policies looking forward.

An overview of the plan from the official Rijeka 2020 website presents the 'programme', 'infrastructure', and 'growing together' as the three points of discussion to inform locals and visitors about what the city is doing to prepare. The main infrastructural projects that will be showcased as key sites of culture in the city of Rijeka include a vast industrial complex known as Rikard Bencic, which includes: H-object complex (Museum of Modern and Contemporary Art), T-object (Rijeka City Library), Brick House (which includes the Art-kino, Rijeka Puppet Theatre, and Youth Council Benčić, and will be available for other users) and the Sugar Refinery (Rijeka City Museum). Also, infrastructure investments will be implemented on the Ex Bernardi building (RiHub ECoC), ship Galeb (historical monument used by the Rijeka City Museum) and the building of Energana (a power station built in 1931 that when built was an innovative steam turbine). Each project is currently ongoing at the time of writing.

### 2020 (eventful) vision

From the infrastructural plans presented above, the production of culture is evident in the plans to restore and transform Rijeka's former industrial spaces. The buildings being restored are part of Rijeka's urban fabric and reflect the transitional journey from its industrial past to its role as a renewed cultural centre. Physical regeneration is in line with Grodach's (2017) point on using culture to drive economic development, but what is important is how engaged and involved the community residents are in this process and what they contribute to Rijeka's longitudinal narratives about urban heritage amid regeneration:

> ECOC is a project whose size and importance overshadows all previous cultural projects in the city. Such an intense endeavour can only be carried out by the entire city, down to each artist, citizen, neighbourhood, team, entrepreneur, company. Everyone. To better understand the way we are going, we need to talk as much as possible and be as direct as possible. We want to hear your expectations and we want to tell you all about our plans. There is no better way than directly, face to face, so we call everyone to visit us every week near Mali Salon on Korzo, as well as occasionally on larger events around town. Until we see each other, here is the greatest question–How will we get to 2020? In phases.
>
> (Rijeka 2020, 2018d)

Now if we consider Glasgow's and Liverpool's plans, both places had succumbed to negative images in previous years, so the ECoC was part of a much wider vision to recreate the image of both cities (Smith, 2012; Spirou, 2011). But in the opportunity to renew both cities, beyond image transformation and place perception among outsiders, was the need to increase civic pride and pride in place among residents, a goal which for the most part was deemed successful (Connolly, 2013; Liu, 2016).

### Regeneration initiatives: place (in general) or placemaking (for the community)

Regenerating city spaces corresponds with reimaging industrial areas eroded by time, impacted by changing industries. Glasgow 1990 is a benchmark for event-led regeneration from an ECoC perspective (Richards & Palmer, 2010), because Glasgow put emphasis on cultural-led regeneration to reuse industrial spaces by transforming them into new places for opportunity, culture, and entertainment – each supporting the growth of the service sector of the city's renewed economy. But the challenge, and critique, of physical regeneration is the question: is it holistically inclusive (see Bailey et al., 2004; Clark and Wise, 2018; Cowen, 2016; Low, 2017)? Cowen (2016) goes so far as to call new tourist areas and events spaces 'islands'. Although new tourist areas and events spaces are transformed and often times aesthetically pleasing (relating to Chapter 16 in this book), they are often times exclusive, and exclude people who cannot afford to consume in such higher amenity spaces. Whilst physical infrastructures can enhance the image of a place (in general) and make a city attractive to prospective visitors, it is important to acknowledge how transformations are planned for the community by the community so that placemaking can happen. Low (2017) is also critical of placemaking because it does not always happen organically. Planners and policy-makers decide and set strategies for how they envision a city, and the developments happen around these visions. But for placemaking to occur, physical presences the define a place need to reflect local resident values. The community needs to come together and celebrate spatial transformations, and then give new meaning to regenerated places. It is important that Rijeka does not succumb to lessons learnt from the literature when regenerating physical spaces, where they find themselves excluded (Cowen, 2016).

Much of the discussion that Rijeka conveys when it comes to regeneration is in line with reshaping its image. Building on discussions offered in the previous section, the main form of regeneration that Rijeka is concerned about is image regeneration by adding the city to the European and international tourist map. The city is framing this emphasis on image around two goals:

The first one is to contribute to the internalisation and opening up of the city and county, to create strategic international partnerships, to position Rijeka as a relevant regional centre for cultural policies and management in culture, and to promote Rijeka, Primorje-Gorski kotar County and Croatia through a system of targeted mobility for experts in arts and culture, cultural and creative industries and other sectors connected to culture–through international events co-organised and hosted in Rijeka, and through promotions abroad.

The second aim of Cultural Diplomacy is to shift the international public's attention to the year 2020 and Rijeka as a destination, including Croatia as a place with a high quality cultural-touristic offer, and to build a positive image abroad through promotions, emphasising promotions in collaboration with diplomatic representations of the Republic of Croatia outside of the scope of regular media and programming activities.

(Rijeka 2020, 2018c)

These two goals are complicated in several ways because they are broad in scope and suggest that the city has an established international reputation. While these goals fit the regeneration narrative, there is still a need to motivate and involve the community locally.

### *Motivating and involving the community: addressing social impacts*

Community participation is essential for regeneration to have a purpose and for the sustained use of transformed spaces (Wise & Perić, 2017) after hosting an event (Liu, 2014). It is noted that:

> The aim of the programme is to actively involve citizens in creating cultural and social programmes, and to improve the production and organisational capacities of informal civilian groups and individuals. A system of micro-supports will be used to support citizens' cultural and social initiative, informal civilian groups, and associations, based on decisions made by committees formed by representatives of various groups of citizens. This kind of model enables the active participation of citizens in the production of cultural programmes, and at the same time allows for some decision-making responsibility on the relevance of the applied cultural programmes for the community in general.
>
> Rijeka 2020 (2018b)

The Rijeka 2020 website states: 'The aim of the programme is to actively involve citizens in creating cultural and social programmes, and to improve the production and organizational capacities of informal civilian groups and individuals' (Rijeka 2020, 2018b). But defined efforts are difficult to locate. The need for clear policies, based on parallel relationships across stakeholders and inclusive involvement (through work, education, training, participation, and understanding of legacy) is necessary if socially sustainable outcomes are to be achieved. But as Chalip (2014) argues, managing how such impacts are leveraged remains a persistent challenge.

Tangible change is clearly noted on the Rijeka 2020 website, with an outline that regularly updates the progress of infrastructural projects. But more importantly perhaps is the need to consider social regeneration initiatives that aim to include and involve locals in culture-led regeneration. The Rijeka 2020 website attempts to motivate residents, to get them involved and encourage them to share their ideas. Moreover, residents are encouraged to be 'agents of culture', with this message proposed to locals:

> How can I participate? Here are the answers for two important groups of partners.
>
> ECOC is a unique opportunity to develop all aspects of the culture scene. The programme primarily entails investing in all cultural institutions, cultural associations and people who work in culture in the city.

Our hope is that all of them will exponentially grow, both in terms of programmes and human resources. When selecting programmes, we will take the custodian approach, but we also plan to include participative decision-making.

(Rijeka 2020, 2018d)

The emphasis here needs to concentrate on 'how do I participate?' This an attempt by organizers to get people involved, but policies of participation could be clearer. It is possible to interpret this as implying that the community has not been fully involved in the decision-making from the start. What is also mentioned:

ECOC is a project whose size and importance overshadows all previous cultural projects in the city. Such an intense endeavour can only be carried out by the entire city, down to each artist, citizen, neighbourhood, team, entrepreneur, company. Everyone. To better understand the way we are going, we need to talk as much as possible and be as direct as possible. We want to hear your expectations and we want to tell you all about our plans.

(Rijeka 2020, 2018d)

This is followed with a submission area where those interested can add contact details. But it is not clear how they will be informed and encouraged to participate in future projects.

Another creative way to involve the business sector and attract support for ECoC projects was through the creation of Business Club Rijeka 2020. This initiative aims to motivate local entrepreneurs, getting them to participate in events and other activities related to Rijeka 2020:

Business club Rijeka 2020 is necessary because, once developed, it will have the power of a large community of entrepreneurs, from the micro to mid-level all the way to big. Their power and their visibility are what make the collective what it is. Business club is an opportunity for networking both amongst themselves and with the cultural sector and this networking is also an excellent opportunity for mutual benefit. The club provides an opportunity for entrepreneurs to actively involve themselves with Rijeka 2020 ECOC project, to help it financially, by providing services, or in other ways. The finances are not a primary concern and are not the main reason for the initiative: what is important is to promote and spread the culture of philanthropy which is at a very low level in Croatia, where similar initiatives do not exist.

(Rijeka 2020, 2018a)

Involving the private sector in Rijeka is essential to ensure longer-term financial sustainability of cultural projects and ECoC impacts, as well as

maintenance and further (subsequent) developments. The mere creation of
the 'business club' can be critiqued, because without any specific objective
or clear vision of what actual activities this club is going to conduct, it represents yet another work in progress when it comes to building local partnerships. Despite initial criticisms, it is encouraging that representatives of
this business club are dedicated to successful cooperation. But without
establishing clear leadership for implementing action plans and identifying
responsibilities, everything will remain just a 'good idea' in theory, without
practical benefits and actual social impacts. Another sign that suggests
a clear/common goal is missing can be found in the following statement of
the Rijeka 2020 management organization:

> We'd like Business club Rijeka 2020 to act independently from RIJEKA
> 2020, to use and assign its resources in a transparent and self-sufficient
> manner, with, of course, our help. The emphasis would definitely be on
> projects that are extremely visible in the community – projects dealing
> with children, the elderly, ecology, civics, and all the values we believe
> are important for us, our business community, and everyone in Rijeka,
> and which make Rijeka recognizable.
>
> (Rijeka 2020, 2018a)

With the matter of identifying cooperation among different organizations/
sectors, as well as decision-making patterns, such partnerships will continue
to be a complex and challenging process. But without it, ECOC organizers
are clearly more oriented on poetics than on politics concerning stakeholder
management.

Barrera-Fernández and Hernández-Escampa (2017) found that the
emphasis on the tourist experience are considered before impacts on placemaking locally. This concentrates power based on the influence of a few
stakeholders and investors who many not be interested in placemaking so
much as a means to build local capacity or increase civic pride in the longer
term. Placemaking initiatives that will result in financial returns during the
delivery of the event(s) are essential but will depend on initiatives such as
the Rijeka Business Club (discussed above). Friedmann (2010) tried to warn
us that there is too much focus on the bigger picture, as it is the resident
communities that define a place's fabric. If the community as a stakeholder
is not fully immersed in directions of change and has little influence on
policy-making, then the notion of placemaking and disseminating cultural
activities organically is more a false prose. The community residents, as the
makers of place, are who come to define local creativity. Placemaking is
reinforced through elements of local culture and traditions that have been
sustained over the decades. Cultures may have been altered due to wider
social and economic forces, but motives for placemaking need to be guided
by the urban community, its neighborhoods, and residents (Friedmann,
2010; Salzman & Yerace, 2018).

García (2005) was also critical of this concerning the case of Glasgow, because the impact of regeneration is often spatially limited. Similarly, Liverpool's concentration of tangible developments was oriented to the docks and central shopping district, and what was established were exclusive high-consumption areas and upscale residences (Spirou, 2011). Rijeka's development is similar, but much less extensive than Glasgow's or Liverpool's. Therefore, planners in Rijeka have the potential to create more inclusive spaces for locals to celebrate their city's renewal and contribute to building local meaning and capacity. Stakeholders will also express a range of concerns and aspirations when it comes to planning for events and event-led regeneration. When we consider placemaking, the social impact to consider is local involvement (Richards, 2017; Smith, 2012). While such insight offered by Smith (2012) would be interpreted as involvement at the time of events, Richards (2017) would suggest the process is continuous from initial regeneration, to preparation and legacy plans. The same points of involvement are just as crucial so that residents gain not only from the spectacle, but from the complete regeneration journey.

## Going forward: towards 2020

The ECoC is meant to be a celebration of place, and for the communities that call that place home, new infrastructures and initiatives will impact them beyond the event. As Rijeka's ECoC draws nearer, a legacy plan will evolve, and stakeholders will get a sense of longer-term ambitions and growth beyond 2020. While this chapter was an opportunity to evaluate Rijeka's plans and visions, future research will engage with different stakeholders to understand impacts of social regeneration strategies. There is also a need to conduct research directly with the local community to gain an understanding of destination competitiveness going forward. This will help us review the role of cultural- and event-led regeneration in transforming the image of Rijeka. It also allows us to look at more specific strengths and weaknesses. If we refer once again to Glasgow and Liverpool, both cities have benefited from extensive physical regenerations and have continued to develop event-led placemaking going forward. Wider urban transformations have established sustainable visitor attractions where events are continually staged, such as new venues built around the Albert Dock in Liverpool and along the Clyde River in Glasgow. These continue to attract international visitors. While the ECoC was an image makeover for both cities, it worked to transform both the image and imaginations of Glasgow and Liverpool. Rijeka can also benefit from physical regeneration to give the city a new awareness, but we need to also understand this from a community participation point of view.

Rijeka is a large city in Croatia, but in terms of a cultural capital, Zagreb, Split, and Dubrovnik are more synonymous with Croatian culture and tourism. Rijeka's geographical advantage is its location proximate to the popular resort area of Optaija and the Istrian Peninsula. With Rijeka's maritime and shipbuilding (industrial) legacy, and its status now as an emerging post-industrial city, the service sector economy in the lead up to 2020 will define the new direction of the city. But it is important that an intangible legacy, reinforced through placemaking and community involvement, persists as the destination develops during and post-ECoC. Going forward towards 2020, it is important to plan for the long term, as opposed to channelling business groups that will not have an expanded city-wide or regional impact. In this manner, legitimacy acquired through the ECoC shall be maintained only if social and cultural capital is improved for the benefit of its residents beyond 2020.

## References

Agha, N., Fairley, S., & Gibson, H. (2012). Considering legacy as a multi-dimensional construct: The legacy of the Olympic Games. *Sport Management Review*, 15(1), 125–139.

Agnew, J.A. (1987). *Place and politics*. Boston: Allen and Unwin.

Bailey, C., Miles, S., & Stark, P. (2004). Culture-led urban regeneration and the revitalisation of identities in Newcastle, Gateshead and the North East of England. *International Journal of Cultural Policy*, 10(1), 47–65.

Barrera-Fernández, D., & Hernández-Escampa, M. (2017). Events and placemaking: The case of the Festival Internacional Cervantino in Guanajuato, Mexico. *International Journal of Event and Festival Management*, 8(1), 24–38.

Chalip, L. (2014). From legacy to leverage. In J. Grix (Ed.). *Leveraging legacies from sports mega-events*. London: Palgrave Macmillan (2–12).

Clark, J., & Wise, N. (Eds.) (2018). *Urban renewal, community and participation: Theory, policy and practice*. Berlin: Springer.

Connolly, M.G. (2013). The 'Liverpool model(s)': Cultural planning, Liverpool and Capital of Culture 2008. *International Journal of Cultural Policy*, 19(2), 162–181.

Cowen, A. (2016). *A nice place to visit*. Philadelphia: Temple University Press.

Cresswell, T. (2014). *Place—An introduction*. Oxford: Wiley Blackwell.

Crouch, G.I. (2011). Destination competitiveness: An analysis of determinant attributes. *Journal of Travel Research*, 50, 27–45.

Derrett, R. (2003). Making sense of how festivals demonstrate a community's sense of place. *Event Management*, 8(1), 49–58.

Evans, G. (2001). *Cultural planning: An urban renaissance?* London: Routledge.

Evans, G., & Van Huer, B. (2013). European Capital of Culture – Emancipatory practices and Euregional strategies: The case of Maastricht via 2018. In G. Richards, M.P. de Brito & L. Wilks (Eds.). *Exploring the social impacts of events*. London: Routledge (73–83).

Friedmann, J. (2010). Place and placemaking in cities: A global perspective. *Planning Theory & Practice*, 11(2), 149–165.

García, B. (2004). Urban regeneration, arts programming and major events. *International Journal of Cultural Policy*, 10(1), 103–118.

García, B. (2005). Deconstructing the city of culture: The long-term cultural legacies of Glasgow 1990. *Urban Studies*, 42(5/6), 841–868.

Ginsburg, N. (1999). Putting the social into urban regeneration policy. *Local Economy*, 14(1), 55–71.

Grodach, C. (2017). Urban cultural policy and creative city making. *Cities*, 68, 82–91.

Hixson, E. (2013). Achieving significant event impacts for young residents of the host community: The Adelaide Fringe Festival. In G. Richards, M.P. de Brito, & L. Wilks (Eds.). *Exploring the social impacts of events*. London: Routledge (203–215).

Keofoed, O. (2013). European Capitals of Culture and cultures of sustainability–The case of Guimaraes 2012. *City, Culture and Society*, 4(3), 153–162.

Liu, Y.-D. (2014). Socio-cultural impacts of major events: Evidence from the 2008 European Capital of Culture, Liverpool. *Social Indicators Research*, 115(3), 983–998.

Liu, Y.-D. (2016). Cultural event and urban regeneration: Lessons from Liverpool as the 2008 European Capital of Culture. *European Review*, 24(1), 159–176.

Low, S.M. (2017). *Spatializing culture: The ethnography of space and place*. London: Routledge.

Mooney, G. (2004). Cultural policy as urban transformation? Critical reflections on Glasgow, European city of culture 1990. *Local Economy*, 19(4), 327–340.

O'Callaghan, C., & Linehan, D. (2007). Identity, politics and conflict in dockland development in Cork, Ireland: European Capital of Culture 2005. *Cities*, 24(4), 311–323.

Ooi, C.-S., Håkanson, L., & LaCava, L. (2014). Poetics and politics of the European Capital of Culture project. *Procedia—Social and Behavioral Sciences*, 148, 420–427.

Palmer, R. (2004). *European cities and capitals of culture: Study prepared for the European Commission (Part 1)*. Brussels: Palmer-Rae Associates.

Richards, G. (2017). From place branding to placemaking: The role of events. *International Journal of Event and Festival Management*, 8(1), 8–23.

Richards, G., de Brito, M.P., & Wilks, L. (Eds.) (2013). *Exploring the social impacts of events*. London: Routledge.

Richards, G., & Palmer, R. (2010). *Eventful cities: Cultural management and urban revitalization*. London: Elsevier.

Richards, G., & Wilson, J. (2007). The impact of cultural events on city image: Rotterdam, cultural capital of Europe 2001. *Urban Studies*, 41(10), 1931–1951.

Rijecki Karneval. (2018). A short history of a great carnival. Retrived from: www.rijecki-karneval.hr/en/short_history.

Rijeka 2020. (2018a). Ahead of the "Pogled prema 2020: EPK i HNK" gala concert, an initiative was presented, titled "Business club Rijeka 2020", a great opportunity for structural changes in the city. Retrieved from: http://rijeka2020.eu/en/ahead-of-the-pogled-prema-2020-epk-i-hnk-gala-concert-an-initiative-was-presented-titled-business-club-rijeka-2020-a-great-opportunity-for-structural-changes-in-the-city/.

Rijeka 2020. (2018b). Civil initiatives: Active citizens of an active city. Retrieved from: http://rijeka2020.eu/en/program/civil-initiatives/.

Rijeka 2020. (2018c). Cultural diplomacy. Retrieved from: http://rijeka2020.eu/en/program/cultural-diplomacy/.

Rijeka 2020. (2018d). Growing together. Retrieved from: http://rijeka2020.eu/en/growing-together/.

Rose, G. (1995). Place and identity: A sense of place. In A.D. Massey & P. Jess (Eds.). *Place in the world*. Oxford: Oxford University Press (87–132).

Salzman, R., & Yerace, M. (2018). Towards understanding creative placemaking in a socio-political context. *City, Culture and Society*, 13, 57–63.

Smith, A. (2012). *Events and urban regeneration*. London: Routledge.

Spirou, C. (2011). *Urban tourism and urban change*. London: Routledge.

Tuan, Y.-F. (1974). *Topophilia: A study of environmental perception, attitudes, and values.* Englewood Cliffs: Prentice Hall.

Wise, N. (2016). Outlining triple bottom line contexts in urban tourism regeneration. *Cities,* 53, 30–34.

Wise, N. (2018). Towards a more enabling representation: Framing an emergent conceptual approach to measure social conditions following mega-event transformation in Manaus, Brazil. *Bulletin of Latin American Research.* Retrieved from: https://onlineli brary.wiley.com/doi/10.1111/blar.12775.

Wise N., & Harris, J. (Eds.) (2017). *Sport, events, tourism and regeneration.* London: Routledge.

Wise, N., Mulec, I., & Armenski, T. (2017). Towards a new local tourism economy: Understanding sense of community, social impacts and potential enterprise opportunities in Podgrađe Bač, Vojvodina, Serbia. *Local Economy,* 32(7), 656–677.

Wise, N., & Perić, M. (2017). Sports tourism, regeneration and social impacts: New opportunities and directions for research, the case of Medulin, Croatia. In N. Bellini & C. Pasquinelli (Eds.). *Tourism in the city: Towards and integrative agenda on urban tourism.* Berlin: Springer (311–320).

# 6 Cinematic sense of place

## Embodied celluloid spectres on the red carpet in Cannes

*Dorota Ostrowska*

## Introduction

Second only to the Oscars, the Cannes International Film Festival is one of the world's most widely mediatized and visible film events (Ostrowska, 2017). In 2018 there were about 4,500 accredited journalists at the Cannes International Film Festival from 88 countries around the world. Television and print press journalists accounted for 27% (1,228 persons) and 26% (1,166 persons), respectively; and those attending the festival to spread the message through various online and social media platforms came to 18% (787 persons) (Festival-Cannes, 2018c). In comparison, this same year, 2018, Berlinale (the Berlin International Film Festival) was attended by 3,688 journalists representing 84 countries (Berlinale, 2018a). The presentation of these figures at the start, while not directly in line with the focus of this chapter, is an attempt here to signify the press presence at a film festival to locate the scope of media attention on the film market and international film festivals (positioning press presence as an important measure of the significance and impact of international film festivals). In 2017 there were 12,324 industry representatives attending the Marché du Film (the business counterpart of the Cannes International Film Festival) in Cannes where there were 3,820 films on sale (Festival-Cannes, 2017). In the same year the European Film Market (in Berlin) was attended by 9,536 film industry participants and there were 728 films screened (Berlinale, 2017).

For the duration of the festival, and in the minds of the broader public throughout the year, the place signifies the event: the city of Cannes is the festival. The global media which first arrived in Cannes following the (mostly American) film stars, have always been key in establishing and perpetuating the dynamics between the location of the Cannes festival and the festival itself. It is the focus of the media on the red carpet, the main visual trope signifying the festival, which has led to this absorption of the city of Cannes and the wider Riviera region into the festival event. At the same time, considering the media coverage during the film festival event, the red carpet together with the actors and celebrities parading it, remains more important than the films shown on the festival screens. Interviewed in 2018, Thierry Frémaux, the director of Cannes film festival, remains emphatically enthusiastic in regard to the centrality of the red carpet ceremony for the festival. He says: "They [the Red Carpet Steps] are our flagship! No doubt they are the part of the festival that draws the most media attention" (Festival-Cannes, 2018d).

This also draws the attention of those not accredited at the festival, and following its progress only remotely are the local members of the general public, who are not able to attend screenings because no tickets or accreditations are available to those who are not part of the film industry (see Czach, 2010). This creates social exclusion locally, something that has been observed in recent collections from the events (e.g. Richards et al., 2013; Wise & Harris, 2017) and urban studies (e.g. Clark & Wise, 2018) literature, relating to how events and festivals can impact local wellbeing and sense of place connection (see Gellweiler et al., 2017; Smith, 2012; Wise & Harris, 2016; Yolal et al., 2016). For those interested non-attenders, films screened at the festival, mostly premiers, are reduced to a title and a few lines of the summary of the plot. The actors starring in the films and their director, available for various photo opportunities with the red carpet being the key one, are the only tangible manifestation or the embodiment of the films during the film festival event. The films' invisibility only compares with the hypervisibility of the red carpet and its participants which is perpetuated by the festival itself through a number of media outlets during the festival and the year round through its online archives (Festival-Cannes, 2018b). These archives are a repository of the selected media coverage of the festival event obtained from Association France Presse and Getty Images (Festival-Cannes, 2018a).

The aim of this chapter is to examine how the representations of stars on the red carpet have changed over time based on material from the Cannes International Film Festival online archive, which arguably has modulated the image of the city of Cannes created in the process. These photographic renditions document the only "live" or performative element of the Cannes Film Festival, the actors on the red carpet, which further strengthens the relationship between the live film festival performed on the red carpet and the city of Cannes. The changes in the photographic accounts of the red carpet is the only variable impacting the image of the city of Cannes generated in the minds of the festival's global public. The city of Cannes is only mirrored in the representation of the red carpet, which in itself is interrelational and changeable.

While work on film festivals has looked at organiztional and management approaches among others (see Connell, 2012; Rüling & Pedersen, 2010), this chapter offers conceptual insight on place, identity, and imaginary. Massey (1991, p. 28) proposes an interpretation of place where "what gives a place its specificity is not some long internalized history but the fact that it is constructed out of a particular constellation of social relations, meeting and weaving together at a particular locus". For Massey (1991, p. 28) places "can be imagined as articulated moments in networks of social relations and understandings". The red carpet ceremony in Cannes is an expression of a place understood as a complex architecture of relationships between stars, photographers, media crews, festival organizers, different film industry members, and the public (both real and virtual). Furthermore, Massey (1991) points out that her conception of a place is dynamic and changeable or in her words "progressive". As the relationships that are an expression of the place have evolved over time, becoming processes, so the place of which they are an expression is a process as well. This idea of how the place changes over time through the relationships that embody it is important in this historically grounded view of the Cannes red carpet representations, as examined through the Cannes visual online archive. The representations of stardom on the red carpet are subject to change that depends on several factors: technology, communications, and relationship to the film, each contributing to the creation of a cinematic sense of place in Cannes.

## Sense of place, identity and imaginary

Massey's (1991) idea of a "global sense of place" is met with some criticism, with regards to an absence of a stable foundation in her conception of a place. Without a stable foundation, place is conceptualized as floating, blurry, and porous, and for this reason, potentially disruptive when trying to comprehend what a cohesive sense of local identity means. Massey's (2006) response to this critique is relevant to the discussion of Cannes' identity. Massey (2006) discusses how what is intuitively perceived as solid expression of a place's identity – as Skiddaw is in relation to the Lake District – is in fact mobile and changeable. Rocks are not immobile and always there; rather, science tells us they are immigrant rocks and thus part of the moving and global sense of place. In the case of the red carpet ceremony at Cannes film festival it is the red carpet which appears to be at the first sight the least changeable and stable backdrop to any star and celebrity guest appearance at the festival. Yet, this red carpet is something which is part of the fabric of Cannes only during the festival, with one of the most famous images pre-dating any edition of the festival being the rolling out of the red carpet on the stairs of the Palais des Festivals. The origins of the red carpet ceremony are most commonly traced back to an instance of its appearance in a Greek tragedy where:

> a path of dark red tapestries was rolled out (...) in the Aeschylus play Agamemnon, when the King's vengeful wife Clytemnestra prepares for the triumphant welcome home of her husband from the Trojan War. Even the King hesitates to walk on the "crimson path" laid before him, because he is "a mortal, a man" and not a god.
>
> (Baker, 2016)

It is perhaps more appropriate to associate the red carpet at a film festival with the flying carpets that appear in Arabic tales and are associated with garden spaces (see Ostrowska, 2017). The carpets are efficient means of transport to different realms and locales which may be imaginary or real. Like Massey's (2006) immigrant rocks the red carpets of film festivals are magic carpets taking us to the imaginary-scapes opened by films shown on festival screens. As will be considered later, the red carpet is thus effectively a conduit between the real life of the festival event and the imaginary life projected on screens. Stars belong on the red carpet because their identity is also dual – both real and imaginary – they are "embodied celluloid spectres" (Benjamin, 2004; Cavell, 2004).

The online archives of the Cannes International Film Festival are analyzed in this chapter (it is important to note that the archives are being updated quite regularly with new material and are thus subject to change). At present they cover the period 1946–2017 (all the post-war editions of the festival). They include mostly visual material in the form of posters and photographs, as well as partial scans of film festival documents (only for the early editions of the festival), and also the list of films which were presented in different sections of the festival and the ones that won various film festival prizes. From 2001, the archives also include some audio-visual material. This study is based on the section called "The Festival's Media Library" where both photographic and audio-visual material have been gathered and analyzed. Photographic material has been very carefully selected, but overall the entire collection is quite modest and in many ways underwhelming as it seems to suppress certain aspects of the film festival history. That means that it has some rather strange omissions. For example, there is not a single photograph of Brigitte Bardot, whose career path from a starlet to a star was forged during the festival (Schwartz, 2007).

Numerous scholars and writers have recognized stars as part and parcel of the festival mediascape (Bazin, 1947, 1955, 2009; Morin, 2005). Writing about Cannes film festival and taking a cue from Edgar Morin, Schwartz (2007) argued that the festival not only developed the star system as a symbolic order beyond the economic one, but it also transformed the visual tradition of the representation of stardom. As is widely known, Cannes was a place where the classic star photography was juxtaposed with seemingly impromptu and spontaneous photo shoots of stars, thus creating unauthorized and natural images of a star (Schwartz, 2007). Schwartz (2007) noted that Morin (2005) had missed the link between the new type of naturalistic star photography and the magnetic power of the presence of stars as real people in the context of a film festival. Moreover, according to Schwartz (2007), Morin (2005) was focussed on the immediate and startling effect that the presence of real stars at the festival had in relation to the films in which they starred and which were screened at the festival. He was interested in the double-bind of a real person and her screen representations in the context of the festival. At the same time Morin didn't really address the issue of the stylized star photography in relation to the naturalist images generated by paparazzi in the context of the festival. In other words, he did not talk about differences in the ways in which star image was mediatized in the context of the film festival.

Both Edgar Morin and André Bazin were contemporaries who frequented the Cannes film festival around the same time in the 1940s and 1950s and both wrote very perceptive and striking pieces about the festival and the presence of the stars there. Whilst Morin was focussing on the nature of the stars and their relationship to the festival event and the films screened there, Bazin was reflecting on the way in which critics like himself responded to the experience of encountering a star live and on screen in the context of a film festival. The concept of the embodied celluloid spectres can be thus explored from these two different perspectives while drawing on the material in the online Cannes archives. On the one hand, this chapter refers to Morin's argument about the relationship between the stars and the film festival event. One hypothesis is that the star photography in the Cannes online archives captures and conveys in a very precise way the dual nature of a star's existence in the context of the film festival, as both a real person and a cinematic image (emphasized over and over again). The photographs in the archives also expand on the star imagery by incorporating the figure of an auteur director who gains the status of a star comparable to that of a star actor. In this way not only actors, but also directors, are embodied celluloid spectres in the context of a festival event.

Additionally, this chapter will also draw on Bazin, who articulates the experience of the members of the public when it comes to the encounter with stars in the context of the festival. The drama of the festival could not be fully played out without the participation of the public who are drawn to the festival precisely because it offers an opportunity to experience the duality of the stars' existence. But this is where the embodiment of the celluloid spectres becomes painful beyond measure, as the public is haunted, just like Bazin, by the star spectres who are present and illusive and can never be possessed in real life. The fragmentary and incomplete nature of the Cannes online archives exacerbates this experience, creating another barrier to the stars through the imperfect digital interface.

Ultimately, this chapter is interested in the ways in which these two perspectives on stardom are represented in the star photography of the Cannes online archives and how they become the expression of "Cannes" in the minds of the wider public, linking the notions of events, places, and societies. The circumstance which has shaped these photographic representations mirrors complex relationships that create Cannes' cinematic sense of place, captured in the trope of the red carpet.

## Edgar Morin: film festivals are where stars belong

According to Morin (2005) a star is not just an actor and not just a role. Rather, the star is a result of a dynamic relationship that exists between the two. Morin (2005, p. 27) argues that: "actor and role mutually determine each other. (…) The star is more than an actor incarnating characters, he incarnates himself in them, and they become incarnate in him". Star is created from the union of the two. It is a "composite created who participates in both, envelopes them both", as stars are modern day "superhuman beings, heroes and gods" (Morin, 2005, p. 29). Thus, Morin (2005) sees stardom not as a finished product but as a dynamic and ongoing process of mythmaking. Film festivals provide both the time and space where this process can fully unfold. With its dual dynamics of the real life of stars unravelling on the beaches and streets of Cannes, and on the screen where the same actors are present, film festivals are a unique playground for the stars. The actors and the characters are there in the closest possible proximity and it is from that intimacy that the star is born. This is also the time and space when "the confrontation of myth and reality" takes place (Morin, 2005, p. 48).

For Morin, the most important ritual of the film festival is the red carpet ceremony, which is like a rite of ascension of the virgin from the earth into the temple. This is the transformative moment for the actor, who is in the transitional space between reality and the imaginary realm created on screen. The process of divinization unfolds in front of the eyes of the mortals – the fans and photojournalists. Morin (2005, p. 50) writes: "the star is *there*, at her moment of extreme magic efficacy, between the limousine and the movie theatre where she will double herself, between the screen and the temple". Such moments are privileged ones and may only happen during the festival. In fact, the festival is needed for the red carpet ceremony to take place. This moment of transformation is mediated across the world through the images taken by photographers and more recently TV crews. For this reason, the red carpet ceremony is "the key photograph of the festival (and) the one that seizes her [the star] in this radiance and this glory at the apogee of the ceremonies" (Morin, 2005, p. 50). By focussing so strongly on the red carpet ceremony Morin emphasizes the staged aspect of the stars photographed at the festival. That is why the props of the red carpet ceremony are very important. They are the crowds, the building of the Palais des Festivals, photographers, and the stars – which are among the central tropes to be found in the photographic representations of the festival. These are also the necessary elements to create an embodied celluloid spectre, which is a star photographed in a film festival environment.

We find the images of the Palais in the section of the Cannes archives covering the 1952 edition. The red carpet is unfolded before the Palais des Festival which leads to the building where the screening takes place (the actual steps were inside the building at that time). The crowds constitute another important prop, but there are few pictures of the anonymous crowds in the archives. That means that the stars, rather than the crowds, are important for the archives. There are also images of the stars who have their backs to the sea and who are walking towards the Palais. But these images are only included in the archives from the early 1970s. What connects the stars and the crowds is the direction of their gaze. What is striking is that all of them are photographed looking up. The crowds are presumably looking up to the top of the stairs where the red carpet finishes and where the stars enter the building. The stars are also looking up while walking up towards the Palais. The direction of the gaze of the crowds (the proto-audiences) and of the stars supports Morin's (2005) thesis about the centrality of the screening and of the red carpet in the context of the festival for the creation of the embodied celluloid spectre of the star at a festival.

In the same way, the intensity of the stars' gaze is a very prominent feature of the festival. We can find the tense look of anxiety and anticipation on the faces of the actors, as they are distracted and looking around or even making rude gestures intended as a joke. Yet, the intensity of their gaze is gone and the behavior is less poised and formal. In light of this, a photograph of Sophia Loren from 2014 stands out as we can see there the same look that was present on the faces of many actors and actresses throughout the decades, which is rare when it comes to younger actors.

This change in the nature of the gaze raises questions as to whether the embodied celluloid spectre is just a manifestation of stardom at a particular moment in cinematic history (which was dominated by celluloid technology, now obsolete with the advent of the digital). Or, is it that the star's look is distracted because they don't know where to focus, which camera is going to deliver their defining image of the festival? The gesture therefore, rather than the gaze, becomes the central attraction of the scene for both the photographers and the viewing public. The last point is worth considering more carefully, especially in light of the most recent activity on the part of the Cannes Film Festival, whose archive now includes some carefully crafted and immaculately executed portraits of stars, not on the red carpet, but in the intimate surroundings of plush hotel rooms.

As mentioned, the red carpet ceremony is only featured in the online archives from the early 1970s. Importantly, there are few photographs which represent actors only. Rather, they mostly feature a combination of the cast and the directors. The presence of the directors complicates Morin's (2005) argument about stars in an interesting way and adds another dimension to it. Whilst most of the time the director does not feature on screen, s/he becomes a star of the festival, on an equal footing with the actors, in the context of a festival like Cannes. In this way a director becomes subject of the same divinization as the stars. In other words, directors come to share in the stardom of their actors. It is a result of their benefiting from the continuous attention offered them by the festival. A disproportionately high number of male directors have won Palme d'Or, which leads to an association of film authorship with men rather than women (see Quick, 2018). A trio of good examples here is Roman Polanski, Lars von Trier, and Pedro Almodovar, who are among the star-directors and thus represent a variation of the embodied celluloid spectres. There is always something quite pristine and immaculate in the images of the directors at the festival, which gives them an air of authority and innocence.

For Morin, the presence of mythical creatures such as star-actors at the festival is crucial in shaping the perception of the festival event. Their images need to communicate that:

> the stars lead a festival existence: the Festival leads a life of star – a movie life. Ceremonies, receptions, battles of flowers, bathing suits, evening dresses reveal them: décolleté, half-naked under a perpetual sun (…). Everything contributes to the image they present of life as Elysium.
>
> (Morin, 2005, p. 48)

These images belong to the realm of the "spontaneous" and "natural" rather than being staged and crafted. By referring to them Morin does in fact recognize their importance for capturing and conveying the liveness of the stars' festival existence. In this way Morin also closes the gap in his analysis of stardom at a film festival, for he recognizes the importance of both staged and spontaneous elements in the star photography at a film festival, and gestures towards the embodied celluloid spectres.

When talking about the spontaneous aspects of star photography Morin identifies three different kinds of images which dominate the media coverage of the festival. The first type of images refers to mirroring, which takes place between the life of the stars at a film festival and the stars' representations in the films that are screened there. Elements of films in which the star-actors have appeared are mirrored in the festival existence of the stars. In turn, the way they live their lives at festivals has already been doubled on screen. The result is a creation of something that Morin refers to as a "festival film" which is an amalgam of the film festival reality and cinema itself, with the star-actor being the glue that holds the two together. Another type of festival imagery identified by Morin focuses on parties, receptions, and get togethers, which are full of poses that "express the plenitude and ecstatic joy of life" (Morin, 2005, p. 50). There is a sense of affection and intimacy which these images exude. Finally, there are images of star-actors as beacons of hope and help for the weakest and most innocent – children. The festival film is about deepest human emotions and longings, which the star-actors embody in their on-screen and off-screen existence.

The way in which Morin (2005) described festival film as being made up of all three types of image is played out in the context of the Cannes online archives. In the first instance that assumes we will have to think of these archives as a type of festival film itself. Whilst the interface is designed to offer a smooth and easy access to the festival history, creating the impression of the richness and plenitude of the material reality is quite different. For the archives are heavily redacted and limited, leaving the contemporary user disenchanted much in the same way that a Bazinian critic is when experiencing the real film festival. This chapter now turns to Bazin to further understand the disappointment of the Cannes online archives.

## André Bazin: a film critic at a film festival

Whilst Morin is focused on the dynamics of the relationship between the star and the film festival, Bazin's (1947, 1955) analysis presents a different voice, which articulates the relationship between the film-going public and the stars, in the context of a film festival, as a different dimension of the embodied celluloid spectre. As an established and respected film critic, Bazin represents a particular section of this general public. Nonetheless his analysis of the relationship with the embodied celluloid spectre of a star has broader application and appeal beyond his individual case or the case of his professional group. Much of Bazin's argument helps us understand the allure and attraction of the voyeuristic star photography at a film festival, and by extension the relationship we have with the Cannes online archives in our role as member of the public interested in film festival culture.

Bazin's (1955) main reflection on the Cannes Film Festival can be found in his well-known piece "The Festival Viewed as a Religious Order", but it began nearly a decade earlier in a 1947 article in *Esprit* entitled "Cannes-Festival 47". The *Esprit* article describes a confrontation between the world of beautiful people, with athletic tanned bodies, money, and cars – the world of stars and millionaires – and the reality of a film critic who is attending the film festival in Cannes. The stars and starlets who normally inhabit the cinema screens stepped down to walk the surface of the earth – on the beaches of Cannes. You can call them "goddesses" and "heroes", or "Tarzans" and "pin-ups" – the critic is among them on the beach. This critic, the mortal, is awfully intimidated and experiences bouts of an inferiority complex in relation to the creatures who surround him. He is an imposter, a stranger, and feels damned. He is not part of their world and not part of their paradise.

The confrontation with the luxury lifestyle, money, and stars on screen is different from experiencing any of that in the real life. It is the film festival in Cannes which allows for such confrontation to happen and it is painful for the critic. While the experience of the luxury and beauty in cinema allows the critic to possess it, seeing all that in real life, where it is "even nicer than in the Technicolor" (Bazin, 1947, p. 774), makes him realize that he will never in his life possess the object of his desire. It is on the Cannes beach that the critic understood that "cinema was a dream" (Bazin, 1947, p. 774). In the cinema all women were available because (you) the spectator was Clark Gable, Humphrey Bogart, or Spencer Tracy (or any other multimillionaire). The spectator is painfully aware of the impossibility of becoming such a cinematic hero, by encountering a film star on the beaches in Cannes, where even the critic's untanned white body conspires against him and prevents him from becoming part of the cinematic universe in real life. He must clad this imperfect body in a tuxedo, which, as we read in his other piece on Cannes, is like the attire of a monk for whom carnal pleasure is contained to the realm of fantasy in the cinema theatre.

## Conclusion

The photography of stars on the red carpet contained in the Cannes online archives is a carefully selected and catalogued representation of the embodied celluloid spectres. The photographs of the stars capture and convey the duality of the star at a film festival as a real person and as a cinematic image. The photographs in the archives are arranged into an unfolding photo reel whose design evokes the duality of the stars' image. On the one hand it seems that the images in the archives are accessible and at our fingertips. We can choose them by clicking on them, then pause them, cut them, and download them. But on the other hand, and on closer inspection, we become aware of their fragmentary and incomplete nature and of the controlling and imposing curatorial policy of the festival, which creates an image of its own past. We are like Bazin, whose desire to possess the festival past is only equal to the painful disappointment of realizing how inaccessible it is to us. The online Cannes archives is just another version of the Cannes media strategy, rather than an archive in any true sense of the word.

To conclude, and briefly returning to how Massey's writing on Skiddaw are evocative of the red carpet itself, the red carpet signifies different sets of relationships depending on the film festival event. If the Oscars could be considered a film festival then the role that the red carpet plays there resembles closely the red carpet of Cannes. The red carpet is different for a film festival like Berlinale where, unusually for film festivals that normally have only one red carpet as the focal point of the media, Berlinale has a number of red carpets rolled out in front of various cinemas in the city used by the festival. The red carpet in front of the Berlinale Palast, which shows the premiers of the main competition, is the most important one from the point of view of the global media. Other red carpets serve a different function as they are displaced across the cinemas of Berlin including the suburbs (Berlinale, 2018b). They democratize access to stars and premiers, and allow members of the Berlinale festival-going public to enjoy the red carpet ceremony – not broadcast on a TV screen, but live (and followed by watching the film together with the crew sitting in the same cinema). The multiple red carpets at Berlinale are a way to communicate the identity of the festival and of the city of Berlin – they are diverse, inclusive, and open to the public.

Two archival film festivals taking place in the Italian cities of Pordenone and Bologna have a very unique take on the red carpet. Pordenone is a film festival of silent cinema, which does not have any actors or directors attending, because they are dead. However, the festival organizers make a point of rolling out the red carpet in front of the main theatre used for the festival screenings. This carpet attracts the attention of any festival participant, even though there will never be a red carpet ceremony. In Pordenone, only celluloid ghosts walk the red carpet. In a similar way there is no red carpet in Bologna, either, replaced instead by the daily public screenings of the highlights of the festival – restored film classics – on a mega-sized screen in the main piazza of Bologna, Piazza Maggiore. This is the instance when the red carpet turns into a cinema screen and the two merge (together) as one. The celluloid spectres of film stars becoming an expression of a new set of relations involving film archivists, historians, critics, cinephiles, and members of the general public are present on the Piazza Maggiore at the time of the screening. For the duration of the festival in Bologna, these live public screenings define the city and its civic culture, the unique sense of place it has through cinema, for those attending the festival.

To host a film festival means that certain cities, Cannes, Berlin, Bologna, and Pordenone, among others, develop a cinematic sense of place which is unique and individualized, depending on the relationship the film festival has with the red carpet ceremony. Not surprisingly, the less intense the media attention on the festival, the more variations there are on the theme of the red carpet.

# References

Baker, L. (2016). Where does the red carpet come from? *BBC Culture*, 22 February, available at: www.bbc.com/culture/story/20160222-where-does-the-red-carpet-come-from (Accessed 19th April 2018).

Bazin, A. (1947). Cannes-festival 47, *Esprit*, November, pp. 773–774.

Bazin, A. (1955). "The Festival Viewed as a Religious Order" *Cahiers du Cinéma*. June. Translated by Emilie Bickerton. Reprinted 2009 in Dekalog 3: On Film Festivals, (ed.) R. Porton. London: Wallflower, pp. 13–19.

Bazin, A. (2009). "The Festival Viewed as a Religious Order" in R. Porton (ed.) *Dekalog 3: On Film Festivlas*. London: Wallflower, pp. 13–19.

Benjamin, W. (2004). "The Work of Art in the Age of Mechanical Reproduction" in L. Braudy and M. Cohen (eds.) *Film Theory and Criticism*. Sixth edition. New York and Oxford: Oxford University Press, pp. 791–811.

Berlinale (2017). Berlinale annual archives facts & figures 2017, available at: www.berlinale.de/en/archiv/jahresarchive/2017/01_jahresblatt_2017/01_jahresblatt_7.html#Zahlen2017.

Berlinale (2018a). Berlinale annual archives facts & figures 2018, available at: www.berlinale.de/en/archiv/jahresarchive/2018/01_jahresblatt_2018/01_jahresblatt_2018.html#Zahlen2018.

Berlinale (2018b). Berlinale Goes Kiez, available at: www.berlinale.de/en/das_festival/sektionen_sonderveranstaltungen/berlinale_goes_kiez/index.html.

Cavell, S. (2004). "From the World Viewed" in L. Braudy and M. Cohen (eds.) *Film Theory and Criticism*. Sixth edition. New York and Oxford: Oxford University Press, pp. 344–352.

Clark, J. and N. Wise (eds.) (2018). *Urban Renewal, Community and Participation Theory, Policy and Practice*. Berlin: Springer.

Connell, J. (2012). Film tourism – Evolution, progress and prospects. *Tourism Management*, 33(5), 1007–1029.

Czach, L. (2010). Cinephilia, stars, and film festivals. *Cinema Journal*, 49(2), Winter, 139–145.

Festival-Cannes (2017). Marché du Film 2017 Key Figures, available at: www.march edu film.com/en/quisommesnous/chiffrescles.

Festival-Cannes (2018a). Credits, available at: www.festival-cannes.com/en/credits.

Festival-Cannes (2018b). La Média Thèque de Festival, available at: www.festival-cannes.com/en/mediatheque/.

Festival-Cannes (2018c). Press area statistics, available at: www.festival-cannes.com/en/press/.

Festival-Cannes (2018d). The festival in 2018, interview with Thierry Frémaux, available at: www.festival-cannes.com/en/qui-sommes-nous/festival-de-cannes-1.

Gellweiler, S., T. Fletcher and N. Wise. (2017). Exploring experiences and emotions sport event volunteers associate with 'role exit'. *International Review for the Sociology of Sport*. doi:10.1177/1012690217732533.

Massey, D. (1991). A Global Sense of Place., *Marxism Today*, June, 24–29.

Massey, D. (2006). Landscape as a provocation. Reflections on moving mountains. *Journal of Material Culture*, 11(1/2), 33–48.

Morin, E. (2005). *The Stars*. Minneapolis: University of Minnesota Press.

Ostrowska, D. (2017). Cosmopolitan spaces of international film festivals: Cannes film festival and the French Riviera. *Alphaville: Journal of Film and Screen Media*, 14, 94–110.

Quick, M. (2018). The data that reveals the film industry's 'women problem'. *BBC*, 9 May, available at: www.bbc.com/culture/story/20180508-the-data-that-reveals-the-film-industrys-woman-problem.

Richards, G., M. de Brito and L. Wilks (eds.) (2013). *Exploring the Social Impacts of Events*. London: Routledge.

Rüling, C-C. and J.S. Pedersen. (2010). Film festival research from an organizational studies perspective. *Scandinavian Journal of Management*, 26(3), 318–323.

Schwartz, V. (2007). *It's So French! Hollywood, Paris and the Making of Cosmopolitan Film Culture*. Chicago: University of Chicago Press.

Smith, A. (2012). *Events and Sustainable Regeneration*. London: Routledge.

Wise, N. and J. Harris. (2016). Community, identity and contested notions of place: A study of Haitian recreational soccer players in the Dominican Republic. *Soccer & Society*, 17(4), 610–627.

Wise, N. and J. Harris (eds.) (2017). *Sport, Events, Tourism and Regeneration*. London: Routledge.

Yolal, M., D. Gursoy, M. Uysal, H. Kim and S. Karacaoğlu. (2016). Impacts of festivals and events on residents' well-being. *Annals of Tourism Research*, 61, 1–18.

# 7 Qingdao International Beer Festival

## Place identity and colonial heritage

*Xiaolin Zang, Bouke van Gorp, & Hans Renes*

## Introduction

Tsingtao Brewery opened in 1903 as the *Germania Brauerei* and was part of the German colonial enterprise on the Chinese coast. It is now the second largest brewery in China, claiming about 15% of domestic market share and selling beer in over 50 countries worldwide. Almost a century later, in 1991, the Qingdao International Beer Festival was launched. The festival was conceived to promote beer sales domestically and internationally. However, the local authorities, who supported the festival, recognized the opportunity this festival offered to brand the city as well. Since 1991 the beer festival has expanded into the largest of its kind in Asia and is now a major tourist attraction for Qingdao (Rogerson & Collins, 2015). The festival is modelled after the archetypical Bavarian beer festival: the Munich Oktoberfest. The Qingdao festival lasts a fortnight and is hosted at six different sites dispersed throughout city of Qingdao (Figure 7.1), attracting over 4 million visitors. The majority of these visitors come from China, but international tourists find their way to the festival as well. The slogan of the event "Ganbei (Cheers) with the World!" reflects its international aspirations.

Festivals and hallmark events like the Qingdao International Beer Festival have been implemented as part of larger marketing and branding efforts. Events and festivals are recognized as opportunities to draw visitors, redevelop/regenerate cities, and reimagine the brand of a city (Getz, 2008; Richards & Palmer, 2010; Smith, 2012; Wise & Harris, 2017). Apart from the expected economic benefits and improvements in infrastructure, events offer the possibility to reframe the narrative of the city. Black (2007) describes events and festivals as "unrivalled place promotion opportunities"; this is also true for Qingdao International Beer Festival. The present city of Qingdao was known in the early twentieth century as Tsingtao, which is still the name of the brewery. The whole German concession was known as Kiautschou. In this chapter, Qingdao is used to refer to the city, and Tsingtao for the brewery.

However, the transformation of local celebrations and traditions into festivals that can accommodate many tourists, has come with concerns about commodification of the local culture, with questions around the authenticity of the

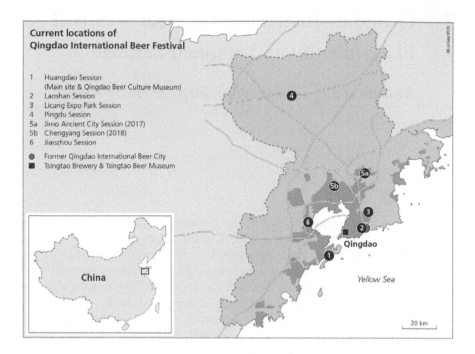

*Figure 7.1* Map of the city with the locations of the festival, brewery, and museum. (Map created by Margot Stoete, Faculty of Geosciences, Utrecht University).

rituals performed on stage. This concerns issues of ownership and economic exploitation of cultural events (Hall, 2005). Ma and Lew (2012) highlight that concerns raised by the increasing festivalization are particularly acute in China since every city in China hosts several events as parts of their marketing efforts. Despite the popularity of festivals as marketing and branding instruments, not all festivals in China are actually successful. After government involvement ceases, many festivals fade away. Ma and Lew (2012) explain the success and failure from the perspective of contextualization: to what extent is a festival rooted in local history and local sense of place? Local roots and local atmosphere are what makes a festival unique and also provide opportunities for branding a city (Hernández-Mogóllon et al., 2018). From this perspective, the Qingdao International Beer Festival proves an interesting case study on city and place branding. On the one hand, the beer itself is rooted in local history; on the other hand, although the beer festival is slowly receiving the status of a tradition, it is still an invented tradition – copied from beer festivals elsewhere in the world (notably Germany).

Questions about the suitability of a festival as a branding instrument may be heightened when the product celebrated has an unmistakably colonial history. The brand, the custom of drinking beer and the beer festival all relate to the history of Qingdao as a former German colony. During the First World War, when the colony changed hands from Germany to Japan, so did the brewery. The brewery thus reflects the colonial histories of Germany and Japan in Qingdao. Ongoing research by the authors makes it clear that in Qingdao the era of Japanese colonization evokes stronger and more negative feelings than does the German period. Moreover, in the past the "German-ness" of the beer has been used as part of its brand, as a quality measure. The historical connection with Germany can therefore be used as a unique characteristic of the city – something that has shaped not only its drinking culture (beer) but also the landscape of the city. Still, the colonial nature of the connection between Qingdao and Germany can also be seen as part of a past that is unwanted, and therefore discarded.

Combined, these issues, from dissonant heritage to lack of authenticity, make the Qingdao International Beer Festival an interesting case to study, since the festival has been successful in attracting huge crowds. This chapter focuses on several questions, concerning how the beer festival is represented and the degree to which it is seen as part of the Qingdao brand. It looks at how the colonial origins are negotiated in projected images, and will analyze the way the festival is officially promoted on the festival's website and in policy documents. This study will also consider how visitors describe the festival in their reviews. The main method that will be applied is textual analysis, combined with fieldwork and desk research. The chapter starts with an introduction on the themes of city branding and the role of festivals in this context. It then continues with a brief description of the colonial history of Qingdao and the Tsingtao Brewery. This is followed by an introduction to beer tourism and an analysis of the Qingdao International Beer Festival as a part of the city's branding strategy.

## Place branding and festivals

City marketing became increasingly popular since the 1980s. Boisen et al. (2011, p. 139) note that "the marketing and branding of cities, regions and countries is positioned firmly on contemporary policy agendas". They further claim that in Western Europe rising entrepreneurialism and re-scaling of statehood has led to a quest for marketing-driven development strategies for cities (see Boisen et al., 2011, 2018). Policy-makers and consultancy firms alike perceive place marketing as instrumental in attracting tourists and investors to achieve economic growth (Maheshwari et al., 2011). Similarly, branding has increasingly been applied to places, as a consequence of the increased (or at least perceived) competition between cities.

Marketing and branding policies are aimed at strengthening the competiveness of a place on regional, national, and global scales (Boisen et al., 2011). Although strongly associated with promotional activities, marketing is more than just advertising. It encompasses a variety of initiatives aimed at improving the competitiveness of a city, such as urban planning and design, regeneration schemes, infrastructural improvements, restoration of heritage, and the hosting of mega-events and cultural festivals (Maheshwari et al., 2011; Wise & Harris, 2017).

Although place marketing and place branding are often used in combination, the two differ. Place marketing is defined by Maheshwari et al. (2011, p. 199) as "the strategic planning procedure undertaken by a place's brand developers with the main aim of satisfying diverse needs of target markets". Place branding is an element of place-marketing strategies that aims at adding value to the brand, in this case: the city. It attempts to influence the perceived qualities of the city (Boisen et al., 2011). The perceptions that target audiences hold of a city are important – as these influence spatial behavior (whether people visit or not) and how one experiences a place. Kavaratzis (2004, p. 66) adds that "all encounters with the city take place through perception and images". As a consequence, place marketing and branding should revolve around planning and managing the image of the city (Vanolo, 2015). Of course, places are different from consumer goods, and therefore branding a city is not the same as branding shampoo, beer, or cars. However, many scholars in the field of place marketing and branding have explained how place branding can apply insights from product branding (Runyan & Huddleston, 2006). A brand consists of two elements: its image and its positioning, or how it is communicated to target audiences such as stakeholders and customers (Runyan & Huddleston, 2006). Image, meanwhile, comprises the overall impression and is what differentiates a city from other places (Runyan & Huddleston, 2006). Brand image is thus represented through positioning statements such as symbols, slogans, and logos, all meant to communicate the uniqueness of a place (McDaniel & Gates, 2010).

Kavaratzis (2004) distinguishes three types of communication through which the image of the city is communicated: primary, secondary, and tertiary communication. Primary communications result from landscape strategies, infrastructure projects, the city's governing structure, and what he terms the city's behavior: the vision and strategy of the city's leaders and the resulting services provided by the city. Image communication is the effect of whatever measures the city thus takes. Events and festivals are part of this primary communication. Secondary communication refers to the intentional representation of the city through promotion by the formal (destination) marketing organization. Here one would expect to find the positioning statements mentioned above. Tertiary communication, on the other hand, relates to all "unintentional" communication – image communication that is not controlled by the formal marketing organizations such as news media representations, tourism guidebooks, and word-of-mouth. Increasingly, internet and social media (in particular blogs, vlogs, and reviews), play a part in these tertiary communications.

As part of the primary communication, events and festivals have become a prominent instrument in branding and marketing strategies, to such a degree that some authors speak of "event strategies" and "the festivalization of city politics" (see Preuss, 2015). Events and festivals are organized and supported to attain dual goals: attracting tourists and fostering a positive city (place) image (Richards & Palmer, 2010; Smith, 2012; Wise et al., 2015). When carefully planned, events and festivals can yield intangible legacies such as enhanced reputation, opportunities for community building, shared memories, and strengthened cultural identity (Getz, 2008; Richards et al., 2013; Preuss, 2015). However, using events and festivals as development, urban regeneration, or marketing strategies are not without problems. Upscaling events to host larger crowds can lead to (temporary) displacement, overcrowding, excess noise, and pollution. Furthermore, transforming local cultural festivals into tourist attractions may lead to commodification of culture and change traditions and rituals into staged performances that lose local meaning (Backmann, 2018).

Ma and Lew (2012) distinguish four types of festival, based on how they rank on a spatial and temporal scale. Their question is the extent to which a festival is based in local tradition or history and in local (sense of) place. Their framework then discerns four types of festival, which each score differently on local identity and uniqueness, authenticity, and liminality: local heritage festivals; local modern festivals; national heritage festivals; and global modern festivals. The Qingdao International Beer Festival is considered a "local modern" festival: "being local, these events still contribute to local identity, but instead of focusing on authentic replications of traditions, there is more of a focus on entertainment and the experience of fun or liminality" (Ma & Lew, 2012, p. 5). As with many contemporary festivals in China, the development of the Qingdao International Beer Festival mainly relied on the sponsorship of national and municipal authorities (Ma & Lew, 2012). This raises questions about the sustainability of festivals, and particularly the extent to which they can connect to the local population. In this case of an event with German roots and a beer drinking culture, Ma and Lew (2012) claim that the festival is only loosely related to sense of place – as there was no prior tradition of a beer festival. The festival may simply be a clever attempt to increase sales and secure a spot in the growing international market of beer tourism (Rogerson & Collins, 2015). This case therefore raises questions of how the festival is perceived by locals and tourists alike, and how it is embedded and received by the local community.

## Colonial Qingdao and Tsingtao beer

Today, Qingdao as a brand is associated with beer and German architectural heritage, and a clear example of German architecture can be seen in Figure 7.2. Ji (2011) analyzed the projected image of the city in 2009 and found that the main ingredients of the Qingdao brand were natural scenery, urban landscape (both the modern skyscrapers and the European architecture), and events. These associations come together in the positioning statement used for several years to promote the city: "red roofs of buildings, surrounded by green trees with green sea and blue sky as natural backdrop"

*Figure 7.2* The original site of the Tsingtao Brewery.
(Photograph by Jichuan Zang).

(Ji, 2011: 77). Not part of this slogan but definitely part of promotional materials analyzed by Ji (2011) were the events the city hosted: the sailing competition in the 2008 Olympics and the International Beer Festival.

Perhaps one of the most interesting aspects of the association of the city with beer is its colonial connection. Qingdao was founded by the German navy as part of the efforts to bring the unified German state in line with its European competitors by building a colonial empire. Arriving late to the game at the end of the nineteenth century, Germany had to build its colonial empire from a few dispersed parts of Africa, some islands in Oceania, and a concession on the Chinese coast. Searching for a foothold on the Chinese coast, the German government followed the advice of the geographer Ferdinand von Richthofen, who had travelled widely in China and had written a standard reference work in four volumes on the country (see Von Richthofen, 1882). He was particularly interested in exploitable resources such as coal, but in the meantime also had a keen eye for possibilities for a German colony and pointed to Kiautschou Bay as a good location (Schrecker, 1971). The bay provided an excellent harbor and was close to exploitable (but disappointing in quality) coal reserves (Conrad, 2016). It gave Germany a foothold on a coast that during the final decades of the nineteenth century gained importance for international trade and, hence, for European expansion. Kiautschou might be seen as the German reaction to the British foothold in Hong Kong (Schrecker, 1977). The navy was interested in a supply harbor for its increasingly world-wide ambitions and used the bay as a home base for their East Asia Squadron.

The navy was determined to develop Kiautschou into a model colony. The earlier town of Tsingtao was developed into the administrative centre of the concession. The town was rebuilt with wide streets, solid housing areas, government buildings, electrification throughout, a sewer system, and a safe drinking water supply. Schools were founded by the German state as well as by Protestant and Roman Catholic missions (Schultz-Naumann, 1985). Germany invested more in Qingdao than in any other of its colonies. The town developed quickly and so did the harbor. However, the German colonizer itself derived little profit from its investment (Conrad, 2016). Moreover, the German period was full of conflicts between the German government and the local Chinese population, worsened by continuous tensions between the Catholic missions and Chinese civilian authorities (Lu, 2008).

In November 1914, after Japan's declaration of war on Germany, Japanese troops conquered Qingdao. In the Versailles Treaty (1919), the old concession was not restored to Chinese rule but left to Japan. The city reverted to Chinese rule (the Republic of China) in December 1922, but Japan maintained its economic dominance of the railway as well as the brewery. Japan re-occupied Qingdao in 1938. In 1945 the town returned to the Republic of China and in 1949 became part of the People's Republic of China.

Today, Tsingtao beer is seen as quintessentially Chinese, but its roots are colonial. In 1903 a German-style beer brewery, operating as the Anglo-German Brewing company, started to produce German-style beer called Germania, or Tsingtao Beer in Chinese (Matzat, 2003). The brewery mainly catered for Germans and other Westerners living in Qingdao and other Chinese cities (Yang, 2007). The factory was originally equipped with German machinery, and even the brewing process followed the German *Reinheitsgebot* to ensure the quality and taste of the beer. As a consequence, ingredients were brought in from Germany (Yang, 2007). According to Yang (2007, p. 32), the beer was adopted by the German colonial authorities "as part of their effort to promote the city of Qingdao".

Yang (2007) has demonstrated how over time the meaning of beer was renegotiated to attract Chinese customers not used to drinking beer. After the First World War, the German client base had dwindled, so the new owners of the brewery had to find new markets for the product. These consumers were partly found in Hong Kong. However, the new Japanese owners of the brewery also attempted to brand the beer as Asian to attract Chinese customers. When the brewery was handed over to Chinese management in the aftermath of World War II, it became even more important to brand the beer as "Chinese". The source of water used to brew the beer (Laoshan mineral water) became an important element in the advertisements, although the German origin was also still mentioned as proof of its authenticity (Yang, 2007).

While in the early days of the brewery the survival of the brand had been at stake a number of times, today Tsingtao is a major brand selling over 7 million kilolitres of beer annually to local, national, and international markets. The subsequent owners of the brewery have found ways to spur Chinese consumers to drinking beer and have also established a position in the international beer market. The brand even withstood allegations of poor quality in the 1990s, when the barley cultivated in China was said to contain unsafe quantities of fertilizers and pesticides. Tsingtao has become a global brand that has a high level of international familiarity and is seen as an ambassador of China (Ille, 2009). This international recognition of the brand results not just from the export of the beer to over 50 countries, but also from sponsoring mega-events such as the Olympics in Beijing and other events such as the Asia-Pacific Economic Cooperation (Finance People, 2017). The International Beer Festival is another important platform to showcase the brand.

## The Qingdao International Beer Festival

### Beer tourism

Tsingtao beer has more than a century of history in Qingdao, and part of the production is still at the original location of the Germania Brewery. A beer museum opened in 2003 to mark 100 years of beer brewing in Qingdao – tapping into the new niche market of beer tourism (Rogerson & Collins, 2015). According to Plummer et al. (2005) beer tourism fits in the broader development of food and beverage tourism, which allows tourists to get a taste of local culture, for a unique and authentic experience (see also Chapter 8 by Gillespie & Hall). Bujdoso and Szucs (2012) distinguish between beer tourists that travel to taste specific beers and beer tourists that travel to places connected to brewing and drinking beer. Whereas the first group will join in beer-themed meals, beer routes and beer tastings, the latter will visit breweries, beer museums, and brasseries to get a taste of local culture or heritage. The museum and the Qingdao International Beer Festival mainly seem to cater to this latter group of beer tourists.

The first beer festival in Qingdao was hosted in 1991. Its aims were to market Qingdao, promote the brewery's products, explore potential markets, increase sales, foster relationships with customers, and attract tourists (Du & Qu, 2011; Yang, 2007). The first edition of the Qingdao International Beer Festival hosted several Chinese brewing companies and organized beer tasting and drinking contests. The success of the first edition of the festival led to the decision to turn it into a yearly event. The city immediately recognized the festival as a way to communicate its image to its target audiences. The latest tourism plan states that the beer festival, together with the sailing festival and large international conferences, can be used to attract (Western) visitors to the city. The International Beer

*Figure 7.3* Qingdao International Beer Festival by night in 2017.
(Photograph by Ruizheng Gao).

Festival has grown to become the largest beer festival in Asia. Figure 7.3 shows an image of one of the main gathering points at the festival. According to Ille (2009) the festival received 3.4 million visitors in 2005. Between 2010 and 2013, the number of out-of-town visitors to the festival increased dramatically and the festival also attracted relatively more overseas tourists (Yu & Fu, 2010; Travel Sina, 2013). The large number of visitors are said to have generated the city a revenue of 3.8 billion Yuan, and according to estimates this contributed to a GDP growth of 0.52% (Travel Sina, 2013). The success of the festival has also resulted in the development of International Beer City – a permanent theme park in the Laoshan district (Yang, 2007). In recent years, the festival has moved to the Huangdao district, to a site of 1,115 acres (Xinhuanet, 2018), to accommodate the increasing number of visitors. On the site of the Huangdao theme park, a second beer museum was opened showcasing architectural settings resembling a small Bavarian town (QDGJBEER, 2017).

### German roots, international standing, local flavor

The Qingdao International Beer Festival was modelled after the famous Oktoberfest in Munich. Several "traditional" activities were adopted from Munich Oktoberfest, such as tapping the first barrel of beer, beer tents with long tables where people sit in rows, barbeques, and a carnival. For those who want a keepsake to remember their time at the festival, a variety of curiosities are on sale, including Bavarian-style stone mugs and a pet rooster in lederhosen. On closer inspection these items present an interesting mixture of Bavarian and Chinese signs and symbols. The pottery may be Bavarian in its shape and size, but the landscape depicted on the mugs is Chinese. Similarly, wearing the lederhosen is a semblance of Bavarian traditional wear, while the rooster wearing it represents the Chinese year of the rooster (2017). References to Oktoberfest can also be seen in pictures from TripAdvisor reviews and on the festival website. Images show festival sites with several beer tents, each from different (inter)national brands. The front entrances of the tents are decorated with brand specific logos and symbols and Chinese characters, with neon lights and laser beams lightning up the place. Bavarian elements are evident in the decorations. The Paulaner tent, for example, is themed in Bavarian style, with the Paulaner logo and Bavarian blue and white flags. The decoration of the event site also evokes a Bavarian atmosphere, for example though the *Maibaum*, which is placed on a green between the tents. A *Maibaum* (in English: a maypole) is a central European symbol for spring (a fertility symbol) that is usually put on the village green around the 1st of May each year. The relation to beer is unknown, but the tradition of maypoles is very strong in Bavaria, and so this symbol has made its way to Qingdao for the event.

Looking at TripAdvisor and Mafengwo comments, one entry literally compares the two festivals: "touted to rival the one in Munich. While it isn't necessarily the same, the venue is great!" and also notes the visible references to Oktoberfest: "Everything, lookswise, is German styled". Another reviewer also makes the comparison, but feels the comparison falls short: "it is not like Octoberfest, just a pearl chain of big tents with stages and seatings on benches". Few Chinese reviewers also mention that the festival is a copy of the Munich Oktoberfest. One reviewer draws a connection between the Oktoberfest style arrangements and German colonial rule: "the colonial German culture still embedded in the Qingdao Beer Festival as the festival imitates traditions from the Bavaria Oktoberfest". Few other reviewers (Chinese or international) mention this connection in their reviews. "Beautiful German architecture still found in this part of Qingdao, which was used to be a German enclave until 1919" and a "Nice place to visit. To know the history of Germany and Japan who started their beer business in Qingdao".

Although the German connection seems to be present in the decoration of the festival, it is a superficial hotchpotch of generic Bavarian stereotypes and not local German colonial history that is expressed in this way. However, the colonial history of the beer is mentioned on the official website of Qingdao International Beer Festival. From the perspective of branding, it becomes clear from the review entries that people associate the beer and the festival with the city. One reviewer claims: "if you want to visit Qingdao city, you have to visit the May Fourth Square and the Beer Festival". Other reviews see Qingdao as the birthplace of beer: "Tsingtao beer is authentic beer" and "Qingdao as original place of Chinese beer". The brand Tsingtao apparently has international recognition and international visitors: "finally saw the place where Tsingtao beer is brewed, which my friends in China enjoyed so much in drinking".

Some reviews even go as far as comparing the people of Qingdao with the Tsingtao beer: "We took pleasure in the Beer City, and admired to the great-hearted and straightforward Qingdao people as the same as the cold and refreshing beer". Such local connections linking beer, festival, and city are strengthened by the opening show performed every year. This huge spectacle narrates the history of the city. Some local reviews even express an attachment to the festival and the beer: "I am a native-born Qingdao people. I visited the Beer Festival every year ever since I can remember. [...], I feel a very strong personal attachment with the beer festival".

The above comments show how the festival contributes to the image of the city. However, it is important to explore not only the associations made by reviews, but also how they evaluate the festival. Overall reviews are positive and recommend others to visit: "if in China definitely a must do if you can make it in the area by august" or "Well it is one of those places that is really compulsory". Other reviewers would not recommend an adjustment to the traveling schedule with the sole purpose of visiting the festival: "it is fun in a way and worth to visit once, but not worth to come to Qingdao only for that". Domestic tourists mainly express a desire to experience the festival in their reviews: "Qingdao is my dream destination. [...], I want to visit the Beer City" or "I have been to Qingdao out of the festival, it was interesting. I can imagine how lovely it would be during the festival". The opportunity to taste different brands of beer, the entertainment (singing, dancing, and acrobatics) and the overall atmosphere are praised: "it was amazing overall because of the atmosphere" and "at night though EVERY-THING is lit up like the Northern Light".

There are also more critical reviews recommending readers not to go there, with complaints about the food quality, prices, sanitation, and noise. One reviewer is unpleasantly surprised by the price of beer at the festival and exclaimed: "And Qingdao has a beer factory, so I really don't get how they can have the most expensive beer ever". Others seem to have had an overall bad experience: "loud, irritating and crowding" and "The area is generally crowded and the smells are unpleasant and the atmosphere is no different than a very average county fair". These latter two reviews seem to voice concerns that resonate with potential negative impacts mentioned in the academic literature on festivals. There are several reviews, international and domestic, that feel the festival is overcrowded or too commercial. One review sees this as a recent problem: "before beer festival was quite a nice place. Since last 3–4 years more and more people are coming from all China, [...]". From the contents presented here in the above paragraphs, we begin to see that the complexities of using festivals to enhance a place's brand become clear when assessing consumer reviews.

## Discussion and concluding remarks

This chapter started with a question concerning how a product deeply connected with its colonial history would be negotiated today. Heritage in general has been known to cause dissonance, and colonial heritage in particular is prone to different readings and meanings for various stakeholders (Yeoh, 2001; Graham, 2002; Jones & Shaw, 2006). Such issues may be engraved when they become part of a large-scale commercial festival catering to outside consumers who may be unaware of local history. This chapter has demonstrated that the "German-ness" of the beer festival is clearly present in the way it refers to Oktoberfest. The beer festival mimics the Munich Oktoberfest both in decoration and activities organized. References to Germany are mainly there to provide a themed experience: invoking a "generic" Bavarian atmosphere by using Bavarian flags, lederhosen, and symbols like maypoles. The Bavarian stereotypes used to decorate the beer festival and the theme park are wholly unconnected to the German architecture and urban planning actually present in the city. As such, the festival sites are rather placeless, themed areas are not rooted in a local sense of place (Ma & Lew, 2012).

The original brewery museum is the only clear connection between Tsingtao beer, the festival, and colonial times. The museum is housed in the original brewery. In this museum, visitors learn about the history of the beer and the brewery and thus the German and Japanese "occupation" are mentioned. Visitors share these insights on review sites, thus creating an awareness of this part of Qingdao's history. However, the reviews hardly evoke the impression of a contested heritage. On the contrary, the German history is partly seen as a mark of quality assurance for the beer. Visitors today marvel at the fact that the original German equipment is, one-hundred years later, still in operation. In the past, the German original of Tsingtao beer has been used in marketing campaigns as proof of the beer's authenticity (Yang, 2007).

Associations between the colonial history of the city and beer are limited. There are parallels here with how the city deals with its colonial past. The German architecture is used in projected images of the city as well (Ji, 2011), and may contribute to what makes the city stand out from other Chinese cities. Ongoing research by the authors has, moreover, found that German architecture and urban planning in Qingdao are valued. It is still clearly present in the historic city. On the other hand, professionals are somewhat reluctant to deliberately call it colonial heritage. They prefer simply "German heritage" and stress how objects represent local history and not some national ideology. The German colonial rule meanwhile is also described as a rather short interval in a long history of the city. This is in sharp contrast with the Japanese remains in the city. Factories built under Japanese rule are abandoned and decaying (Zang & Van Gorp, 2018). Professionals hinted at the national trauma that is still felt with regard to the Japanese occupations of parts of China. However, the latest tourism development plan does see opportunities for industrial tourism in Qingdao, and calls for an inventory of industrial heritage. Time will tell how this pans out for the textile mills erected during Japanese rule.

To conclude, Ma and Lew (2012) label the beer festival as a "local modern" festival contributing to local identity, but clearly focused on entertainment and fun instead of an authentic tradition. The reviews we analyzed confirmed this label for the festival. Locals do feel an attachment with the festival, and several reviewers express a notion of how the festival and the beer culture it represents are part of the local place identity. Events and festivals are increasingly used as part of city marketing and branding strategies. The Qingdao International Beer Festival may have originated in the early 1990s as a Bavarian-style Oktoberfest imitation to promote the sales of beer, but it has since developed into Asia's largest beer festival.

## Acknowledgements

We would like to thank the Chinese Scholarship Council for providing the Ph.D. scholarship.

## References

Backmann, K. (2018). Event management research: The focus today and in the future. *Tourism Management Perspectives*, 25, 169–171.

Black, D. (2007). The symbolic politics of sport mega events: 2010 in comparative Perspective. *Politikon*, 34(3),261–276.

Boisen, M., Terlouw, K., Groote, P. & Couwenberg, O. (2018). Reframing place promotion, place marketing and place branding – Moving beyond conceptual confusion. *Cities*, 80, 4–11.

Boisen, M., Terlouw, K. & Van Gorp, B. (2011). The selective nature of place branding and the layering of spatial identities. *Journal of Place Management and Development*, 4(2),135–147.

Bujdoso, Z. & Szucs, C. (2012). Beer tourism – From theory to practice. *Academica Turistica*, 5(1),103–111.

Conrad, S. (2016). *Deutsche Kolonialgeschichte*. 3rd Ed. München: Beck.

Du, J. & Qu, R. (2011). The birth of Qingdao International Beer Festival. [青岛国际啤酒节的诞生历程]. *Shandongdangan*, 1, 55–56.

Finance People. (2017). *Tsingtao Beer is designated to service in the summit of the Shanghai Cooperation Organization*. [青岛啤酒加入上海合作组织"朋友圈" 成为官方指定用酒]. http://finance.people.com.cn/n1/2017/0615/c153179-29342174.html [accessed 19 June 2018].

Getz, D. (2008). Event tourism: Definition, evolution and research. *Tourism Management*, 29(3),403–428.

Graham, B. (2002). Heritage as knowledge: Capital or culture?. *Urban Studies*, 39 (5–6), 1003–1017.

Hall, C. (2005). *Tourism, rethinking the social science of mobility*, London: Pearson Educational.

Hernández-Mogóllon, J., Duarte, P. & Folgado-Fernández, J. (2018). The contribution of cultural events to the formation of the cognitive and affective images of a tourist destination. *Journal of Destination Marketing & Management*, 8, 70–78.

Ille, F. (2009). Building Chinese global brands through soft technology transfer. *Journal of Chinese Economic and Foreign Trade Studies*, 2(1),47–61.

Ji, S. (2011). *Projected and perceived destination images of Qingdao, China*. PhD diss., University of Waterloo.

Jones, R. & Shaw, B.J. (2006). Palimpsests of progress: Erasing the past and rewriting the future in developing societies - Case studies of Singapore and Jakarta. *International Journal of Heritage Studies*, 12(2),122–138.

Kavaratzis, M. (2004). From city marketing to city branding: Towards a theoretical framework for developing city brands. *Place Branding*, 1(1),58–73.

Lu, H. (2008). *Taking Qingdao*. [话说青岛]. Qingdao: Qingdao Publishing House.

Ma, L. & Lew, A. (2012). Historical and geographical context in festival tourism Development. *Journal of Heritage Tourism*, 7(1),13–31.

Maheshwari, V., Vandewalle, I. & Bamber, D. (2011). Place branding's role in sustainable Development. *Journal of Place Management and Development*, 4(2),198–213.

Matzat, W. (2003). *Germania Brauerei und ihre Angestellten 1903–1914*. tsingtau.org. www.tsingtau.org/matzat-wilhelm-dr-prof-1930-2016/ [accessed 29 June 2018].

McDaniel, C.D. & Gates, R.H. (2010). *Marketing Research*. Oxford: Wiley.

Plummer, R., Telfer, R., Hashimoto, A. & Summers, R. (2005). Beer tourism in Canada along the Waterloo-Wellington Ale Trail. *Tourism Management*, 26, 447–458.

Preuss, H. (2015). A framework for identifying the legacies of a mega sport event. *Leisure Studies*, 34(6),643–664.

QDGJBEER. (2017). *Experiencing beer culture by 5D*. [5D带你体验啤酒文化]. www. qdgjbeer.com/a/xinwendongtai/jiaodianxinwen/2017/0626/46.html [accessed 19 June 2018].

Richards, G., de Brito, M. & Wilks, L. (Eds) (2013). *Exploring the social impacts of events*. London: Routledge.

Richards, G. & Palmer, R. (2010). *Eventful cities: Cultural management and urban Revitalization*. London: Elsevier.

Rogerson, C. & Collins, K. (2015). Developing beer tourism in South Africa: International Perspectives. *African Journal of Hospitality, Leisure and Tourism*, 4(1),1–15.

Runyan, R. & Huddleston, P. (2006). Getting customers downtown: The role of branding in achieving success for central business districts. *Journal of Product & Brand Management*, 15(1),48–61.

Schrecker, J. (1971). *Imperialism and Chinese Nationalism: Germany in Shantung*. Cambridge: Harvard University Press.

Schrecker, J.E. (1977). Kiautschou and the problems of German colonialism. In J.A. Moses & P.M. Kennedy (Eds). *Germany in the Pacific and Far East, 1870–1914*. St. Lucia: University of Queensland Press (185–208).

Schultz-Naumann, J. (1985). *Unter Kaisers flagge: Deutschlands schutzgebiete im Pazifik und in China einst und heute*. München: Universitas.

Smith, A. (2012). *Events and urban regeneration: The strategic use of events to revitalize cities*. London: Routledge.

Travel Sina. (2013). *Over 4 million visitors came to the 23rd Qingdao International Beer Festival*. [第23届青岛啤酒节闭幕接待400万人]. http://travel.sina.com.cn/china/2013-08-26/1114211841.shtml [accessed 11 May 2018].

Vanolo, A. (2015). The image of the creative city eight years later: Turin, urban branding and the economic crisis taboo. *Cities*, 46, 1–7.

Von Richthofen, F. (1882). *Das nördliche China*, vol. 2 of *China: Ergebnisse eigener reisen und darauf gegründeter studien*. Berlin: Reimer.

Wise, N., Flinn, J. & Mulec, I. (2015). Exit festival: Contesting political pasts, impacts on youth culture and regenerating the image of Serbia and Novi Sad. In T. Pernecky & O. Moufakkir (Eds). *Ideological, social and cultural aspects of events*. Wallingford: CABI (60–73).

Wise, N. & Harris, J. (Eds) (2017). *Sport, events, tourism and regeneration*. London: Routledge.

Xinhuanet. (2018). *Enjoying the Qingdao Beer Festival in Huangdao*. [沉醉西海岸, 尽在青岛 啤酒节]. www.xinhuanet.com/expo/2018-06/13/c_1122977317.htm [accessed 6 July 2018].

Yang, Z. (2007). "This beer tastes really good": Nationalism, consumer culture and development of the beer industry in Qingdao, 1903–1993. *The Chinese Historical Review*, 14(1),29–58.

Yeoh, B.S. (2001). Postcolonial cities. *Progress in Human Geography*, 25(3),456–468.

Yu, H. & Fu, Y. (2010). The research on the current status and future development of the Qingdao International Beer Festival. [关于青岛国际啤酒节目前发展状况及 其发展前景的调查研究]. *Internet Fortune • Theory Studies*, 6, 154.

Zang, X. & Van Gorp, B. (2018). Assessing the potential of resident participation in local heritage conservation, the case of Qingdao, China. In J. Clark & N. Wise (Eds). *Urban renewal, community and participation*. Berlin: Springer (141-159).

# 8 A taste of place

## The Hokitika Wildfoods Festival in New Zealand

*Alexandra Gillespie & C. Michael Hall*

### Introduction: Food, place and events

Food is a powerful expression of place that has long been associated with the hosting of events (Hall & Sharples, 2008). For much of the history of food events the justification for their being held has been primarily dominated by religion and/or the celebration of certain times of the agricultural cycle, such as harvest (Corsale & Vuytsyk, 2018; LaPan & Barbieri, 2014). Food-related events are therefore deeply embedded in the fabric of many cultures and communities (Timothy, 2016). However, with the industrialization of agriculture and the global food system, food events have become increasingly commodified and focused on promoting place, and in particular their produce, as attractions and destinations for trade and tourism (Hall & Sharples, 2008).

Food events lie at the intersection of numerous stakeholder demands (Hall & Sharples, 2008). From a business perspective their primary marketing function is to provide products, sponsors, and destinations with an opportunity to secure high prominence in the market place whilst also adding brand value and building consumer relationships (Chang et al., 2014; Girish & Chen, 2017). However, because of the nature of food as a product and the daily part it plays in personal consumption and economic systems, food events are more than just retailing, marketing, and promotional opportunities but also coincide with a number of other economic, political, and social concerns (Hall & Gössling, 2013, 2016). These include the nature of contemporary agricultural systems, conservation and maintenance of rural landscapes and lifestyles, notions of community, and concerns over food quality (Chung et al., 2018; Hall & Gössling, 2016; Roy et al., 2017).

Food events can therefore be understood on multiple, interconnected levels. Food events are not just about external promotion to visitors and/or consumers outside of the host region, but they can also have substantial internal drivers that relate to the consumption and production of food from particular locations and communities, and to the maintenance of those communities (Hall, 2016). Food events are therefore strongly connected to senses of place and community pride in local products and can contribute substantially to an understanding of local and regional identity (Timothy, 2016). Interestingly, such notions of identity may be reinforced by appellations and geographically protected products that serve to connect identity with place and global production processes (Gössling & Hall, 2016). However, the emotions and necessities that surround food are significant for producers and consumers, and have potential implications for identities and lifestyles. Therefore, a reading of events that have been held over time may provide clues to understanding how social and economic change is reflected in the hosting, management, and promotion of events (Hall & Sharples, 2008).

This chapter discusses the hosting of the Hokitika Wildfoods Festival in Hokitika on the west coast of the South Island of New Zealand. The festival celebrates the rugged, wild nature of the Westland District and the wider West Coast Region (Leung-Wai et al., 2012). The festival has been held since 1990 in a township that was first developed by European settlers in connection with the discovery of gold in the region. The mining and pioneering spirit has become integral to the region's identity and has become an important element in the promotion of regional products. However, at the same time there is a strong sense of self-identity associated with the region's heritage, which also becomes an element in the sense of place that the festival has sought to promote.

The festival has become integral to regional tourism and place promotion as it is now a recognized brand both domestically and internationally, and receives significant media exposure in travel guides, magazines, newspapers, websites, and television news programmes (Leung-Wai et al., 2012; Wilson, 2014). Promotion of both physical features, including the natural environment, and cultural aspects such as the welcoming community, small seaside town, and the party atmosphere associated with the festival, has also mutually reinforced the positioning of the festival as an authentic New Zealand, and West Coast, experience (Modlik, 2015).

*National Geographic Traveller* magazine placed the festival on their 'World's best food festivals celebrating local tastes' list, claiming the 'globe's gutsiest diners alight on the South Island at Hokitika's Wild Foods Festival to feast on the world's most extreme cuisine' (Stone, 2011). The event was also favored with the tag of the most 'outrageous food experience' in New Zealand, a claim that won it a place in Frommer's top 300 unmissable festivals in the world (The Age, 2011). Lonely Planet endorse the festival as offering weird and wild fare 'for the intrepid eater' (Whitmay, 2016), while Bucketlistmap (2017), recommend that 'it is definitely worth doing at least one time in your life'. The *Straits Times* placed the festival on its 'Eating your way around the world' list of best food festivals, asserting that savoring local food is a simple and pleasurable way to discover a different culture (Vasko, 2017). This report also suggested that a food festival is an ideal opportunity to discover local culture, as this is when a community's favorite food is celebrated and shared among locals and visitors (Vasko, 2017). However, the issue of whether the 'wild' in the festival's title represents local heritage and identity, or whether it is part of an attempt by a relatively peripheral and tourism-dependent community to achieve a profile in a highly crowded food event and tourism marketplace is a matter of considerable debate. For example, the festival's infamous 'stallion semen' shots prompted an international media frenzy (Deidre, 2014), from the Australian media claim that: 'in the world of extreme food, shots of stallion semen are the treat du jour—across the Tasman at least' (The Age, 2011) to a Belgium newspaper's playful mocking that 'a glass of fresh stallion sperm will undoubtedly be a hit at the Hokitika Wildfoods festival' (Het Laatste Nieuws, 2011).

## Context

The discovery of gold in the Taramakau Valley brought about an influx of prospectors and traders in the 1860s to Hokitika's River mouth, the closest anchorage to the diggings (Nathan, 2009). Miners ventured to the Hokitika township for supplies, recreation, and to sell gold. Hokitika's population peaked at over 4,000 during the gold rush, however it had dropped to 2,000 by the end of the nineteenth century as the mining industry declined (Nathan, 2009). For most of the twentieth century, agriculture and forestry sustained the regional economy, for which Hokitika remained a service municipality (Hegele, 2011). In 1965 a tourism market developed with the opening of State Highway 6 through South Westland and over Haast. This allowed the development of a circular tourist route from the gateway city of Christchurch whereby tourists follow a route over Arthur's Pass, through Hokitika to the glaciers, and then cross back to the east coast over Haast Pass to connect through to Christchurch or, increasingly, Queenstown. The growth of accommodation and outdoor recreation opportunities has therefore seen Hokitika become an important tourist centre, with a population of approximately 3,000, in a region in which tourism is becoming increasingly significant especially given the decline of traditional extractive industries such as mining and forestry (Hegele, 2011).

The Hokitika township has developed a distinct identity as a major tourist destination (Nathan, 2009). Given its position as a gateway to the Westland World Heritage Park (Hegele, 2011), and location on the Tasman Sea, Hokitika exemplifies a remote regional tourist enclave. Nevertheless, few of its buildings now face water, with the main street business district, the hub of the goldminers' trade, set back from the beach and the river (Romano, 2016), and the harbor, once one of New Zealand's busiest during the gold rush era, closing in the 1950s. Rail traffic has also been closed to passengers although a freight rail link remains in use for the transport of milk products. The region's boom-bust economy is exemplified by an historical dependence on extractive industries and international commodity prices have undoubtedly contributed to a particular local identity that is promoted as being slow-going and nonchalant. It is connected to a New Zealand notion of a 'Wild West', with the area often described in tourism promotion materials as the 'Wild West Coast' (Romano, 2016). Significantly, this identity has been utilized in the promotion of various South Island and West Coast regional products since the 1990s. Perhaps foremost amongst these is the portrayal of 'Southern Man'.

The 'Southern Man' identity represents the rural and high country areas of the South Island as a nostalgic ideal, the last bastion of treasured New Zealand values of a bygone era (Law, 1997). Described as 'a rugged, outdoor, hard-working folk hero', the 'Southern Man' is steeped in genuine values and a sense of regional pride derived from an ancestry of colonial masculinity and authority over the animal world manifested in New Zealand's pioneering history (Gee & Jackson, 2010; Law, 1997). However, this heroism is tinged with dry, self-mocking humour, where southern men are also quirky, with a personality and an attitude of not taking things too seriously (Law, 1997). Ironically, such mythical images of idealized New Zealand rurality are used to contrast with city dwellers, and commercialized and commodified culture (Gee & Jackson, 2010), in order to sell products, usually beer, to urban dwellers in what is a highly urbanized society.

Another strong regional brand identity is that of the official Hokitika Wildfoods festival sponsor Monteith's, which brews a range of beer advertised as embodying pioneer heritage values (Le Heron & Pawson, 1996). A leading boutique New Zealand beer brand, Monteiths promote themselves as being dedicated to a 'follow no one' approach, characterized by producing original, high quality products (see Monteiths, 2017). An open vat fermentation (which can attract wild yeasts), the use of coal-fired boilers, and batch brewing distinguishes Monteith's products from other breweries. This vision is in line with that of the Hokitika Wildfoods Festival, thus it is unsurprising Monteith's appeared at the first Wildfoods Festival in 1990 and became an official sponsor in 1995 (Glass, 2011), a position it still holds today. The wider commercial and regional context of place identity and heritage is integral to the development and continued existence of the event, which has served to try and balance commercial and community needs from the outset.

## History

Claire Bryant, a local Hokitika woman, initiated the original celebration of foods from the South Island West Coast (Hokitika Wildfoods Festival, 2017). The festival was originally tied in to the commemoration of 125 years of goldfields history in the region in 1990 (White, 1997) by the opening of a quayside development on the site of the old port, the main access point during the West Coast gold rush. Bryant suggested that holding a festival on the quayside would be a unique way to promote the area to visitors, as West Coast wild foods, including her gorse-flower wine and rose-petal brew, were already receiving awareness among locals and visitors.

The first Wildfoods Festival was officially opened at midday on March 24, 1990 (West Coast Times, 1990), with 28 food stalls selling a range of fare, from possum and smoked eel pates, to goat's yoghurt and chamois goulash (West Coast Times, 1990). Although many such products are now regarded as relatively 'normal', at the time the Hokitika Wildfoods Festival was challenging culinary convention in New Zealand (Timaru Herald, 2010). Winning a West Coast Tourism Award of Excellence for the original event (Dorothy, 2006), the Hokitika Wildfoods Festival has become an annual iconic event in New Zealand (Hokitika Wildfoods Festival, 2017). The rare opportunity to celebrate and sample a variety of locally grown, hunted, and gathered 'wild foods' not readily available outside of the festival (Leung-Wai et al., 2012) has stressed the uniqueness of the West Coast as a place to visit (West Coast Times, 1990).

## The festival

### Cuisine

The gastronomic creations served at the Hokitika Wildfoods Festival present an experience that cannot be found on supermarket shelves. Festival-goers are encouraged to expose their palate to 'a taste of the wild', from delicacy to disgusting and everywhere along the spectrum in-between (Hegele, 2011). The festival has always been about 'different foods that are right on our back door', with every realm of wild foods explored, from sea to bush, plains to mountains (Modlik, 2015). Often presented in an innovative fashion (Hegele, 2011), dishes include, what is to some people's palates, extremely adventurous cuisine, with foods such as mutton bird or sheep's testicles prepared in stews, puddings, and kebabs (Hochmanjan, 2002; McCarthy, 2004). One chef spent weeks collecting baby wasp larvae from Canterbury for a larvae compote on polenta, served with organic honeydew in a reduction of balsamic vinegar (Hochmanjan, 2002). Every year new innovative culinary assortments are offered, such as deer semen shots and camel-milk coffee in 2017, to attract (or repulse) new and returning customers (Carroll, 2017). Nonetheless 'tried and true' regional 'classics', including huhu grubs, whitebait, and mountain oysters, return year after year (Carroll, 2017). Tallyrand (2003) pinpointed something of the event's philosophy when he suggested that the festival is about being a hunter and gatherer, that if you can hunt it, shoot it, spear it, or dig it up, it will be cooked and served.

The wild fare of the festival, such as barbequed seagull legs (Hochmanjan, 2002), and cow udders (Mussen, 2012) challenges many taste buds (Romano, 2016; Whitmay, 2016). An early assessment of the festival suggested that if it looks bizarre, wiggles, squiggles, or squirms, odds are it is on the menu and that nothing is off limits in culinary terms (Nicholson & Pearce, 2001). More recently, Modlik and Johnston (2017) argued that the culinary offerings materially and symbolically exemplified the fascinating yet repulsive nature of wild foods. While some are up for the challenge, insisting they 'just can't think about what it is' as they scull back a shot of horse semen, others face abjection at the idea of swallowing a goat's testicle (Modlik, 2015). However, such academic observations fail to acknowledge the long tradition of food foraging in New Zealand and its association with indigenous, pioneer, and post-colonial migrant identities. Earlier New Zealand cookbooks often included recipes for animals, such as possum or mutton bird, which are now considered exotic but, significantly, have long been regarded as part of the local foodways of the West Coast. Nevertheless, such offerings have often created tensions in terms of what the festival represents and its attraction to visitors. For example, the seventeenth festival saw festival organizers eliminating much of the 'gross' fare in favour of more 'gourmet' offerings, in the hope of attracting a more 'mature' audience by offering more appealing food (The Press, 2007). It was reported that goat testicles and other things people were 'very reluctant' to eat had turned the festival into a 'fear factor' competition of unpalatable food, as opposed to a celebration of west coast culinary cuisine (The Press, 2007). Therefore, there has been growing emphasis on classic 'good old bush tucker', such as game meats or a Maori hangi (Christian, 1998; Vasko, 2017), or 'West Coast icons' such as whitebait and venison (Hegele, 2011). Other more refined offerings include honeycomb pieces, Kowlua and milk (homemade coffee liqueur with unpasteurised cow's milk), fresh strawberries with real cream, and spit roasted venison kebabs are also usually on offer (Adams, 2009). 'Westcargots', indigenous snails in garlic and white wine, are collected from local gardens by girl guides (Tyrell-Kenyon, 2002). However, in consciously seeking to offer more 'acceptable' food, the festival faces interesting choices with respect to the mix of local foods that are a formal part of food supply chains, such as fish and wild game, to those that are informal and not readily sold for consumption, but which nevertheless are part of local foraging and food traditions and those that represent potential food innovations.

Given the tensions that surround food offerings, it is therefore not surprising that some controversy has also arisen at Hokitika Wildfoods when certain foods have been sold. For example, Fish and Game, the collective brand name of 12 regional Fish and Game Councils and the New Zealand Fish and Game Council, which administers sports fishing and gamebird resources in New Zealand, provided samples of barbecued pukeko and paradise duck, both protected species that can only be culled a few months each year (Mussen, 2012). As a result, some people labelled Fish and Game 'rednecks' for offering samples of the birds, even though the Fish and Game Council had authorized the cull (Radio New Zealand, 2010).

Nevertheless, the wider notions of what is acceptable (and respectable) in food consumption is something that changes over time. For example, W. Barton (1999) observed that there was once a time when the reaction of most New Zealanders to a photograph in the *Dominion* (a daily newspaper) of two women eating the private parts of a bull at the Hokitika Wildfoods Festival would have been one of horror. Instead, 'today many people would rather consider "I wonder what it tastes like". Throwing culinary caution to the wind, in favour of a new-found sense of adventure' (W. Barton, 1999). As W. Barton (1999) noted, tried simply because they are available, the different types of foods available at the festival are part of a food revolution driven partly by adventurous young chefs, partly by producers, as well as increasing exposure through travel and migration to other cuisines that would not otherwise be experienced.

*Atmosphere*

The food offerings serve to complement the festival's theme, and the popularity of the festival is not just the exotic fare, but also the entire atmosphere and entertainment package. Roving entertainers meander amidst the crowd, from belly dancers and acrobats to magicians and clowns, entertaining congregations while multiple bandstands and buskers provide music throughout the day (Adams, 2009). Cowboys, duck shooters, cows, glamour queens, zombies, and almost any other costume imaginable are also donned by some attendees, contributing to a 'carnival' atmosphere (Mussen, 2013), with a ratio of the fancy-dressed to the non-costumed sometimes so high that Brown (2009) observed that plain clothed patrons almost look out of place. Such an atmosphere is encouraged by a costume competition that rewards the best (or perhaps wildest) dressed (Vasko, 2017), while there is also a range of carnival games and rides available. Specific entertainment such as the 'Kids Korner' and animal farm (Hokitika Wildfoods Festival, 2017) cater to children and help create a family friendly atmosphere. Additional festivities that have been included over the years include a Wild Warmup comedy show (Carroll, 2017) and Saturday and Sunday markets, which are also family friendly.

For the food-oriented visitor there are demonstrations by local and international 'celebrity chefs', in addition to seminars and competitions about unusual foods (Hegele, 2011). As well as being entertainment, these provide consumer exposure to new or emerging regional food products. Another contribution to supporting local products has been 'O'Feral Fashion at the Foods', a competition supported by designer Annah Stretton, which encourages attendees to don fur, feathers, or flora and fauna, the wilder the better, with classes for feral beauty/beast, Wild West, and animators (Deidre, 2014). Apart from the fashion component, such a competition helps support the use of animal skin and fur products, many of which are pest species.

The atmosphere that draws in the party crowd is created by the combination of food, music, young people and the availability of alcohol at the festival (Modlik & Johnston, 2017). Further, the festival also hosts an official afterparty (originally a barn dance) to keep the festivities going all night long (Nicholson & Pearce, 2001). Spatially, the festival atmosphere is not restricted to Cass Square, a public sports ground where the festival is now held, but takes over the entire downtown area, with full accommodation and hotels, as well as freedom campers and campervans in many of the streets (Davis, 2000; Modlik, 2015). Potentially, therefore, the festival also provides a temporary liminal space removed from the normal atmosphere and happenings in the town, which reinforces the 'wild' brand (Modlik, 2015). However, it is worth noting that such a 'circus' has been regarded as a potential negative for serious 'foodies' (Timaru Herald, 2008).

*Community*

A 2012 Economic Impact Assessment found that the Hokitika Wildfoods Festival attracted 9,700 visitors to the district who stayed an average of 2.5 days (Leung-Wai et al., 2012). Total expenditure attributed to the festival in the Westland District is estimated at NZ $6.5 million, contributing to the local tourism industry, employment, and community group fundraising in the Westland District economy (Leung-Wai et al., 2012). Raising money for local community groups has supported community benefits including the upgrading and building of community facilities and maintenance of membership fees for facilities used by local groups (Leung-Wai et al., 2012). The Westland District Council took over management of the festival in 1993 (Dorothy, 2006). Although the council employs an event management team for the event, who, among a range of other roles, prepare a marketing plan, update the festival website and Facebook page, and work with customer service staff to promote the festival (Westland District Council, 2016), the community remains an essential element in the management and promotion of the festival. The Hokitika Wildfoods festival is regarded as giving local people a sense of belonging and pride; not only does it provide an economic injection into the area, but it is also one of the most buoyant days for the local community (Modlik, 2015) and has long been perceived as being a celebration of community (Timaru Herald, 2010).

The event was originally established through the creativity and entrepreneurship of a local person who has had a profound effect on her local community and businesses (N. Barton, 2016). From the very first festival, which coincided with the Hokitaika quasquicentennial, regalia including flags, banners, and windsocks set a community scene, with community volunteers helping set it up (West Coast Times, 1990). Family and community stalls remain a feature of the event despite a growth in commercial operations over the life course of the event (White, 1997). After 25 years community groups make up almost half of the stalls, taking advantage of the influx of visitors and using the festival as a significant fundraiser (Brown, 2009; Carroll, 2017, The Press, 2007). The festival also offers high school catering and hospitality students exposure to the experience of a live food event (Smith, 2005). Fundraising is also sometimes externally oriented. For example, the Christchurch earthquake of 2011 saw the community come together to support victims, from one stall donating all their mutton bird (*tītī*) southern delicacies for the funerals of several people killed in the February 22 earthquake (Mussen, 2013), to The Holy Smoke Cafe stall run by parishioners in nuns' habits, raising money for St Mary's, the local Catholic church that closed because of earthquake risk (Deidre, 2014).

Wildfoods is not without community controversy though. There have been tensions between residents and tourism providers over the years due to the excessive alcohol consumption that goes hand-in-hand with the event. While the visitors leave behind millions of dollars in Hokitika, they have also, at times, left damaged property, litter, upset residents, and worn-out police (Booker, 2005). According to Tyrell-Kenyon (2002):

> The streets were strewn with rubbish from overflowing bins, and there were people sitting or lying in every shop doorway. The supermarket looked as if it was being looted—those still able to stand peered over huge crates of beer cradled in their arms as they stumbled out into the road. The beach was already littered with bodies and, occasionally, a naked man rushed past, somersaulting into the crashing (freezing) surf. There were plenty of fires to warm up by afterwards, dotted all along the beach.
>
> (Tyrell-Kenyon, 2002)

At some festivals in the late 1990s and early 2000s the streets and beach were repeatedly left littered with broken glass, resulting in several injuries and disturbance to the residents on Beach Street (The Press, 2003).

In 2006, Co-organizer Sue Hustwick claimed that although Hokitika loves its annual influx of visitors, it was 'getting too wild, even for us' (New Zealand Herald, 2006). Thus, a feature that challenged all West Coast stereotypes, a liquor ban, was brought in to try and 'tame' the festival, and ensure a more peaceful, clean and safe, family-oriented event. The ban sought to cut down on drinking in public places including the streets, beach, and downtown attractions, with an exemption for the town's camping grounds. Alcohol is still sold and drunk alongside the wild foods, however the number of stalls selling alcohol was substantially reduced and hard liquor 'shooters' banned. According to Hokitika Mayor Maureen Pugh, 'We wanted to take the focus off the alcohol but put a bit more emphasis on the family kind of day out ... and also the food, it is Wild Food Festival after all' (One News, 2006).

While residents and police are generally supportive of the ban due to the chaos and the mess created, hoteliers were against alcohol bans, claiming that many genuine visitors would not get the complete festival experience with a liquor ban in place (Booker, 2005). Interestingly, Monteiths Brewing Company, the premier alcohol sponsor of the event supports the ban, as they consider themselves as a brand that is more about refined drinking and a range of different tastes and beer and food matching, rather than getting drunk. Nevertheless, while the festival is often blamed for encouraging intoxication in patrons, an event organizer claimed that 'the real issue was with people preloading before even heading to the festival. And then the festival gets labelled with getting everyone drunk' (Whangarei Northern Advocate, 2014).

## Conclusions and futures

The Wildfoods Festival is widely credited with raising the profile of Hokitika and the wider West Coast region (Leung-Wai et al., 2012), while creating a sense of place attachment and belonging for the local community and of place identity to the domestic and international audience (Modlik, 2015). The 'Wild West Coast' identity existed long before the Hokitika Wildfoods Festival, but the festival has served to reinforce this. Nevertheless, managing the commodification of this identity involves varying issues, each with their own positive and negative aspects.

Although the 'Southern Man' identity is idealistic, specifically in the West Coast, social and technological change perhaps makes this identity less relevant (Gee & Jackson, 2010). Once considered a potential threat to the steadfast frontiersman form of hegemonic masculinity, a consumer-based contemporary society is now reality, and consumerism marked by contemporary tourism in particular has spread into even small West Coast communities (Gee & Jackson, 2010). In New Zealand, use of the 'macho man' stereotype is no longer an everyday expectation, especially when the country's substantial mental health issues require sensitivity rather than the 'silent stanch' pressures promoted in this image (Yates, 2015).

Importantly, the festival emerged from within the community as part of the celebration of the region's heritage and it has retained a strong community feel and support. However, like many events the festival is experiencing changes in its management and organisation as a result of broader shifts in society and governance. Although managed by the local council (N. Barton, 2016), in 2015 the festival was outsourced to an external organizer due to the closing of the council's events department (O'Connor, 2015). The Wildfoods brand is valuable in the New Zealand context; selling the festival brand would be potentially lethal to Hokitika, specifically considering the experience of the selling of Nelson's Wearable Arts awards, a festival previously held in Nelson at the top of the South Island, which led to the new owner moving the festival to Wellington to increase profits (O'Connor, 2015). Yet the festival does face considerable challenges, from varying food trends to fluctuating festival attendance and stall numbers, and much in between. Prior to 2003, attendance figures were not always recorded, however various sources (Leung-Wai et al., 2012; Modlik, 2015) assert 2003 to be the peak festival, with numbers slowly declining since. This is due to a variety of factors, including ticket capping (The Press, 2003), alcohol restrictions (The Press, 2003), the Canterbury earthquakes (O'Connor, 2015), and the global financial crisis. The number of stalls has also fluctuated since 1990, starting at 28 (White, 1997), peaking at 91 in 2005 (Smith, 2005), and currently capped at 50 (Carroll, 2017). The menu, which once was pure wild bush tucker fare including venison goulash, possum pate, smoked eel, and whitebait patties (White, 1997), has shifted towards more gourmet specialties, as well as 'fare factor' type eating, vegetarian and vegan food, and more sustainable cooking.

Emerging as significant events for tourism development, food festivals have long been recognized as providing not only strong economic benefits to often peripheral locations, but also a platform to celebrate cultural heritage and identity (Hall & McArthur, 1993; Hall & Sharples, 2008; Timothy, 2016). With a proliferation of wine and food festivals around New Zealand, the Hokitika Wildfoods Festival provides something very distinctive in the country's food event and tourism offerings that serves to attract many people from outside of the region in which it is held.

Arguably the most important consideration for the longer-term wellbeing of the festival is for the place-based nature of the event to be recognized as its greatest strength (Modlik, 2015). By focusing on the sense of place that was intrinsic to the festival from the beginning, it becomes extremely difficult for the event's core attributes to be replicated. Perhaps, ironically, one of the best examples of this comes from the event's premier beer sponsor and a leading regional beer brand: 'If you follow someone, you risk imitating them. But if you strike out on your own, there's no such risk' (Monteiths, 2017).

## References

Adams, M. (2009), 'Wildfoods Festival fare wild fun', *Bangor Daily News*, 9 April, http://bangordailynews.com/2009/04/09/news/wildfoods-festival-fare-wild-fun/?ref=relatedBox.

The Age (2011), 'Feeling seedy? One sip will get you racing', *The Age*, 19 February.

Barton, N. (2016), 'Greymouth local heroes honoured for services to the community', *The New Zealander of the Year Awards*, 7 December, http://nzawards.org.nz/news/greymouth-local-heroes-honoured-services-community/.

Barton, W. (1999), 'Food's wild new wave', *The Dominion Post*, 18 March.

Booker, J. (2005), 'Alcohol ban aims to tame Wild West Coast festival', *New Zealand Herald*, 7 October, www.nzherald.co.nz/nz/news/article.cfm?c_id=1&objectid=10349190.

Brown, G. (2009), 'Organisers raise fees to save Hokitika Wildfoods Festival', *The Press*, 28 August.

Bucketlistmap (2017), 'Hokitika Wildfoods Festival', www.bucketlistmap.com/en/166-hokitika-wildfoods-festival.

Carroll, J. (2017), 'Deer semen and huhu grubs on offer at Hokitika's Wildfoods Festival', *Stuff*, 12 March, www.stuff.co.nz/national/90327150/deer-semen-and-huhu-grubs-on-offer-at-hokitikas-wildfoods-festival.

Chang, S., Gibson, H., & Sisson, L. (2014), 'The loyalty process of residents and tourists in the festival context', *Current Issues in Tourism*, 17(9), 783–799.

Christian, P. (1998), 'Wild delights fill body and soul', *The Press*, 19 March.

Chung, J. Y., Kim, J. S., Lee, C. K., & Kim, M. J. (2018), 'Slow-food-seeking behaviour, authentic experience, and perceived slow value of a slow-life festival', *Current Issues in Tourism*, 21(2), 123–127.

Corsale, A. & Vuytsyk, O. (2018), 'Jewish heritage tourism between memories and strategies. Different approaches from Lviv, Ukraine', *Current Issues in Tourism*, 21(5), 583–598.

Davis, L. (2000), 'The wild wild west', *Metro*, 227, 102–106.

Deidre, M. (2014), 'New tasty treats to try from festival's menu', *The Press*, 7 March.

Dorothy (2006), Hokitika Wildfoods Festival – What is it and why do they have to limit ticket sales? *NZine*, 31 March, www.nzine.co.nz/features/hokitika_wildfoods.html.

Gee, S. & Jackson, S. J. (2010), 'The Southern Man city as cultural place and speight's space: Locating the masculinity-sport-beer 'holy trinity' in New Zealand', *Sport in Society*, 13(10), 1516–1531.

Girish, V. G. & Chen, C. F. (2017), 'Authenticity, experience, and loyalty in the festival context: Evidence from the San Fermin festival, Spain', *Current Issues in Tourism*, 20(15), 1551–1556.

Glass, A. (2011), New sponsor named for coast wild-food event', *The Press*, 20 January, www.stuff.co.nz/the-press/news/4563694/New-sponsor-named-for-Coast-wild-food-event.

Gössling, S. & Hall, C.M. (2016), 'Conclusions: Food tourism and regional development – New localism or globalism?' In C.M. Hall & S. Gössling (eds.) *Food tourism and regional development: Networks, products and trajectories* (pp. 287–294). Abingdon: Routledge.

Hall, C.M. (2016), 'Heirloom products in heritage places: Farmers markets, local food, and food diversity'. In D. Timothy (ed.) *Heritage cuisines: Traditions, identities and tourism* (pp. 88–103). Abingdon: Routledge.

Hall, C.M. & Gössling, S. (eds.) (2013), *Sustainable culinary systems*, Abingdon: Routledge.

Hall, C.M. & Gössling, S. (eds.) (2016), *Food tourism and regional development: Networks, products and trajectories*, Abingdon: Routledge.

Hall, C.M. & McArthur, S. (eds.) (1993), *Heritage management in New Zealand and Australia: Visitor management, interpretation and marketing*, Auckland: Oxford University Press.

Hall, C.M. & Sharples, L. (eds.) (2008), *Food and Wine Festivals and events around the world: Development, management and markets*, Oxford: Butterworth Heinemann.

Hegele, H. (2011), *Hokitika Wildfoods Festival*, www.newzealand.com/ie/article/hoki tika-wildfoods-festival.

Het Laatste Nieuws (2011), 'Paardensperma wordt hit op 'extreem voedingssalon'', *Het Laatste Nieuws*, 18 February, www.hln.be/hln/nl/959/Bizar/article/detail/1224457/2011/02/18/Paardensperma-wordt-hit-op-extreem-voedingssalon.dhtml.

Hochmanjan, D. (2002), 'The call of the wild foods', *The New York Times*, 13 January, www.nytimes.com/2002/01/13/travel/the-call-of-the-wild-foods.html?mcubz=0.

Hokitika Wildfoods Festival (2017), *Hokitika Wildfoods Festival*, www.wildfoods.co.nz.

LaPan, C. & Barbieri, C. (2014), 'The role of agritourism in heritage preservation', *Current Issues in Tourism*, 17(8), 666–673.

Law, R. (1997), 'Masculinity, place, and beer advertising in New Zealand: The Southern Man campaign', *New Zealand Geographer*, 53(2), 22–28.

Le Heron, R.B. & Pawson, E. (1996), *Changing places: New Zealand in the nineties*, Auckland: Longman Paul.

Leung-Wai, J., Stokes, F., & Dixon, H. (2012), *The 2012 Wildfoods Festival: An economic impact assessment*, www.parliament.nz/resource/0000215342.

McCarthy, P. (2004), 'Real WILD ones', *The Southland Times*, 20 March.

Modlik, M. (2015), 'Let's get wild': Sensuous geographies of Kāwhia Kai and Hokitika Wildfoods Festivals in Aotearoa New Zealand, Doctoral dissertation, University of Waikato.

Modlik, M. & Johnston, L. (2017), 'Huhu grubs, bull semen shots and koki: Visceral geographies of regional food festivals in Aotearoa', *New Zealand Geographer*, 73(1), 25–34.

Monteiths (2017), 'Follow no one', www.monteiths.co.nz/Follow-No-One.

Mussen, D. (2012), 'Grubs and EQC jokes shake blues', *The Press*, 12 March.

Mussen, D. (2013), 'Wild and weird come out to play on West Coast', *Sunday Star-Times*, 3 March.

Nathan, S. (2009), 'West Coast places', *Te Ara - the Encyclopedia of New Zealand*, www.TeAra.govt.nz/en/west-coast-places/page-12.

New Zealand Herald (2006), 'Booze bans means festival not so wild', *New Zealand Herald*, 18 January.

Nicholson, R. E. & Pearce, D. G. (2001), 'Why do people attend events: A comparative analysis of visitor motivations at four South Island events', *Journal of Travel Research*, 39, 449–460.

O'Connor, S. (2015), 'Loss jeopardises Wildfoods Festival', *The Press*, 28 March.

One News (2006), 'Options vary wildly at food fest', *One News*, 11 March, http://tvnz.co.nz/content/680274/2591764.xhtml.

The Press (2003), 'Wildfoods crowd may be capped at 18,000', *The Press*, 21 August.

The Press (2007), 'Gourmet flavour to Wildfoods Festival', *The Press*, 5 March.

Radio New Zealand (2010), 'Thousands flock to Wild Foods Festival', 13 March, www.radionz.co.nz/news/national/53217/thousands-flock-to-wild-foods-festival.

Romano, E. (2016), '10 tasty food festivals around the world', *D'Marge*, 27 June, www.dmarge.com/2016/06/worlds-best-food-festivals.html.

Roy, H., Hall, C.M., & Ballantine, P. (2017), 'Trust in local food networks: The role of trust among tourism stakeholders and their impacts in purchasing decisions', *Journal of Destination Marketing and Management*, 6, 309–317.

Smith, M. (2005), 'Wildfoods fans start salivating', *The Southland Times*, 4 March.

Stone, G.W. (2011), 'Where's the party?', *National Geographic Traveller*, 28(7), 110–111.

Tallyrand (2003), Hokitika Wildfood's Festival 2003, www.hub-uk.com/interesting/hokitika2003.htm.

Timaru Herald (2008), 'A circus sideshow for the real foodies', *The Timaru Herald*, 7 March.

Timaru Herald (2010), 'Grub's up', *Timaru Herald*, 19 March.

Timothy, D. (ed.) (2016), *Heritage cuisines: Traditions, identities and tourism*, Abingdon: Routledge.

Tyrell-Kenyon, V. (2002), 'Grubs treat', *The Spectator*, 22 June.

Vasko, L. (2017), 'Eating your way around the world', *The Straits Times*, 12 July, www.nationmultimedia.com/detail/world/30320477.

West Coast Times (1990), 'Fine weather promised for Hokitika celebrations', *West Coast Times*, 23 March, http://ketewestcoast.peoplesnetworknz.info/en/site/images/show/394?view_size=large.

Westland District Council (2016), 'Position description. Role: event manager: Hokitika Wildfoods Festival 2018', www.westlandc.govt.nz/sites/default/files/PD%20-%20Event%20Manager-%202018%20Hokitika%20Wildfoods%20Festival%20Fixed%20Term%20August%202017.pdf.

Whangarei Northern Advocate (2014), 'Wild West Coast delicacies beckon', *Whangarei Northern Advocate*, 8 March.

White, A. (1997), 'Tastebud tickling on the wild side', *Sunday Star-Times*, 16 March.

Whitmay, T. (2016), 'New Zealand's best foodie events', *Lonely Planet*, www.lonelyplanet.com/travel-tips-and-articles/new-zealands-best-foodie-events/40625c8c-8a11-5710-a052-1479d2763c46.

Wilson, R. (2014), 'New Zealand, celebrating everything from wines to wild foods', *Washington Post*, 8 May, www.washingtonpost.com/lifestyle/travel/new-zealand-celebrating-everything-from-wines-to-wild-foods/2014/05/08/d8a259c6-d473-11e3-95d3-3bcd77cd4e11_story.html?utm_term=.1da81774840b.

Yates, S. (2015), 'Male ideals put pressure on Kiwi blokes', *Stuff*, 1 August, http://i.stuff.co.nz/life-style/life/70572718/male-ideals-put-pressure-on-kiwi-blokes.

# 9 Durban and the forfeiture of the 2022 Commonwealth Games

## A bid won and lost by default

*Brij Maharaj*

### Introduction

The Commonwealth Games (CWG) were first held in 1930 in Hamilton, Ontario, Canada, and was known as the British Empire Games, in which 400 athletes from 11 countries (including South Africa) participated. In the 21st century, 71 teams from 53 member countries are eligible to participate in the CWG (Kobierecki, 2017). One city that bid to host the games in 2022 was Durban, South Africa's third largest city, situated on the east coast with a population of 3.6 million and an unemployment rate of 27 per cent (Apelgren, 2017). In the post-apartheid democratic era, Durban has attempted to market itself as a sporting mecca. This is basically an entrepreneurial approach to marketing to attract international investment to Durban. Durban's climate, hotel infrastructure and spatial configuration of various sporting codes in one locality, the King's Park Sport Precinct (KPSP), was believed to put the city in an advantageous position to host international events like the Commonwealth Games and Olympic Games (Maharaj et al., 2006).

Durban's Commonwealth Games 2022 (CWG2022) bid is a unique case study of an event that was "won by default" because the only other competitor, Edmonton, withdrew their bid in February 2015 – citing economic woes, especially the fall in global oil prices (Akinadewo, 2015). Other cities that had expressed an initial interest in hosting CWG2022 but did not follow-up with a bid included: Hambantota (Sri Lanka); Singapore; Christchurch (New Zealand); Cardiff; Bristol; London; and Birmingham. There was concern among the Commonwealth Games Federation (CFG) that there was very little interest amongst its member countries to bid for the games, and the main reason was the exorbitant costs (McLaughlin, 2014).

Despite winning the bid by default, Durban subsequently lost the bid (also by default) because of failure to meet critical deadlines, as well as a reluctance by the South African government to honor certain contractual responsibilities and provide financial guarantees. Now the 2022 Commonwealth Games will take place in Birmingham, England. This chapter will focus on Durban's sporting ambitions; its reasons for making the CWG2022 bid and the promises made; the first casualty – the closure of the Stables;

the deviations from the bid and attempts to compromise with the CGF; and the fallout after the default. The data for this paper was collected from various documentary sources, including: the summarized bid book (54 pages from a total of 600 pages); the economic assessment report for the Durban games; various media releases by South African Sports Confederation and Olympic Committee (SASCOC) and the CGF; parliamentary presentations; and newspaper reports.

## Durban – South Africa's sporting mecca

The marketing of Durban as a sporting destination started in 1991 with the staging of the first leg of the International Powerboat Racing Grand Prix in the city's harbor. The city used the campaign name: "Durban for Sport". The event was viewed in about 70 different countries and it was estimated that over 150 million people worldwide became more aware of Durban following this event (Dayanand, 1995). Durban's focus on sport was largely influenced by the increasing recognition that an entrepreneurial approach to sport and recreation could help boost investment and generate economic growth (Lauermann, 2018).

In 1991, three cities (Durban, Cape Town and Johannesburg) submitted bids to the National Olympic Committee of South Africa (NOCSA) to host the Olympic Games in the year 2004. To promote the city's image, several catch phrases were coined including "Welcome to Durban: Africa's Hottest Favorite" and "Olympics for the People". However, in January 1994 Cape Town was chosen as the South African candidate city for the 2004 Games bid, which was subsequently awarded to Athens (Maharaj, 1998).

As early as September 2008, there were suggestions that Durban would consider a bid for the 2020 Olympics, although an IOC decision would not be made until 2013. The initial strategic decision was to host the International Olympic Committee's (IOC) 123rd Congress in 2011. According to Durban's city manager, Mike Sutcliffe:

> We have a "2010 and beyond" strategy that involves looking at potential events, whether they be Commonwealth Games or Olympics, coming to what we believe is a world-class African city. At the same time I must stress that we haven't officially put our hat in the ring as far as the Olympics are concerned because that decision must take place at national level.
>
> (Admin, 2008)

After South Africa successfully hosted the 2010 Football World Cup, there were persistent reports that Durban was considering a bid for the 2020 Olympics. However, in May 2011 the South African government decided not to bid for the 2020 Olympics as the country had far more urgent social and welfare priorities (Mackay, 2016). Then in February 2014, sports minister

Fikile Mbabula said South Africa intends to bid for the 2024 Olympics and host the Commonwealth Games prior to build a mega-sporting events legacy (IOL Sport, 2014). However, after Durban was awarded CWG2022, the intention to bid for 2024 was postponed. Durban's bid for CWG2022 was initiated by SASCOC in 2013.

## Why South Africa and Durban?

In its rationale for supporting the bid for hosting CWG2022, the South African government argued that the event would promote national pride and social cohesion, and advance local economic development (in line with national development goals/plans). The benefits included job creation (especially in the construction, hotel/catering, transport and security sectors), attracting tourists and promoting positive perceptions of the country for investors. However, Wa Azania emphasized:

> the reality that after an hour of "unity" at a stadium, the socio-spatial dialectic remains the same. Everyone returns to their lives: poor working-class blacks to their townships, the middle class to their rented complexes, and wealthy whites to the suburbs ... What kind of nation-building is this?
>
> (Wa Azania, 2015, p. 1)

The government believed that Durban would be the most appropriate city to host CWG2022 because the weather in July would be good, it could deliver a compact games without any major capital expenditure (most of the major sporting codes and events would take place within a radius of 2.5km of the Moses Madiba Stadium), and the upgrading of facilities would help the city to bid for future events like the Olympic Games. The proposed athletes' village in Conurbia would also provide housing for middle-class families after the event (Department of Sport and Recreation, 2015).

According to the CWG2022 Bid Committee (Executive Summary, 2015, p. 4) the

> City of Durban still remains the most favoured sports centre for many of South Africa's iconic annual sports events, such as the famous Comrades Marathon; the Dusi Canoe Marathon; several rugby test and super XV matches; one day and T20 international and domestic cricket matches; national team, Bafana, and premier soccer league matches; and the Amashova Cycle Race.

Furthermore, Durban had successfully hosted several international events including: 2010 Football World Cup matches; international cricket and rugby matches; 1999 All Africa Games; as well as other international events such as the Commonwealth Heads of Government Meeting in 1999; 2000 XIII

World Aids Conference; the World Conference on Racism in 2000; and the 123rd IOC session in 2011 (Executive Summary, 2015).

As a result of the extensive list of sporting events Durban has hosted, much of the infrastructure and superstructure requirements for CWG2022 were already available. Hence, it was thought that Durban city would require minimal capital and infrastructure investment ahead of 2022 (Ernst & Young, 2015). Also, as shown in Figure 9.1, over 80 per cent of the necessary sporting facilities are located in KPSP (each within a 2.5km radius of one another). Such spatial proximity of venues creates a unique platform that provides easy maintenance, faster transport and efficient movement between venues.

## "Ready to inspire" – Durban's Commonwealth 2022 bid

Durban's vision for the games was to demonstrate how "reconstruction and development" can be used to:

> accelerate progress and build a more inclusive and an empowered citizenry [...] to showcase how the Commonwealth Games can contribute directly to improvement in the lives of ordinary people and help develop a city to be a better place in which to live.
>
> (Executive Summary, 2015, p. 6)

In terms of legacy, the key focus would be on human settlements, sustainable sport facilities, transport upgrades and human capital development. The intention was to integrate the sport precinct into the city's renewal plans – to create a socially equitable and quality living environment. For instance, the athletes' village would be converted into family units for moderate-income families after the event. Investing in and refurbishing the sports precinct would provide sustainable, multi-purpose facilities for training and practice for athletes. The games would provide another incremental step towards the realization and implementation of the city's Integrated Rapid Public Transport Network. In terms of human capital development, the focus would be on investment in training and skills development to promote Durban as a "smart city" (Executive Summary, 2015).

These legacy initiatives would be realized from the economic benefits that would accrue from hosting CWG2022. Table 9.1 outlines direct, indirect and induced economic impacts for Durban, and according to a report prepared by Ernst & Young, *Economic Impact, 2022 Commonwealth Games, South Africa: Durban Host City*, the benefits included:

- R20 billion being spent in the economy, which would contribute R11 billion to GDP;
- Direct revenues would include sales of approximately 1.3 million tickets to different events over a 11 day period, with multipliers, especially

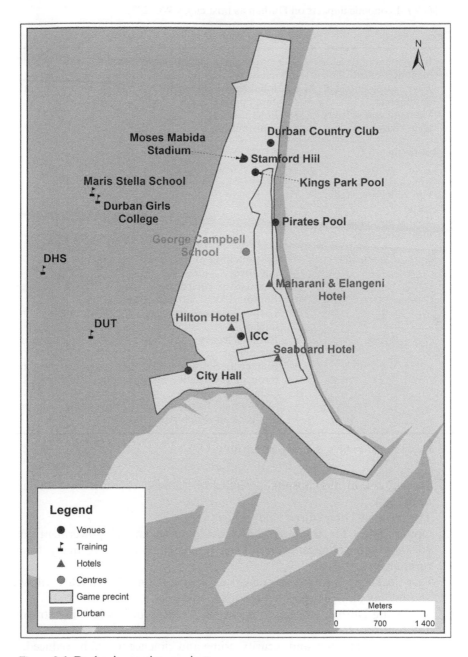

*Figure 9.1* Durban's sporting precinct.
(Source: Adapted from Executive Summary, 2015, p. 56)

*Table 9.1* Economic impacts on Durban as host city, CWG 2022.

| Direct impact | Indirect impact | Induced impact |
|---|---|---|
| • Infrastructure development and refurbishment<br>• Job creation and skill development<br>• Planning and delivery team costs | Increased demand throughout national supply chains<br>• Job creation and skill development<br>• Enhanced tax contributions | Spending across the economy stimulated by additional employment |
| Ticket revenue | | |
| • Match day spending<br>• Fan zones and stadia spend<br>• Tourist spending in local economies | | |
| *Legacy post the Games* | • Fast tracking of national development plan initiatives<br>• Increased participation in sport<br>• Improved local infrastructure<br>• Lasting tourism effects and positive economic impact<br>• Business legacy – profiling of host city for inward investment<br>• Enhancing South Africa's brand of global view in terms of governance, infrastructure, safety, and stability<br>• "Feel-good" factor and the positive outlook in the minds of all South Africans | |

(Source: adapted from Ernst & Young, 2015, p.10).

expenditure in the hospitality industry (hotels, restaurants, tourism, transport);
• The creation 11,650 direct and indirect jobs;
• Opportunities for training, skills development and empowerment for 10,000 youth volunteers (as well as some senior citizens), many from rural areas;
• Fast-tracking housing development e.g. constructing the athletes' village and improving Durban's public transport system;
• Marketing Durban and South Africa as a centre for business investment and tourism; and
• By investing in safety and security, crime and violence would be reduced.

Ernst & Young's (2015) assessment was supported by other prominent auditing and consulting firms. For example, Ruwayda Redfearn from Deloitte in KwaZulu-Natal said:

Hosting the Commonwealth Games 2022 [...] will position the city as an international destination of choice. Although Durban is South Africa's top domestic tourism destination, this will position it perfectly to grow its piece of the international tourism pie [...] South Africa remains justifiably proud of the 2010 FIFA World Cup [...] It is important that we deliver games that are free from any corruption, bribery or unlawful acts whatsoever.

(Maharaj, 2016, p. 1)

According to Gillian Saunders, Head of Advisory Services at Grant Thornton Johannesburg there are many positive benefits attached to hosting CWG2022:

Whether it's the economic impact; national pride; city and country brand development, sports development and health; or improved infrastructure and sports facilities, the Games can be a very effective tool to achieve a host of immediate and legacy elements Durban has a different status to a Cape Town or Johannesburg and hosting such a global event would certainly boost its reputation on the world stage.

(Neethling, 2014, p. 12)

The submission of the bid in London on 2 March 2015 was followed by the CGF's Evaluation Commission in loco visit between 27 and 30 April 2015. The purpose of the four-day evaluation was to obtain more technical information as well as a more practical understanding of the bid details (including transport, security and medical support); visiting the different competition venues and the proposed athletes' village; and meeting local and central government partners who would be integrally involved in ensuring success of the Games (Media Release, 2015a).

After completing the evaluation and assessment, Commission Chair Louise Martin optimistically said:

We conclude our visit inspired by the prospect and potential of Durban's bid to host the first Commonwealth Games on African soil. Plans are emerging well, further informed by the opportunity to hear first-hand the Bid team and stakeholders' strategies and technical proposals to deliver the Games [...] We leave Durban with a clear sense of opportunity – a deeper understanding of how they will optimize their plans and maximize the opportunities for young people, sport, business and communities from hosting Africa's first Commonwealth Games. The alignment of the bid with the Country's National Development Plan and the Province's ambitions for youth engagement is particularly powerful.

(Media Release, 2015b)

According to Mark Alexander, Durban Bid Chairman, there were robust engagements with the Evaluation Commission about the details of the bid. He believed that the Evaluation Commission were impressed by a passionate [bid] committed to hosting the Games in 2022 (Media Release, 2015c). However, there was simply no place for the poor, as noted in previous studies (Maharaj, 2015, 2017), in an aspiring world-class city like Durban, and the first casualty in Durban's CWG2022 plan was the closure of the Newmarket Stables.

## First casualty – the stables

As part of its CWG2022 plans, the city intended to close the iconic Newmarket Stables and the popular Night Market to develop a R300 million international sports development centre, including a football academy to be built in the KPSP by Hoy Park Management (Pty) (Nxumalo, 2015; Pillay, 2017).

The Newmarket Stables formed part of the KPSP along Jacko Jackson Drive in Stamford Hill (see Figure 9.1). The buildings and stables on the property date back to over 100 years ago, when it was first used as a training yard for race-horses (Newmarket Stables, 2011). More recently the stables, which is considered a heritage site by many, offered riding lessons and livery to horse owners and a popular flea market which supports about 270 vendors (Habbib, 2015), as well as accommodating the Metro Police Mounted Unit. Not only did the stables offer a place of recreational fun and a haven for horse lovers, it was also home to the groomsmen who lived and worked on the property (Wolhuter, 2017).

The was uncertainty over jobs, the loss of homes for both groomsmen and horses and the livelihoods of the vendors from the Night Market. The tenants claimed that there was no proper consultation and they had received no corres-pondence from the municipality before eviction notices were issued (Rondgan-ger, 2016). According to Nadine Parker, who runs the stables riding school:

> This has been like a sword of Damocles hanging over our heads. We offer 100 children riding lessons as well as livery. We are a heritage site, catering to disabled riders and able-bodied riders making it affordable for Durban and surrounding areas children to learn ride.
>
> (Habbib, 2015)

The municipality received 164 letters and two petitions with a total of 7,818 signatures objecting to the closure of the stables and the building of the acad-emy and sports precinct, which were ignored (Rondganger, 2016). The tenants have since taken the matter to court and have claimed that that they had a 30-year lease with the Durban municipality. According to attorney Tashya Giya-persad, her "clients were lawful occupants of their premises, and the city had sought to evict them without fair warning or proper notice" and this "would be to the detriment of more than 22,000 local and international people who visited the market monthly, and hundreds of workers" (Pillay, 2017).

Even before Durban was awarded CWG2022 the livelihoods of vendors and groomsmen at the Stables market was threatened. This contradicted Durban's 2022 bid commitment to generate jobs and create a more inclusive city.

Meanwhile, the CGF's Evaluation Commission subsequently recommended that CWG2022 should be awarded to the Durban.

## The award ...

In endorsing Durban's 2022 bid, the Evaluation Commission contended that "Durban's vision supports and contributes to South Africa's 2030 National Development Plan and is rooted in the desire to engage citizens (especially young people), athletes and the Commonwealth" (Media Release, 2015d). On 2 September 2015 the CGF voted unanimously that CWG2022 be awarded to host city Durban.

The usual rhetorical platitudes were regurgitated by those supporting the bid – politicians, bureaucrats and the business elites – "sustainable legacies, world class, African first". In a remarkably candid statement, Durban City Manager, Sibusiso Sithole, contended that: "this decision comes with serious responsibilities and expectations [...] Such Games require careful planning and tight budget controls to make sure that we avoid optimism bias, and cost overruns" (Mthethwa, 2015). However, Durban was no different to the vast majority of other cities in this domain (Rocha, 2016; Wagg, 2015).

There was also the customary condescending reference to wining the bid for Africa. The president of SASCOC, Gideon Sam, was: "an extremely proud South African. We are ready to host the 2022 Commonwealth Games, for the very first time on African soil, in Durban South Africa in 2022" (Media Release, 2015f). Similarly, Durban's mayor James Nxumalo added:

> We will be hosting these games on behalf of the African continent which is about 1 billion people. It is history in the making, as these games will be coming to the African continent for the first time. South Africa is under reconstruction and development, as we are building this new country which is non-racial, non-sexist and democratic.
>
> (Mthethwa, 2015)

A hollow claim, especially against the background of escalating xenophobia and Afrophobia in South Africa (Maharaj, 2017).

Despite such sentiment, bid-committee chairman, Mark Alexander, added that CWG2022 will be a "game changer" for Durban, and will contribute to an "inclusive citizenry [...], greater social cohesion, create opportunities for empowerment, boost prosperity and ensure equality, while also fast-tracking economic growth in our country" (Media Release, 2015f). However, the CWG2022 award to Durban was "subject to the final and timely delivery of a limited number of outstanding Host City Contract requirements" (Media Release, 2015e) and key issues included finalization and underwriting of the total costs, establishing the local organizing committee and signing of the agreement. The failure to comply subsequently led to a fallout and ultimately the withdrawal of the award to Durban as the CWG2022 host city.

### ... and the fallout

A major issue was the lack of clarity about the total cost of hosting the CWG in Durban. An initial figure citing the cost of hosting CWG2022 was R3.4 billion (Manda, 2015), but six months later it doubled to R6.4 billion (Pavitt, 2016). All indicators speculated that South Africa was heading into recession, so the final cost could more than double the R6.4 billion. This posed great concern, considering that the 2014 Commonwealth Games in Glasgow cost R13 billion (Pavitt, 2016). Durban declared its intention to bid for CWG2022 on 22 July 2014 in Glasgow, before this decision had been ratified by national government, with SASCOC's support. In November 2014, the Minister of Sport and Recreation "submitted a memorandum to Cabinet requesting Cabinet's endorsement of South Africa's intention to bid and host the Commonwealth Games in 2022 in Durban" (Durban2022, 2017, p. 3). However, when the national government approved the bid to host CWG2022, they only guaranteed funding of R 4.32 billion. In early June 2016, Minister of Sport and Recreation, Fikile Mbalula, reported:

> We can now confirm that the processes relating to the finance guarantee have been finalised after due consideration of all factors by the fiscal liability committee and the National Treasury as it is required by South African law, specifically Section 66 read with Section 70 of the Public Finance Management Act [...] We have consistently indicated that the South African government was and remains committed to the hosting of these games. We have further highlighted that the South African government in the interest of prudency and fiscal discipline was engaged in an intra-governmental process related to the necessary and required finance guarantee.
>
> (African News Agency, 2016)

More specifically, the R4.32 billion budget would be sourced through an "intra-governmental process" from different relevant departments (at both central and provincial levels): presidency; finance; arts and culture; energy; environmental affairs; international relations and cooperation; human settlements; sport and recreation; police; transport; health; communications; home affairs; justice and correctional services (Durban2022, 2017).

However, as early as March 2016, Belinda Scott, Member of the Executive Committee of KwaZulu-Natal province who was responsible for finance, admitted that the province could not contribute R580 million in funding as initially promised for CWG2022, which was considered a national event. This was because the province had more urgent priorities to serve poor communities. The provincial treasury had notified the national treasury about this decision so that a contingent plan for urgent central government (national) intervention could compensate for the shortfall (Pavitt, 2016; Stolley, 2016). According to the World Bank (2018), in 2015 one quarter of the KwaZulu-Natal population was chronically poor (R647 income per person per month).

On the first anniversary of the award of the 2022 Games, the CGF was concerned that South Africa had not met certain preconditions and contractual obligations within stipulated timeframes. There were further concerns about governance structures, and Durban had missed a number of critical targets. No organizing committee had been established within 180 days, and they had "failed to make their first payment of £1.5 million" by 31 March 2016 to host the event (Mackay, 2016). The chairman of Durban 2022, Mark Alexander, conceded that he had "no idea when the guarantees will be signed, and the money paid" (Pavitt, 2016). Furthermore, the CGF was not happy with the location of the athletes' village in Conurbia and wanted it to be sited closer the KPSP.

Media reports in December 2015 announced South Africa's President, Jacob Zuma, had "fired Finance Minister Nhlanhla Nene" and this had "delayed the signing of a crucial 2022 Commonwealth Games document – one of a series of mishaps that put the Durban showpiece on the road to failure" (Savides & Isaacson, 2017). Tensions then escalated as accusations arose that the South African government was deviating from obligations. There were also allegations that the CGF was changing the goalposts and increasing the budget to R8 billion. However, this figure was not an exaggeration, or escalation, as the Commonwealth Games Evaluation Commission report in June 2015 had in fact suggested a budget of R9 billion (Savides & Isaacson, 2017). Notwithstanding that, in June 2016 the government approved a budget of R4.32 billion for CWG2022, "with the understanding that South Africa is in a constrained fiscal environment" (Botton, 2015). According to Esethu Hasane, spokesperson for South Africa's Department of Sport and Recreation:

> We want value for money for hosting the Games. When the South African government woke up (during the 2010 World Cup), we were footing most of the bills. When there were returns, the government did not get its fair share.
>
> (McCallum, 2017)

SASCOC was the intermediary between the government and the CGF. There were suggestions that the South African government had not included any SASCOC official in its proposed local organizing committee and had effectively "hijacked" CWG2022 from the sport's governing body. All previous international sports events hosted in South Africa were led by officials from the appropriate governing bodies (e.g. rugby, cricket, soccer), and not by governmental or political figures. SASCOC was "too weak to stave off government interference, and they were too silent when it happened" (Isaacson, 2017).

South Africa's Sport and Recreation Minister, Fikile Mbalula, and his director-general, Alec Moemi, had submitted a budget to government that was R2 billion short of the amount needed to host a successful CWG2022 (Isaacson, 2017). One possible reason for this was that the government was more likely to endorse a lower budget (McCallum, 2017). The CGF indicated that if the outstanding matters were not resolved by the end by the end of November 2016, then Durban could lose the CWG2022 event. Louise Martin, president of the CWG, informed the General Assembly of the CGF in Edmonton on 7 October 2016 about the possibility that Durban and South Africa may not meet the pre-conditions, prospectively looking for an alternate host:

> In the past two weeks we have received information from SASCOC and the South African Government that raises doubts in relation to their financial position and their ability to meet the commitments they made through the bid. I acknowledge that there have been and there are challenges. And while there is time to address these challenges, we need to be mindful not to place ourselves in a position where a Games in 2022 are at risk. Therefore, we need to resolve this situation with our colleagues from South Africa expeditiously [...] or look at alternatives.
>
> (Mackay, 2016)

The GCF adopted a motion granting the ruling executive board the power to select a "new host city without a formal bid process if the event is withdrawn from Durban", as "the most important priority was protecting the Commonwealth Games, so it took place in 2022" (Mackay, 2016).

In his response, president of SASCOC, Gideon Sam, said that his organization was negotiating with the various stakeholders, including government, to comply with their obligations. This was reaffirmed by SASCOC CEO, Tubby Reddy:

> Negotiations with national government and Treasury are on-going and we are guided by decisions taken at national level. We have already secured many of the agreements with national government and are working tirelessly to conclude any outstanding matters, including the issue of funding for the Games [...] We reaffirm that SASCOC will deliver a world class Commonwealth Games that would make us all proud. Our partners in government are working with us to ensure that the first ever games in Africa will be a memorable one.
>
> (SASCOC, 2016)

Behind the scenes negotiations continued between the South African government, SASCOC and the CGF. By the end of November 2016, SASCOC sent a revised submission to the CGF. The death knell came on 13 March 2017 when the CGF released the following statement:

> It is with disappointment that the detailed review has concluded that there is a significant departure from the undertakings provided in Durban's bid and as a result a number of key obligations and commitments in

areas such as governance, venues, funding and risk management/ assurance have not been met under the revised proposition. The CGF is fully confident and committed to delivering a successful Commonwealth Games for athletes and fans in 2022 ... and remains committed to realizing the shared ambitions of a future Commonwealth Games in Africa.

(Gleeson, 2017)

Responding to the withdrawal of CWG2022 from Durban and South Africa, Sport and Recreation Minister, Fikile Mbalula, indicated that open-ended guarantees that committed the government to absorbing any budget shortfalls could not be signed. Mbalula emphaszsed:

at this juncture, our country is regrettably not in a position to make huge financial commitments given the current competing socio-economic needs and global economic down turn. In the interests of fiscal discipline and financial prudency, our government has considered all options and remains confident that we have acted in the best interest of South Africa.

(Mbalula, 2017)

Similarly, SASCOC president, Gideon Sam, expressed his disappointment for the country

and for the whole African continent. But without the necessary government guarantees, we couldn't move on [...] Everybody was very excited to see the Commonwealth Games staged in Durban, which was very well equipped to host the event, but once the economics started to play a role, it became difficult. We had hoped to make this a Games for all of Africa, and so this is a very sad day for the whole continent.

(Staff Writer, 2017)

Durban's former mayor, James Nxumalo, who had promoted the initial bid process, lamented the economic loss for the city:

eThekwini would have been in line to receive huge economic spin-offs from hosting the Games, and as we had previously shown when hosting games during the 2010 World Cup and 2013 Africa Cup of Nations, we were convinced of our readiness to host the event.

(Daily News, 2017)

The loss of CWG2022 also created international embarrassment for South Africa. A group of World Rugby delegates arrived in South Africa in March 2017 to assess the country's offer to host the Rugby World Cup in 2023, which was subsequently awarded to France.

Ironically, the withdrawal of CWG2022 from Durban

> will bring back unhappy memories. A South African city was due to host the British Empire Games in 1934 but was forced to hand them back, partly because of economic difficulties but also because a color bar operated in the country.
>
> (Barker, 2017)

On 21 December 2017, the CGF selected Birmingham to host the event in 2022.

## Conclusion

In making the bid for CWG2022, Durban was following a global trend where marketing the city as a mega-event destination was a prominent neo-liberal urban promotion strategy (Hall & Wilson, 2016; Vanwynsberghe et al., 2013). There was clearly limited understanding about why far more wealthy cities like Edmonton withdrew from bidding for the event. Perhaps they were being more cognizant of the economic realities, as other cities withdrew their bids to host the Winter Olympics for the same reason. South Africa was using mega-events as a means of distancing itself from Africa, and as part of attempts to reimagine the country and market, which subliminally reflected "a hankering for an association with the world class, international community – in other words, the West" (Maharaj, 2011, p. 53). Ironically, the campaign for CWG2022 was presented as an African bid.

Was Durban was looking for global glory or perhaps an escapist fantasy from its inability to address serious social and economic challenges in its jurisdiction? Clearly, the lessons from the 2010 Football World Cup experience were not being heeded. In many respects the bid was doomed from the start, because of only qualified, conditional support from central and provincial government. In fact, CWG2022 was imposed onto the central government by SASCOC and Durban. There were clearly tensions between national government and SASCOC, with suggestions that the latter wanted to control CWG2022. For instance, the planned closure of iconic establishments such as the Stables to pursue urban sports development, created conflict and tension between those who were affected and those who make the decisions in a place. Various aspects of the residents' daily lives such as housing; employment; leisure activities; transport; human rights violations and democratic participation are affected by intrusive mega-events.

Generally, bids for events like the CWG are promoted by influential, politically connected people and groups in the private and public spheres. These include global corporations such as Ernst & Young, Deloitte, and Grant Thornton, who are actively involved in developing and encouraging governments to bid for these international events. However, such corporate consultants are unlikely to speak on behalf of those who lack power and resources, and for whom benefits are unlikely. The 2010 Football World Cup was used by the Durban municipality as a smoke-screen to remove informal traders and shack dwellers, and to try (unsuccessfully) to destroy the Warwick Market (Skinner, 2009).

There were legitimate concerns that the escalation in the costs of the stadiums and infrastructure for this event resulted in the diversion of public funds from more urgent social priorities such as sanitation, housing, healthcare and education. There is no evidence that CWG2022 in Durban would have been any different. There is an emerging trend of some countries and cities in the global north turning their backs on the hosting of mega sporting events, seeing the need instead to focus on social priorities. For example, the following candidate cities declined to bid for the Olympic Games 2022: Boston, Hamburg, Rome and Budapest. It therefore becomes even more imperative to investigate the impact of these spectacles on the economy of developing countries such as South Africa, Brazil and India, where social and economic indices indicate that inequality is deepening rather than being mitigated.

# References

Admin, G.B., 2008. A 2020 Summer Games bid from Durban possible. https://games bids.com/eng/summer-olympic-bids/future-summer-bids/a-2020-summer-games-bid-from-durban-possible/ (accessed 3 March 2018).

African News Agency, 2016. 2022 Commonwealth Games finance guarantee finalised, says Mbalula. https://mg.co.za/article/2016-06-04-00-2022-commonwealth-games-finance-guarantee-finalised-says-mbalula (accessed 10 March 2018).

Akinadewo, G., 2015. Commonwealth Games 2022: Edmonton withdraws bid. http://freedomonline.com.ng/commonwealth-games-2022-edmonton-withdraws-bid/ (accessed 4 April 2018).

Apelgren, E., 2017. Overview eThekwini municipality, Durban, South Africa. www.mile.org.za/QuickLinks/News/Urban%20Strategic%20Planning%20Master%20Class%202017/Day%201.1-%20Eric%20Apelgren-Overview%20of%20eThekwini%20Municipality.pdf (accessed 12 November 2017).

Barker, P., 2017. When South Africa gave up the 1934 Empire Games. www.insidethegames.biz/articles/1047947/philip-barker-when-south-africa-gave-up-the-1934-empire-games (accessed 12 May 2018).

Botton, W., 2015. Commonwealth Games: Cheque not signed yet. https://citizen.co.za/news/south-africa/678850/games-cheque-not-signed-yet/.

Daily News, 2017. Chad le Clos gutted after Durban loses Commonwealth Games. www.iol.co.za/sport/chad-le-clos-gutted-after-durban-loses-commonwealth-games-8185297 (accessed 6 March 2017).

Dayanand, S., 1995. Local government restructuring and transformation: A case study of Durban. Unpublished Master's Thesis, University of Durban-Westville.

Department of Sport and Recreation, 2015. South Africa's bid to host the 2022 Commonwealth Games. http://pmg-assets.s3-website-eu-west-1.amazonaws.com/170329_commonwealth.pdf (accessed 10 March 2018).

Durban2022, 2017. Presentation to Portfolio Committee. http://pmg-assets.s3-website-eu-west-1.amazonaws.com/170329_commonwealth.pdf.

Ernst & Young, 2015. Economic impact, 2022 Commonwealth Games, South Africa: Durban host city. http://durban-2022.com/assets/files/Commonwealthgames.pdf (accessed 11 November 2017).

Executive Summary, 2015. Durban2022 Commonwealth Games candidate city file. www.durban-2022.com/assets/files/durban-2022-cg-candidate-city-file.pdf (accessed 18 March 2018).

Gleeson, M., 2017. Durban loses right to host 2022 Commonwealth Games. www.reuters.com/article/us-games-commonwealth-durban/durban-loses-right-to-host-2022-commonwealth-games-idUSKBN16K1UN (accessed 6 March 2018).

Habbib, S., 2015. Newmarket stables given eviction notice. https://northglennews.co.za/64170/newmarket-stables-given-eviction-notice (accessed 1 September 2017).

Hall, C.M. and Wilson, S., 2016. Mega-events as neoliberal projects:'Realistic if we want Dunedin to prosper'or 'the Biggest Civic Disgrace … in Living Memory'? In J. Mosedale (ed.), *Neoliberalism and the political economy of tourism*. London, Routledge, pp. 49–66.

IOL Sport, 2014. SA to bid for 2024 Olympics - Mbalula. www.iol.co.za/sport/sa-to-bid-for-2024-olympics-mbalula (accessed 3 January 2019).

Isaacson, D., 2017. The cost of Durban losing the Commonwealth Games. www.businesslive.co.za/bd/opinion/2017-03-14-the-cost-of-durban-losing-the-commonwealth-games (accessed 6 March 2018).

Kobierecki, M.M., 2017. The Commonwealth Games as an example of bringing states closer through sport. *Physical Culture and Sport. Studies and Research*, 73(1), 36–43.

Lauermann, J., 2018. Municipal statecraft: Revisiting the geographies of the entrepreneurial city. *Progress in Human Geography*, 42(2), 205–224.

Mackay, D., 2016. Durban 2022 warned they risk losing Commonwealth Games unless they meet deadline. www.insidethegames.biz/articles/1042406/durban-2022-warned-they-risk-losing-commonwealth-games-unless-they-meet-deadline (accessed 17 March 2018).

Maharaj, B., 1998. The Olympic Games and economic development – Hopes, myths, and realities: The Cape Town 2004 Bid. In R. Freestone (ed.), *Twentieth century urban planning experience*. Sydney, University of New South Wales, pp. 583–588.

Maharaj, B., 2011. 2010 FIFA World Cup: (South) 'Africa's time has come'? *South African Geographical Journal*, 93, 49–62.

Maharaj, B., 2015. The turn of the South? Social and economic impacts of mega events in India, Brazil and South Africa. *Local Economy*, 39, 983–999.

Maharaj, B., 2016. Durban should quit as Commonwealth Games host city. www.dailymaverick.co.za/opinionista/2016-12-05-durban-should-quit-as-commonwealth-games-host-city/ (accessed 3 April 2018).

Maharaj, B., 2017. Durban's FIFA 2010 Beachfront 'beautification'. In N. Wise and J. Harris (eds.), *Sport, events, tourism and regeneration*. London, Routledge, pp. 40–53.

Maharaj, B., Pillay, V. and Sucheran, R., 2006. Durban – A tourism mecca? Challenges of the post-apartheid era. *Urban Forum*, 16, 262–281.

Manda, S., 2015. Commonwealth Games will cost billions. www.iol.co.za/news/south-africa/kwazulu-natal/commonwealth-games-will-cost-billions- (accessed 28 March 2018).

Mbalula, F., 2017. The minister of sport and recreation South Africa, Mr. Fikile Mbalula MP, statement on the recent reported announcement by the Commonwealth Games Federations, 14 March. www.durban.gov.za/Resource_Centre/Press_Releases/Pages/The-Minister-Of-Sport-and-Recreation-South-Africa%2C-Mr.-Fikile-Mbalula-MP%

2C-Statement-On-The-Recent-Reported-Announcement-by-.aspx (accessed 12 March 2018).

McCallum, K., 2017. Crisis meeting for 2022 Commonwealth Games. *The Star*, 21 October.

McLaughlin, C., 2014. Commonwealth Games: Lack of interest in hosting future games. www.bbc.com/sport/commonwealth-games/25832867 (accessed 10 March 2018).

Media Release, 2015a. Evaluation Commission analyses bid for Africa's first Commonwealth Games. http://durban-2022.com/media/evaluation-commission-analyses-bid-for-africas-first-commonwealth-games/ (accessed 10 March 2018).

Media Release, 2015b. 'Inspired by prospect and potential' of bid for Africa's first Commonwealth Games. http://durban-2022.com/media/inspired-by-prospect-and-potential-of-bid-for-africas-first-commonwealth-games/ (accessed 10 March 2018).

Media Release, 2015c. Durban will deliver world class games. http://durban-2022.com/media/durban-will-deliver-world-class-games/ (accessed 10 March 2018).

Media Release, 2015d. Durban on the road to host games in 2022 after endorsement by the Commonwealth Games Federation's Evaluation Committee. http://durban-2022.com/media/durban-on-the-road-to-host-games-in-2022-after-endorsement-by-the-commonwealth-games-federations-evaluation-committee (accessed 10 March 2018).

Media Release, 2015e. Durban 2022's bid preparations enter final straight as evaluation report published. http://durban-2022.com/media/durban-2022s-bid-preparations-enter-final-straight-as-evaluation-report-published (accessed 10 March 2018).

Media Release, 2015f. CGF awards 2022 Games to Durban. http://durban-2022.com/media/media-statement-cgf-awards-2022-games-to-durban (accessed 10 March 2018).

Mthethwa, T., 2015. Press release: Durban wins 2022 Commonwealth Games bid. www.durban.gov.za/Resource_Centre/Press_Releases/Pages/Durban-Wins-2022-Commonwealth-Games-Bid-.aspx (accessed 3 April 2018).

Neethling, T., 2014. 2022 Commonwealth Games for Durban South Africa? www.tourismtattler.co.za/downloads/Tourism-Tattler-December-2014.pdf.

Newmarket Stables, 2011. Welcome to Newmarket Stables. http://newmarketstables.weebly.com/ (accessed 29 August 2017).

Nxumalo, M., 2015. Market project will go ahead. www.iol.co.za/dailynews/news/wrecking-ball-looms-for-stables-2014811 (accessed 30 August 2017).

Pavitt, M., 2016. South African sports minister confirms financial guarantees received from national treasury for Durban 2022. www.insidethegames.biz/articles/1038185/south-african-sports-minister-confirms-financial-guarantees-received-from-national-treasury-for-durban-2022 (accessed 3 January 2019).

Pillay, K., 2017. Stables traders still defiant in face of eviction. www.iol.co.za/mercury/news/stables-traders-still-defiant-in-face-of-eviction-10203884 (accessed 4 March 2018).

Rocha, C.M., 2016. Support of politicians for the 2016 Olympic Games in Rio de Janeiro. *Leisure Studies*, 35(4), 487–504.

Rondganger, L., 2016. Durban stables booted out. www.iol.co.za/dailynews/news/wrecking-ball-looms-for-stables-2014811 (accessed 30 August 2017).

SASCOC, 2016. SASCOC reaffirms commitment to deliver world class 2022 Commonwealth Games. www.sascoc.co.za/2016/03/11/sascoc-reaffirms-commitment-to-deliver-world-class-2022-commonwealth-games/ (accessed 17 March 2018).

Savides, M., & Isaacson, D., 2017. SA warned on Commonwealth Games risk. www.pressreader.com/south-africa/sunday-times/20161009/281487865858610 (accessed 3 January 2019).

Skinner, C., 2009. Challenging city imaginaries: Street traders' struggles in Warwick Junction. *Agenda*, 23, 101–109.

Staff Writer, 2017. Durban loses 2022 Commonwealth Games. https://businesstech.co.za/news/business/164109/durban-loses-2022-commonwealth-games-report (accessed 28 March 2018).

Stolley, G., 2016. No money for Commonwealth Games. www.iol.co.za/sport/no-money-for-commonwealth-games-1996081 (accessed 10 March 2017).

Vanwynsberghe, R., Surborg, B. and Wyly, E., 2013. When the games come to town: Neoliberalism, mega-events and social inclusion in the Vancouver 2010 Winter Olympic Games. *International Journal of Urban and Regional Research*, 37, 2074–2093.

Wa Azania, 2015. We won the games, but lost much more. www.iol.co.za/sundayindependent/we-won-the-games-but-lost-much-more-1915141 (accessed 20 March 2018).

Wagg, S., 2015. *The London Olympics of 2012: Politics, promises and legacy.* London, Palgrave.

Wolhuter, B., 2017. Horse club challenges eThekwini municipality. www.iol.co.za/news/crime-courts/horse-club-challenges-ethekwini-municipality-7737566 (accessed 2 September 2017).

World Bank, 2018. *Overcoming poverty and inequality in South Africa – An assessment of drivers, constraints and opportunities.* Washington, DC, World Bank.

# 10 Cultural sites of tension in the Iditarod of Alaska

*Trine Kvidal-Røvik & Kari Jæger*

## Introduction

> On March 3rd, sixty-six teams from around the world will line up in Anchorage, Alaska to kick off the 40th Annual Iditarod Sled Dog Race. Each team is powered by 16 "Alaskan sled dogs" and one human "musher," who leads the pack across ~1,100 miles of Alaskan wilderness to the Bering Sea town of Nome. The race takes only 8–10 days to complete, with the dogs running ~100 miles a day at speeds between 8 and 13 miles per hour.
>
> (Doucleff, 2012, p. 180)

The Iditarod of Alaska is the world's longest sled dog race. It starts in Anchorage each year on the first Saturday in March, and it ends when the last musher reaches Nome. This chapter uses this annual long-distance sled dog race as a case through which to discuss how events play a role in how places are perceived, consumed and contested.

Contributing to debates on the complexities of events, places and societies, the chapter builds on theoretical perspectives of place to critically evaluate the practice, impacts, legacies and management of events within specific contexts. Anchored in perspectives from event theories and critical cultural theories, this chapter will discuss how an event like the Iditarod is linked to a place's history, and how it directly affects the place(s) today (see map in Figure 10.1). In order to bring forth knowledge on place and event dynamics, we discuss how, in different, yet interconnected and overlapping ways, these Iditarod-relevant sites speak to issues of cultural contestations and power in the Alaskan context. The place, and its societal and cultural contexts, are intertwined and interconnected with global cultural trends.

## Events

Event and festival venues accommodate different activities, creating individual and social values through casual encounters and producing identity for

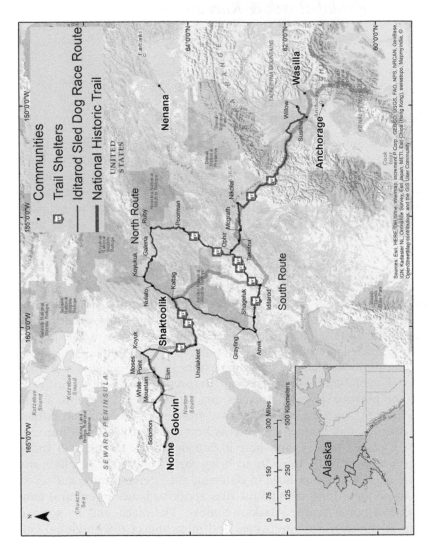

*Figure 10.1* The Iditarod racecourse across Alaska and the towns the event passes through. (Map produced for this chapter by Jennifer Schmidt, Institute for Social and Economic Research, University of Alaska Anchorage).

those involved. Certain events come to play important roles for host cities, wider geographical regions and countries, both in and of themselves (their presence in a landscape) and as a performance arena for those involved (Getz, 2013; Hall, 1989; Jago et al., 2003; Richie, 1984). Moreover, media scholars have found such events interesting and relevant in terms of how they become powerful and effective vehicles for showcasing a place (or places), and functioning as a locus of community affect and identity (Morley, 2001; Pietikäinen & Hujanen, 2003; Silk, 2002). Events and festivals are seen to have an important role in (re)building identities for people and places, and a sense of belonging to that place may develop or become strengthened (Aldskogius, 1993; Ekman, 1999; Lavenda, 1997; Lewis & Pile, 1996; Quinn, 2009; Wise & Harris, 2016). Events could provide new creative spatial practices and provide space for performed identity for visitors and local people, offering opportunities for active participation in an event context (Cloke, 2007). An event might offer the joys and hardship of outdoor living, which sometimes is self-propelled travel, associated with physical engagement in the natural environment over time, nature, passage and comfort (Varley & Semple, 2015).

Events are co-created consumption spaces where the creation of value depends on those who participate. Typically, in events, locals and visitors who participate create value through the consumption of the same services and products, blurring defined roles (Jæger & Olsen, 2017; Perić et al., 2017). Furthermore, the value created during an event can extend beyond the event itself when based on dimensions focusing on individual values and not only on salient desires and wants. For instance, Haanpää et al. (2016, p. 46) point out that these events "clearly create meaning-based value for the people and places, but the monetary value created is often marginal". Furthermore, events contribute to the development of place stories, as event activities and happenings are communicated via television and online during the event, or regularly throughout the year on social media (Jæger & Kvidal-Røvik, 2015).

Events and festivals represent important social and cultural arenas, replacing the historical role of churches, village feasts and gatherings. According to Jepson and Clarke (2016, p. 3), "Festivals and events are the lifeblood of society, they are inseparable and crucial to enhance and maintain community well-being or quality of life". Put another way, events create unique settings where individuals from different cultures and social classes can meet, interact and sometimes find new friends. The number of events and festivals has increased (de Brito & Terzieva, 2016), indicating their social importance. Furthermore, the event's role in a community as a temporary place in a physical place means that events are venues for value co-creation – that is, both the tourists and the local people can use events as value-creating areas (Haanpää et al., 2016). In this dynamic it is worth examining more closely what an event embedded in place entails in terms of social and cultural impacts.

# Place

The concept of place has been widely discussed in a variety of fields such as geography, sociology, economy, anthropology, architecture and planning studies. As part of a critical cultural tradition, relational place perspectives, as first developed within human geography, have been particularly relevant. In light of this, we see place as "a site in space constituted and made meaningful by social relations of power and marked by identifications or emotional investments," and seen as "a bounded manifestation of the production of meaning in space" (Barker, 2004, p. 144). Place, then, is not something fixed, but is given meaning as part of our discursive meaning-making processes and practices. Appadurai (1996) notes that places are "produced" and do not exist *a priori*. Media discourse in and about places impacts on how we see the world as it helps "shape our experience, relationships, interactions, understandings, and knowledge" (Williams & Brandt, 2013, p. 44), influencing political debates and decision making (see Allern, 2001; Neuman et al., 1992; Wise & Mulec, 2012). While ideas and thoughts about place may be very personal, such ideas and thoughts are always shaped within specific contexts, in which social, cultural and economic dimensions play a role. This, of course, does not mean that our thoughts and ideas are determined by such dimensions, but rather, as Kielland (2012, p. 42, *emphasis added*) puts it, "our knowledge and our social practices are structured *through* discourse, while also being productive and thus structuring *of* discourse". This is especially evident in tourism, as Wise and Mulec (2012, p. 59) note: "media communication presents images of places and events, producing knowledge for consumption and interpretation".

Thus, place is always in process, and can be seen as a performance in which bodies, the built and natural environment, and discourses interact (de Certeau, 1984; Middleton et al., 2015). This means, "place is socially constructed but materially conditioned and 'earthed', still without being materially determined" (Granås, 2014, p. 86). For example, "even though every county is a particular locality with its own unique material, symbolic and embodied qualities, every county is also part of a spatial system that links localities into broader social structures and practices" (Endres & Senda-Cook, 2011, p. 259), and such connections linking different localities are important to consider when assessing an event such as the Iditarod of Alaska, spread across such a vast geographical area.

# Examining Iditarod

Building on the above sections, the event, the Iditarod of Alaska, is an important part of such processes related to Alaska as a place. The Iditarod was initiated locally, and when it was started in 1973, 32 dog teams participated. Today, around 65 teams start the race each year. Mushers are mostly from Alaska, but also from other US states as well as from Canada and Europe. In 2016 mushers came from the United States, Switzerland, Norway, Czech Republic, Germany, France, Sweden, New Zealand, England and Hungary. During the race teams are required to stop at check-points (official stopping places). At some check points only official times are clocked; at others the teams are required to lay-over for a certain period of time, allowing for food and rest for the dogs and mushers. At these points mandatory gear is also checked by officials and veterinarians examine the dogs. Iditarod is a journey through a whole state, where most of the trail passes through wild natural landscapes with no access by road. Participants pass through small villages with native people, where the mushers and dogs have their checkpoints for resting. Veterinarians, media and race managers follow the race by plane or snowmobile in the most inaccessible areas.

This chapter is based on research conducted during Iditarod 2014, as part of an international research project entitled "Winter: New turns in Arctic winter tourism". Before and during the race, interviews with people in and around the race organization were conducted, as well with people from local communities, mushers and visitors. Observations were also held at the start, at check-points and at the finish line. Contemporary media texts and historical documents were also examined and support the content presented in this section.

Iditarod represents a rich entry point for discussing an event's impact on a place. Specifically, as an event, the Iditarod constitutes and enables certain cultural processes, providing an "arena" for a place-making performance in which built and natural environment, bodies and media discourses interact. The Iditarod trail runs through the many rough and varied sceneries and climate zones of Alaska, and as such the materiality of Alaska becomes an essential part of the event, both in terms of how participants experience it, and in terms of how it is articulated via media representations. The event brings dogs and mushers through forests and into remote local communities, across windy mountain plateaus and over frozen waters. Through the movement of bodies (human and canine), the event connects parts of this large area. As participants move along on the Iditarod tracks, then, it is not only a process of generating a specific year's winning team, it is also part of a process in which a place is being articulated. The core activity of these sporting events is sled dog racing, but at the same time it is a travel through nature.

Importantly, the Iditarod is closely connected to the construction of Alaska as a place. The Iditarod event is embedded with/in the place of Alaska in several ways, both symbolically and materially. Also, the race is linked to the cultural and geographical heritage of Alaska, as well as cur-rent political and cultural trends. The Iditarod organization (2018) mentions that dog mushing and sled dogs is key to Alaska's frontier spirit. Moreover, the name of the Iditarod event is closely connected to trail history in Alaska and was one of three main routes across Alaska using in the winter, often crosses by dogsleds (Bureau of Land Management, 2018).

The Iditarod as an event serves many purposes for different groups and people. Some of the informants talk about how the race serves to connect different areas of Alaska, bringing visitors to remote villages and places. One informant explains how the event has brought activity to villages that previously had most of their connections during the summer months only. The informant talks about how the event has been central in giving "something more to the villages, and impact the villages in a good way". Also, the Iditarod event has been important in other ways. For instance, from a document from Bureau of Land Management, it becomes clear that the event brings much needed attention, and perhaps also status, to areas in Alaska that might previously have not been seen in this way. From the Bureau of Land Management's perspective, the Iditarod Sled Dog Race is an important influence for the status of the only congressionally designated National Historic Trail in Alaska (Bureau of Land Management, 2018).

Other actors foreground how the event celebrates Alaskan mining history. This is a central part of the information the race organization itself presents on its web page. On its web page, under the titles "Information" and "About," the Iditarod organization presents information about the race divided into several sub-pages: History, The Iditarod Trail, Champions & Records, Mushing Terminology, Veterinary Center, Iditarod Air Force, Trivia & Facts, as well as Other Links (Iditarod, 2017). There is a lot of information presented on the historical aspects of the Iditarod, throughout many of the pages. For instance, stories about the historical use of sled dogs in Alaska, as well as the use and location of (sections of) the Iditarod trail are presented. The web page presents a lot of information about the gold rushes as part of Alaskan history and explains that, with this, the need for year-round mail and freight services to miners in western Alaska led "the federal government to survey and construct a winter trail from Seward to Nome for use by dog sled teams" (Bowers, 2012a).

Additionally, the original Iditarod trail is well-described, and presented information explains that the use of dogs was something native Alaskans mastered particularly well:

> The typical traveler on the Iditarod Trail was a musher driving a team of twenty or more dogs pulling a massive freight sled capable of carrying half a ton or more. These mushers followed in the ancient traditions of Alaska Natives, who mastered the fine art of using dogs for winter transportation many centuries ago. Different Native peoples bred dogs for their particular needs over the centuries. The Malemiut Inupiat people of the Seward Peninsula developed a particularly hardy breed of sled dog that today bears their name: the Malamute.
>
> (Bowers, 2012a)

At the same time, when looking into important arenas for the communication of Native Alaskan history, mushing is not emphasized much. An informant who is a scholarly expert on Native Alaskan perspectives explains that the Native Alaskan–mining link is complex and even a bit problematic, as this history refers to a time during which Native Alaskans were kept from owning land and partaking in the gold rush in the same way as Whites.

The relationship between the event Iditarod and Native Alaskan culture is also brought up in the media. Medred (2016a, 2016b), a journalist in Anchorage who has written extensively about the race over the years, discusses how the participants in the race are changing. While sled dog racing used to be a sport dominated by Alaskan Natives back in the 1950s, with many villages organizing their own races, today sled dog racing does not have a central position among Native Alaskans. Instead, other activities and events have become central to actors in rural Alaska, in particular related to snowmobiling. The increased role of the snowmobile in Alaska is highlighted as a reason why there are almost no native mushers today, while in 1973 almost half of those were Alaskan Natives (Medred, 2016a). Specifically, Medred (2016b) claims that the snowmobiling event "Iron Dog has become rural Alaska's race. Young people in rural Alaska today grow up wanting to be Iron Dog racers, not Iditarod mushers".

In light of these changes in rural Alaska, Medred further explains that the Iditarod has faced challenges:

> Iditarod today enters the real world of rural Alaska as a slow-moving relic of another time. The public face of village Alaska is that it continues to embrace the Iditarod. The Iditarod is an Alaska icon. A village would hardly dare express any other view.
>
> (Medred, 2016b)

This means that even though the event may not be accessible or interesting to a village, it has an iconic status that "requires" villages to support it. Other informants in Alaska speak of similar challenges, but many also explain that it is almost impossible for Alaskans living in native villages to perform at the level that is required in order to do well in today's Iditarod, as it would require a support system and financial resources that few of the people living in the rural villages have access to. The event that brings people and dogs out to the small villages along the Iditarod trail, then, seems to be an event inaccessible for natives to participate in, except as spectators or providers of service or food for the Iditarod participants when they pass through.

There are also other aspects of tension that point to how narratives of events and places are interconnected. In terms of the Iditarod, the narrative of the beginning sparks a bit of discussion. For many people – perhaps in particular people outside Alaska, and outside the US – the first thing they bring up when they hear a reference to the Iditarod is the story of the Serum Run. Examining the discourse on the Iditarod, this is not surprising, as there are several examples of how the Serum Run is implicitly and explicitly connected to this particular contemporary sled dog race. For instance, in a story on Alaskan history and culture in a regional magazine, the story of the Serum Run is linked to the Iditarod trail and the sled dog race several times. After a relatively detailed account of the Serum Run – the "great race of mercy" – the article reads:

> Almost 90 years later, the trail that Goodwin blazed is still making news. The annual Last Great Race, which officially began on March 3, 1973, draws hundreds of well-wishers and dozens of mushers and dogs to Anchorage to take part in a race of stamina, wits and ever-changing technology.
>
> (Bill, 2014, p. 19)

The article goes on to talk about the winner of the previous year's Iditarod, and implicitly links all of this together. At the same time, this aspect of how it all began is challenged by the Iditarod race organization. *The Iditarod Official 2014 Race Guide* even includes an article entitled "Myth Busting: The Iditarod Sled Dog Race Started Because ..." which explicitly explains that the Serum Run and the start-up of the Iditarod sled dog race are not to be seen as connected. This article reads:

> The most common "fact" I have heard since the publication of my book *Champion of Alaskan Huskies* has been "Oh, I know about the Iditarod. It started because of the serum run". This, however, is a misconception that has been perpetuated over the years and never corrected.
>
> (Mangelsdorf, 2014, p. 12)

Despite the race organization's attempt to get rid of this misconception, the Serum Run story is being re-told and reinforced in public discourse, via books, such as *The great serum race: Blazing the Iditarod trail* (Miller, 2006) or *Balto and the great race* (Kimmel, 1999), films (Balto), and in media stories. Even the race organization itself implicitly feeds into the same story that it wants to remove. On its web page, under the titles "Information" and "About," the Iditarod organization includes a section on how "the sled dogs has [sic] one last taste of glory in early 1925 when a diphtheria epidemic [...] threatened isolated, icebound Nome. The nearest serum was in Anchorage" (Bowers, 2012a). As the only pilot in the territory considered capable of braving the unpredictable weather was unavailable, "a Pony Express-type relay of dog teams was quickly organized" (Bowers, 2012a). The web page presents information on how trains rushed the serum to Nenana, from where different mushers took it westward:

> Every village along the route offered its best team and driver for its leg to speed the serum toward Nome. The critical leg across the treacherous Norton Sound ice from Shaktoolik to Golovin was taken by Leonhard

Seppala, the territory's premier musher, and his lead dog Togo. Gunnar Kaasen drove the final two legs into Nome behind his lead dog Balto, through a blizzard hurling 80 mph winds.

(Bowers, 2012a)

It is not surprising that the Serum Run narrative lives on, and that this is what many people bring up when Iditarod is brought up in conversation.

There are also some other narratives about the reason for the Iditarod, and one seems to be particularly strong in the symbols and stories in the Iditarod headquarters in Wasilla. Outside the building there is a statue of Joe Redington, who is referred to as the father of the Iditarod. The foregrounding of Redington can be seen in many of the race organization's texts, and also on their web page. Here it is explained how Joe Redington Sr. had witnessed first-hand a "decline of the need for the sled dogs in Alaska," which inspired him "to dedicate much of his life to the Iditarod Trail Sled Dog Race" (Bowers, 2012a). There is also a page with an extended version of the Joe Redington Sr. story on the site, where the decline in dog sledding is explained in terms of the growing use of snowmobiles:

During the 1960s, however, it was not space travel but the advent of the "iron dog" (or snowmachine or snowmobile) that resulted in the mass abandonment of dog teams across the state and loss of much mushing lore.

(Bowers, 2012b)

According to the Iditarod organization, Redington had two reasons for organizing the long-distance Iditarod race: to save the sled dog culture and Alaskan huskies, which were being phased out of existence due to the introduction of snowmobiles in Alaska; and to preserve the historical Iditarod Trail between Seward and Nome. According to the race organization, the race is really a reconstruction of the freight route to Nome and commemorates the part that sled dogs played in the settlement of Alaska – reinforcing the historical geography of this remote state.

Other informants point to other motives as important for the start of the Iditarod race. For instance, some speak of the role of tourism as a factor, and how some wanted to "bring that race to Nome, and turn it in to tourism" as one informant says. This informant, who works with tourism and was involved with the Iditarod race from the very beginning, underscores how the race now is the reason many people are coming to visit Alaska, and he includes both mushers and spectators in this dynamic, describing how people are "coming up just to see the Iditarod. It is mushers coming in a whole week".

At the same time, there is a slightly different narrative about the beginning of and the reason for the race, and that has to do with a consciousness-raising internally in Alaska. In the October 1979 issue of the *Iditarod Runner*, Dorothy G. Page, who is called the "Mother of the Iditarod", is quoted on her intention for the Iditarod:

To keep the spirit of the Iditarod the same. I don't ever want to see high pressure people getting in and changing the spirit of the race. We brought the sled dog back and increased the number of mushers. It is really an Alaskan event. I think the fact that it starts in Anchorage and then ends in Nome has opened up a whole new area for people in Alaska. I think they appreciate that. It puts them in touch with the pioneer spirit.

(Iditarod, 2018)

Page was a resident of Wasilla and a self-made historian, and was unhappy that in the '60s most people in Alaska did not know there was an Iditarod Trail or that dog teams had played a very important part in Alaska's early settlement. It was then that Page saw the importance of an event to create this awareness, to celebrate time and place and promote the destination.

The last type of narrative that is important to address here in this chapter has to do with the Iditarod as a challenge and an individual accomplishment. In line with this understanding, one informant from Nome points out:

Every single minute there is a story in the race. More people has climbed the Mont Everest in a year, than has been finishing the Iditarod. We want to hear the musher's story, it is about their story. When the banquet starts the last person that came to the finish line, gets up and he talks stories. In sports, it is all about winning, but in the Iditarod, it is a different story. Every musher that participate is a winner. Everybody that is in it has a story.

(Study informant, 2014)

This aspect is underscored by the fact that there seem to be countless books published by people who have participated in the Iditarod. Such stories circulate in the public discourse, feeding into narratives of the Iditarod as the ultimate challenge. Other aspects support this, like the fact that people who have finished the Iditarod can use the "Iditarod finisher" confirmation as an ethos-confirming fact in their tourism business.

At the same time, informants point out that the race is no longer as tough as it used to be, and some seem to look back to the "old days" as the real or authentic race. As another informant mentioned, "the mushers are all Merlot-drinkers these days", indicating that today only a certain kind of musher is able to participate in the race. Similarly, Medred (2016b) writes about the way some look at the Iditarod today, quoting Hans Oettli, a Canadian musher, who says:

The race is about rich, White, folk from somewhere else playing their game in a wilderness where most of the residents are Alaska Natives struggling to find ways to transition from the fading subsistence economy of old to the cash economy of today. There are issues of class and race here that cannot be ignored, and the differences have only grown over the years.

(as cited in Medred, 2016b)

## Concluding remarks

Understanding the intersections of events, place and society, our discussion speaks to an understanding of social and cultural impacts related to the Iditarod event of Alaska. In different, yet interconnected and overlapping ways, the Iditarod relates to issues of cultural contestations and power in the Alaskan context, which are intertwined and interconnected with global cultural trends, regarding understandings of Alaskan history. *Place* as understood in the context of the Iditarod event investigated in this chapter, is an event that is staged, but what this staging entails depends on where you stand in relation to history and place. The findings and discussions from this study help us understand local expectations, needs and experiences, social and cultural impacts related to the event, for both the visitors and the people who reside in Alaska. More broadly, this chapter adds to understandings of event and place dynamics, specifically addressing the cultural complexities and power relations that are part of such intersections.

## References

Aldskogius, H. (1993). Festivals and meets: The place of music in 'Summer Sweden'. *Geografiska Annaler Series B*, 75, 55–72.

Allern, S. (2001). Kildene og mediemakten [The sources and the media power]. *Nordicom Review: Nordic Research on Media & Communication*, 23(1), 17–27.

Appadurai, A. (1996). *Modernity at large: Cultural dimensions of globalization*. Vol. 1. Minneapolis: University of Minnesota Press.

Barker, C. (2004). *The SAGE dictionary of cultural studies*. London: SAGE.

Bill, L. (2014). A line in the snow. Blazing the Iditarod trail. *Alaska: The Magazine of Life on the Last Frontier*, March, pp. 16–19.

Bowers, D. (2012a). *Booms and Busts*. Retrieved 23 April 2015 from: http://iditarod. com/about/booms-and-busts/.

Bowers, D. (2012b). *History*. Retrieved 23 March 2015 from: http://iditarod.com/about/ history/.

Bureau of Land Management. (2018). *Iditarod national historic trail*. Retrieved 20 August 2018 from: www.blm.gov/programs/national-conservation-lands/ national-scenic-and-historic-trails/iditarod.

Cloke, P. (2007). Creativity and tourism in rural environments. In G. Richards & J. Wilson (Eds.), *Tourism, creativity and development* (pp. 37–47, Chapter 2). London: Routledge.

de Brito, M. P. & Terzieva, L. (2016). Key elements for designing a strategy to generate social and environmental value: A comparative study of festivals. *Research in Hospitality Management*, 6(1), 51–59.

de Certeau, M. (1984). *The practice of everyday life* (S. Rendell, Trans.). Berkeley: University of California Press.

Doucleff, M. (2012). Iditarod sled dog race. *Cell, 148*(5), 839–841.

Ekman, A. K. (1999). The revival of cultural celebrations in regional Sweden: Aspects of tradition and transition. *Sociologia Ruralis, 39*(3), 280–293.

Endres, D. & Senda-Cook, S. (2011). Location matters: The rhetoric of place in protest. *Quarterly Journal of Speech, 97*(3), 257–282.

Getz, D. (2013). *Event tourism*. New York: Cognizant Communication Corporation.

Granås, B. (2014). A place for whom? A place for what? The powers of destinization. In B. Granås & A. Viken (Eds.), *Tourism destination development: Turns and tactics* (pp. 79–92). London: Routledge.

Haanpää, M., García-Rosell, J. C. & Tuulentie, S. (2016). Co-creating places through events: The case of a tourism community event in Finnish Lapland. In A. Jepson & A. Clark (Eds.), *Managing and developing communities, festivals and events* (pp. 34–49). UK: Springer Link.

Hall, M. C. (1989). The definition and analysis of hallmark tourist events. *GeoJournal, 19*(3), 263–268.

Iditarod. (2017). The last great race. Retrieved 15 March 2017 from: http://iditarod.com/.

Iditarod. (2018). History. Retrieved 23 August 2018 from: http://iditarod.com/about/history.

Jæger, K. & Kvidal-Røvik, T. (2015). "Du får som fortjent": Destinasjonsmarkedsføring, eventer og sosiale medier ["You will get what you deserve": Destination marketing, events, and social media]. In K. A. Ellingsen & T. Blindheim (Eds.), *Regional merkevarebygging* (pp. 135–150). Oslo: Fagbokforlaget.

Jæger, K. & Olsen, K. (2017). On commodification: Volunteer experiences in festivals. *Journal of Tourism and Cultural Change, 15*(5), 407–421.

Jago, L., Chalip, L., Brown, G., Mules, T. & Ali, S. (2003). Building events into destination branding: Insights from experts. *Event Management, 8*(1), 3–14.

Jepson, A. & Clarke, A. (2016). An introduction to planning and managing communities, festivals and events. In A. Jepson & A. Clarke (Eds.), *Managing and developing communities, festivals and events* (pp. 3–15). UK: Springer Link.

Kielland, I. M. (2012). *Whose stories? Whose place? Place politics and the politics of place stories in Tromsø's Olympic debate*. Unpublished PhD thesis, University of Tromsø.

Kimmel, E. C. (1999). *Balto and the great race*. New York: Random House Books for Young Readers.

Lavenda, R. (1997). *Corn fests and water carnivals: Celebrating community in Minnesota*. Washington: Smithsonian Institution Press.

Lewis, C. & Pile, S. (1996). Women, body, space: Rio Carnival and the politics of performance. *Gender, Place and Culture, 3*(1), 23–42.

Mangelsdorf, K. (2014). Myth busting: The Iditarod Trail Sled Dog Race started because …. *Iditarod Trail Sled Dog Race: The Official 2014 Race Guide*.

Medred, C. (2016a). *A difficult trail shared by all*. Retrieved 15 March 2015 from: https://craigmedred.news/2016/03/15/a-difficult-trail-shared-by-all/.

Medred, C. (2016b). *Iditarod's village problems*. Retrieved 16 March 2015 from: https://craigmedred.news/2016/03/16/iditarods-village-problems/.

Middleton, M., Hess, A., Endres, D. & Senda-Cook, S. (2015). *Participatory critical rhetoric. Theoretical and methodological foundations for studying rhetoric in situ*. London, New York: Lexington.

Miller, D. S. (2006). *The great serum race: Blazing the iditarod trail*. USA: Bloomsbury Publishing.

Morley, D. (2001). Belongings: Place, space and identity in a mediated world. *European Journal of Cultural Studies, 4*(4), 425–448.

Neuman, R., Just, M. R. & Crigler, A. N. (1992). *Common knowledge. News and the construction of political meaning*. Chicago, London: The University of Chicago Press.

Perić, M., Wise, N. & Dragičević, D. (2017). Suggesting a service research agenda in sport tourism: Working experience(s) into business models. *Sport, Business and Management: An International Journal, 7*(1), 58–76.

Pietikäinen, S. & Hujanen, J. (2003). At the crossroads of ethnicity, place and identity: Representations of northern people and regions in Finnish news discourse. *Media, Culture & Society, 25*(2), 251–268.

Quinn, B. (2009). Festivals, events and tourism. In T. Jamal & M. Robinson (Eds.), *The SAGE handbook of tourism studies* (pp. 483–503). London: SAGE.

Richie, B. J. (1984). Assessing the impact of hallmark events: Conceptual and research issues. *Journal of Travel Research, 23*(1), 2–11.

Silk, M. (2002). 'Bangsa Malaysia': Global sport, the city and the mediated refurbishment of local identities. *Media, Culture & Society, 24*(6), 775–794.

Varley, P. & Semple, T. (2015). Nordic slow adventure: Explorations in time and nature. *Scandinavian Journal of Hospitality and Tourism, 15*(1–2), 73–90.

Williams, D. L. & Brandt, E. A. (2013). Sense of place, identity and cultural continuity in an Arizona community. In P. N. Goggin (Ed.), *Environmental rhetoric and ecologies of place* (pp. 42–52). London: Routledge.

Wise, N. & Harris, J. (2016). Community, identity and contested notions of place: A study of Haitian recreational soccer players in the Dominican Republic. *Soccer & Society, 17*(4), 610–627.

Wise, N. A. & Mulec, I. (2012). Headlining Dubrovnik's tourism image: Transitioning representations/narratives of war and heritage preservation, 1991–2010. *Tourism Recreation Research, 37*(1), 57–69.

# 11 Reinventing and reimagining rural Wales

## The case of the World Alternative Games

*Lucia Aquilino & John Harris*

## Introduction

Whilst much work has focused on events and urban regeneration (see Wise & Harris, 2017), events and festivals are also hosted in rural landscapes to celebrate local traditions and to boost the local economy (see Gibson et al., 2011; Sharpley & Jepson, 2011). Indeed, some rural communities have shown a good understanding of emerging niche markets in search of alternatives to well-established tourism offerings (Daugstad, 2008; MacDonald & Jolliffe, 2003; Sharpley & Jepson, 2011; Wilson et al., 2001). This chapter focuses on the case of the World Alternative Games (WAG), a biennial event that takes place in Britain's smallest town. Based on a social constructionist approach, this chapter will look at how participation in event activities contributes to a sense of community and a sense of place.

The second author has been undertaking work relating to this event since 2012 (see Harris, 2013a, 2013b) and the first author undertook an ethnographic study of the event during the third edition of the Games in 2016. By looking at the ways in which people make sense of reality (see Harris, 2006), through spectating, competing and volunteering, we were able to explore the engagement of people in the event. Data presented in this chapter is based on participant observation and interviews with WAG event organizers and those who attended the 2016 event.

Rural areas may look at promoting events to increase tourism as an opportunity to regenerate the local economy (see Daugstad, 2008; Eusébio et al., 2017; Su, 2011). Rurality can be used as a theme, provide stimulating scenery or lend resources to events while defining the place and the community hosting them (see Bertella, 2014; Gibson et al., 2011). Yet it should also be noted that the development of the event itself can also lead to some tension as an increase in tourists visiting to take part in an event can be perceived as disruptive or as a threat to the rural idyll (see Derrett, 2004; Mason & Beaumont-Kerridge, 2004).

## Understanding rurality and creating an event place

Rural landscapes seem to be suited to hosting events that promise a captivating experience in a stimulating natural environment, offering the perfect scenario and resources to design and plan event activities (Bertella, 2014). Rurality can be understood as the result of a process of how a place and its community are socially constructed. In reflecting on the processes driving the development of a place, Tuan (1977) and Proshansky et al. (1983) emphasise the physical aspect as one of the layers contributing to the make up of a place. This can be looked at as a sort of visual reflection of part of the experiences lived by people within it (Adams, 2010; Mendoza & Morén-Alegret, 2012). However, by using and experiencing a physical space (and interacting within it), people tend to create meanings and values that help define a place's identity (Adams, 2010; Proshansky et al., 1983; Tuan, 1977; Wise, 2015a). In doing this, they tend to establish a relationship with the constructed place and develop symbolic connections with it and within social groups (Greider & Garkovich, 1994; Shamai, 1991). Yet, this process is subject to change and different uses of the space can result in changing dynamics of (re)negotiation and meaning (see Greider & Garkovich, 1994; Hay, 1998; Raffaetà & Duff, 2013). The understanding of a place, and the associated place attachment that might derive from it, can vary across different contexts (e.g. temporal, spatial, social, cultural, political) leading to the development of different senses of place (see Greider & Garkovich, 1994; Wise, 2015b).

Raymond Williams is widely regarded as one of the most important cultural theorists of the twentieth century. An area he was particularly interested in was the place of communities within the rural environment (see Williams, 1973). He not only looked at the relationship between the urban and the rural and the ways in which the countryside was viewed as being very much about the past (and different to the forward and modernist impressions of the city), but also included rich descriptors of rural communities in his novels (see Williams, 1960). These works, based on semi-autobiographical accounts of his early experiences in his native Wales, highlighted the ways in which social and economic change impacted upon this country. The work of Williams has been used to look at the importance of mega-events to contemporary Wales (Harris, 2015), but to date little research has incorporated his work into the study of smaller events outside of the large urban centres. The next section briefly looks at the role of events in rural areas.

An event can be understood as a social product built up through interactions of people who organize, manage, host and attend it (see de Geus et al., 2015; Kirkup & Sutherland, 2015; Perić et al., 2016; Pettersson & Zillinger, 2011; Quinn, 2005). As a social product, an event encompasses interactions and emotional connections triggered by certain physical and social components within a specific spatial and temporal dimension (see Picard & Robinson, 2006). Engaging in event activities tends to be linked to the necessity to engage in social relationships (see Crandall, 1979; Kelly, 1981; Kyle & Chick, 2002). This echoes the developmental processes of community, which defines itself through the interrelation between individuals and their physical and social spaces (Delanty, 2010; McMillan & Chavis, 1986; Theodori, 2005). In order to stimulate engagement in such interactions, events are characterized by driving factors, values which sometimes overlap with the values and meanings linked to the physical environment and to the community of the host location (de Geus et al., 2015; Ziakas & Boukas, 2013).

Studies exploring the social content of events and event participation show how culture and related meanings and values emerge across community-based events (e.g. De Bres & Davis, 2001; Quinn, 2005; Yolal et al., 2009). Small-scale events taking place in rural landscapes can offer a learning experience which, through the engagement of all the senses boosted by the peculiarities of the natural setting and of the event activities, tends to shape perceptions of the natural environment and its relative values (cultural and others), and of all the people involved in the same event context, which may bring about senses of place and community (Bertella, 2014; Crouch, 2000; Đurkin & Wise, 2017; Urry, 2002). Forms of identification and engagement, not only with the natural setting of the event but also with other attendees or participants, are shaped through interactions with the surrounding environment and with people within the event context (Kirkup & Sutherland, 2015). The next section will briefly outline some of the background to the creation of the World Alternative Games and will also provide an introduction to the town of Llanwrtyd Wells.

## The World Alternative Games

The World Alternative Games first took place in 2012 in the smallest town in Britain. Presented as an alternative to the London 2012 Olympic Games, the WAG was developed with the aim of putting Llanwrtyd Wells on the map and supporting the local community (World Alternative Games, 2016b). The Welsh Assembly government had recently developed an events strategy aimed at enhancing the reputation of Wales as a tourism destination (Welsh Assembly Government, 2008). Harris (2013a, 2015) has looked at the ways in which Wales has attempted to use large-scale events as a means of developing sport tourism. This work has highlighted some of the challenges faced in (re)positioning Wales within and around a competitive and challenging business environment.

Those involved in promoting Wales as a tourist destination have looked at tourism and sport as tools through which distinctiveness can be shaped in an international context (see Harris, 2013a, 2015; Pitchford, 1995). With the decline of traditional rural work (e.g. farming), tourism has become a new driving force for many local economies and for the regeneration and promotion of rural areas within Wales (Pitchford, 1995; Pritchard & Morgan, 2001). As such, events are increasingly recognized as being key in engaging local communities in leisure and tourism activities and enhancing the reputation of Wales in an international context (Welsh Assembly Government, 2008).

With this in mind, the World Alternative Games may be looked at as more than a small-scale event held in a rural town. It can be considered as a marketing tool that aims to reshape a rural area by attracting tourism and event opportunities (see Harris, 2013a, 2013b). The key aspect of the WAG is the capacity of the local population to come up with wacky ideas which can attract the attention of visitors and media organizations. The natural resources and the endeavors of the host community in planning and ensuring the performance of activities during the event itself are the main drivers of this event. The local community, in a town with a population of around 600 people, plays a leading role in the organization of the event and provides further support through volunteering activities. Furthermore, it draws on developing partnerships with public and private stakeholders, such as the Welsh Assembly government, that support and sponsor the games. As with many of the other events discussed within this collection, those involved in developing the WAG work hard to encourage media coverage with different media outlets from local newspapers through to national television shows like the BBC's *Breakfast* programme covering the event (see BBC, 2012; The Telegraph, 2012; World Alternative Games, 2016a, 2016b).

More than 60 games challenged competitors' skills in different ways during the 2016 event. Some of these were created in the town and the rest were borrowed or inspired by events held in other countries all over the world. Worm charming, backward running, egg throwing, bog snorkelling, wife carrying, and husband dragging are just some examples of the varied activities that make up the WAG (World Alternative Games, 2016a, 2016b). What contributes to making these event activities attractive is the rural environment, which acts as a perfect stage for hosting activities such as the annual Man versus Horse Marathon and the very popular World Bog Snorkelling Championships. These are both key events in an expanding event portfolio within the town, which is an important part of the identity of this place. Both of the above have been taking place in Llanwrtyd Wells for a number of years and were in many ways the catalysts for the development of the World Alternative Games in 2012. The next part of this chapter considers the role of creativity in shaping these events before we then go on to look specifically at some of the ways in which place is important in helping us to understand the particular case of the World Alternative Games.

### Rural creativity

Llanwrtyd Wells has long been a place where wacky event ideas are brought into the community. Some locals shared stories of the childhood of their children to depict a rural reality in which the amount of spare time that people have at their disposal can be filled up with various activities. Exploring nature with the aim of finding objects and reshaping them to create entertainment was something referred to by a number of people. Making obstacles with wood and ropes, jumping on an inflatable boat to glide on snowy steep ground and taking apart an old car to reassemble it into a dune buggy are just some examples referred to. These of course have been a feature of play across the centuries in a range of different cultures.

There seemed to be a connection between creativity and rurality in Llanwrtyd Wells. Rurality was an important aspect of the local events which celebrated the landscape. However, in this particular case, rurality also seemed to be much more than an event component. It seemed to be embodied in a sort of attitude which stimulated a creative process that formed a key part in the development of event activities. The local creativity was a sort of projection of how rurality as a physical and social space was experienced and lived. This reflects the perspectives that Cloke and Milbourne (1992) and Greider and Garkovich (1994) share about the experience of a space and the interaction with a landscape contributing to the construction of its meanings. In addition to this, creativity was not just purposively staged as a form of rurality. Instead, it was nurtured by symbolic connections that locals developed through being immersed in the rural space. In other words, the local creativity was embedded in the rural life of Llanwrtyd Wells, becoming a factor of development in the event portfolio. The success of events such as the World Bog Snorkelling Championships were undoubtedly key in highlighting the ways in which events could be used to develop an awareness of place and provided an activity that people could come together to enjoy. The importance of place is considered further in the next section of this chapter, where we look at how the natural environment shapes the type of activities developed in the town.

### Rurality shaping event activities

Apart from providing a setting for the event experience, the rural landscape was an essential condition for certain games to take place. Harry, one of the participants, explained how some of the physical elements of the surrounding natural environment were essential for the WAG:

> You're gonna have bog snorkelling where there's a bog! You know. And "bog" literally, in the true meaning of "bog" is a peat bog and these two trenches are cut into the peat bog. Peat bogs always float on a lake of water, you jump up and down on that it's like jumping up and down on the mattress on your bed [...] it waves everywhere and you crawl in that, and one or two things happen. Either the whole rock collapses in, or the sticking earth, dense enough would hold itself and, so you do need that! Man vs horse, that couldn't happen anywhere flat because the horse would always win, whereas the terrain here is such that a horse, and this is coming from a horse stoner, would not run down the side of the hill, so the whole thing equalises. So 26 miles, it produces an equal playing field. So, yeah, and most definitely the things that are happening here have evolved because of what we've got where we are.

According to some, certain rural characteristics of the place inspired the development of what many would consider as peculiar competitions. Indeed, many pointed out the fact that the Man versus Horse Marathon could not take place in a flat green area, which would have guaranteed the horses' victory over the runners. Others admitted that when locals were in search of ideas that could attract people to the town "one farmer said having a big bog in the back field, so they thought, 'let's dig a hole and try to swim in', and that is how the bog snorkelling started" (Clara). This supports Bertella's (2014) and Loureiro's (2014) research on how physical elements of a rural area contribute to shaping the setting of tourism and event experiences. The setting of the WAG was not artificially or purposively created for running certain events. The geomorphologic characteristics of the rural area (its physical features), meant that ideas of competitions could develop.

In describing the beauty of the rural landscape, another research participant Jen (an event competitor), suggested that:

> It is just the beautiful countryside. Certainly, the weather is not really reliable but it does not matter. So it's the countryside, the clean air, the hills, I do a lot of running and mountain biking while I am here I go out and explore as well. Yeah, it just, it just feels like a "bolt-hole" what we call a "bolt-hole" is somewhere to run to and have two weeks away from everyday life and stress and work, it feels like, I cannot think of a word now … refuge, a refuge somewhere you go to get away from everything and that is what this town looks to us.

Feeling completely immersed in the green lands and in the wilderness while hiking or cycling tended to be the main aspiration of many people. They would spectate or participate in certain activities like ditch racing, stone skimming and hay bale throwing. Certainly, some event activities stimulated the sensorial experience of people triggering emotional processes (see also, Bertella, 2014). Participants would dive in the dirty water of the bog, they would make a stone skim on the pond or throw a hay bale. A sort of subliminal connection to the rural landscape of Llanwrtyd Wells and the natural elements shaping it were such that a strong attachment to it developed.

The interaction with the rural space in these activities, instilling a sense of attachment to it and defining a sense of rurality, reflects arguments that Tuan (1977) and Proshansky et al. (1983) made to describe how the engagement with a space contributes to the development of place-identity (see also, Williams, 1973). In particular, bog snorkelling, ditch racing and stone skimming gave people the opportunity to become familiar with different parts of the area surrounding the town.

This is certainly a different way of connecting to the landscape, when compared to what many of the more commodified rural tourism areas offer. In line with the arguments that Daugstad (2008) offers, explaining how locals and visitors negotiate their views of the rural, these perspectives seem not to present the focus on tourism development in rural areas and on the landscape as an asset.

### Rurality and events shaping a sense of place

The attraction of living in a small town with a focus on community was something that a number of people referred to. Another research participant Lucy explained:

> I think people connect with what's happening, with the atmosphere that's here and if you connect with it you want more of it [...]. I wonder if, if you were in a certain point of your life when you think you can make a change and you have, maybe, just a small sense of adventure of doing things a little bit differently, just a little bit and this attracts people. People do not stay if they don't feel they fit in.

The local way of life and the daily interactions within the place seemed to be the main factors attracting people. Here people found they could (re) shape their lives, while contributing to the development of bonds and a sense of attachment to Llanwrtyd Wells. The way of life of many of the local population tended to turn the town into a place where event activities drove relationships and interactions with the surrounding space and the people. Certainly, this is a process that did not affect all the inhabitants of Llanwrtyd Wells, especially those who preferred not to be involved in event activities. Social meanings deriving from symbolic interactions between people and spaces, and between individuals, were not the only points driving discussions related to the development of a sense of place (e.g. Hay, 1998; Shamai, 1991). Other factors, such as enacting a rural place-making process and the development of a sense of rurality or a sense of natural landscape also help explain meaningful interactions in this case. This is of course not unique to Llanwrtyd Wells and has also been identified as important elsewhere (see Greider & Garkovich, 1994; Halfacree, 1993).

Many of the local population within Llanwrtyd Wells seemed to detach themselves from the stereotyped image of the rural based on a certain use of the natural environment. Where farming was not the main activity, locals engaged in other activities that reshaped their way of connecting to the area and of making sense of their life within it. As Lucy noted:

> we live with beauty on our doorsteps that you can just go and enjoy. We can do a few hour-type of work and there some other [...] people who move here, they do a little bit of gardening, a bit of this, a bit of that and they manage to make just enough to hold body and soul together. And that's all the people here are interested in, a very simple life we have here and nobody is really interested in, in high life of any sort. We just want

to be able to keep going, gather together occasionally. Yeah, it's just a quite inspiring place to live, actually.

In such a place-making process, the interrelationship between social components, practices and physical elements, generated a rurality which could make Llanwrtyd Wells appear to some as a very unusual place. Cloke and Milbourne (1992) commented upon the construction of a rurality which still remains clinging onto past values, regardless of the scale where meaning production occurs (i.e. nationally, regionally, locally). For Williams (1973), this connection with the past in an increasingly dynamic and changing world was one of the reasons that some people found such a strong sense of identity tied to place (see also, Williams, 1960). The case of Llanwrtyd Wells clearly shows how meanings locally (re)negotiated tend to undermine, and sometimes prevail over, those idyllic representations of the rural environment based on the traditional uses of the land (e.g. farming). Many people in Llanwrtyd Wells appeared to be reshaping their way of connecting to the rural area and of making sense of their life within it. This process seemed to be purposively fostered by constructs emerging from practices and activities. These constructs seemed to create a rurality that had almost nothing to do with traditional meanings related to, for example, agricultural activities. This is a process that reflects the results of the study that Galani-Moutafi (2013) conducted on a small Greek village, where events and other tourism practices were adopted to overturn the local traditional meanings derived from idyllic representations of the Greek rural landscape. The case of Llanwrtyd Wells clearly shows how meanings locally negotiated (and renegotiated) tend to undermine and prevail over those idyllic representations of the rural environment based on the past traditional uses of the land such as farming.

The physical aspects of the town, the local activities and people's interactions defining their sense of place can be also considered as spatial and interactional components nurturing a sense of community (see McMillan & Chavis, 1986; Minar & Greer, 1969). In line with Philo (1993) and Jones's (1995) reflections related to the connection between rural place and social life, the sense of rurality emerging from the interconnection of all spatial and interactional components discussed above seemed to nurture a bond within the community of Llanwrtyd Wells.

## Concluding remarks

The case of the WAG sheds light on the meanings of the rurality of Llanwrtyd Wells, emerging from the encounter between people and the landscape. Moreover, the interdependency between people and landscape is mediated by event activities which act as vehicles in the process shaping the rural place and its local identity. As a place made up of meanings resulting from the encounters, interactions and participation of people within a particular space, the rurality of Llanwrtyd Wells can be viewed as a constantly changing process. Through this process, the meanings attached to the town tend to change—making it difficult to define its image once and for all. In an event-tourism context, certain values are used to shape a destination image, which stands out and distinguishes itself from others. This characteristic rurality could itself be a source of inspiration for ideas boosting the development of rural areas and tourism activities, which could certainly offer a different experience of rurality based on the changing values and meanings of place. Williams (1960, 1973) highlighted the ways in which people create an understanding of place and how places and people change. A strong sense of community and identity was central to his writing about a particular part of rural Wales.

Perceived by many as a 'wacky' place, Llanwrtyd Wells has positioned itself as a town where events are an important part of its identity. For some time now, the town has been known for bog snorkelling and various other activities that are focused on the unusual. The success of these events and the World Alternative Games has been driven by the dedication of a small number of local residents who have recognized the potential of events in developing tourism and a sense of community. The town is an interesting site for looking at the ways in which events contribute to a sense of place. Further research will continue to explore the ways in which these can be important to developing business opportunities and contributing positively to community development.

# References

Adams, P.C. (2010). A taxonomy for communication geography. *Progress in Human Geography*, 35(1), 37–57.

BBC. (2012). Llanwrtyd Wells stages alternative Olympic games. *BBC*, available at: www.bbc.co.uk/news/uk-wales-mid-wales-19208440.

Bertella, G. (2014). Designing small-scale sport events in the countryside. *International Journal of Event and Festival Management*, 5(2), 132–145.

Cloke, P. & Milbourne, P. (1992). Deprivation and lifestyles in rural Wales. -II. Rurality and the cultural dimension. *Journal of Rural Studies*, 8(4), 359–371.

Crandall, R. (1979). Social interaction, affect and leisure. *Journal of Leisure Research*, 11(3), 165–181.

Crouch, D. (2000). Places around us: Embodied lay geographies in leisure and tourism. *Leisure Studies*, 19(2), 63–76.

Daugstad, K. (2008). Negotiating landscape in rural tourism. *Annals of Tourism Research*, 35(2), 402–426.

De Bres, K. & Davis, J. (2001). Celebrating group and place identity: A case study of a new regional festival. *Tourism Geographies*, 3(3), 326–337.

de Geus, S., Richards, G. & Toepoel, V. (2015). Conceptualisation and operationalisation of event and festival experiences: Creation of an Event Experience Scale. *Scandinavian Journal of Hospitality and Tourism*, 16 (3), 274–296.

Delanty, G. (2010). *Community*. London: Routledge.

Derrett, R. (2004). Festivals, events and destinations. In I. Yeoman, M. Robertson, J. Ali-Knight, S. Drummond & U. McMahon-Beattie (Eds.) *Festival and events management*. Oxford: Butterworth-Heinemann (32–50).

Đurkin, J. & Wise, N. (2017). Managing community stakeholders in rural areas: Assessing the organisation of local sports events in Gorski kotar, Croatia. In A. Clarke & A. Jepson (Eds.) *Power, construction and meaning in festivals & events*. London: Routledge (185–200).

Eusébio, C., Carneiro, M.J., Kastenholz, E., Figueiredo, E. & Da Silva, D.S. (2017). Who is consuming the countryside? An activity-based segmentation analysis of the domestic rural tourism market in Portugal. *Journal of Hospitality and Tourism Management*, 31, 197–210.

Galani-Moutafi, V. (2013). Rural space (re)produced - Practices, performances and visions: A case study from an Aegean island. *Journal of Rural Studies*, 32, 103–113.

Gibson, C., Connell J., Waitt, G. & Walmsley, J. (2011). The extent and significance of rural festivals. In C. Gibson & J. Connell (Eds.) *Festival places*. Bristol: Channel View Publications (3–43).

Greider, T. & Garkovich, L. (1994). Landscapes: The social construction of nature and the environment. *Rural Sociology*, 59(1), 1–24.

Halfacree, K.H. (1993). Locality and social representation: Space, discourse and alternative definitions of the rural. *Journal of Rural Studies*, 9(1), 23–37.

Harris, J. (2006). The science of research in sport and tourism: Some reflections upon the promise of the sociological imagination. *Journal of Sport & Tourism*, 11(2), 153–171.

Harris, J. (2013a). Sporting events, image, and identities in contemporary Wales. *North American Journal of Welsh Studies*, 8, 100–112.

Harris, J. (2013b). Conclusion: From London and Llanwrtyd to Glasgow and Gleneagles. In J. Harris (Ed.) *Sport, tourism and national identities*. London: Routledge, pp. 97–100.

Harris, J. (2015). Keeping up with the Joneses: Hosting mega-events as a regenerative strategy in nation imaging, imagining and branding. *Local Economy*, 30(8), 961–974.

Hay, R. (1998). Sense of place in developmental context. *Journal of Environmental Psychology*, 18, 5–29.

Jones, O. (1995). Lay discourses of the rural: Developments and implications for rural studies. *Journal of Rural Studies*, 11(1), 35–49.

Kelly, J.R. (1981). Leisure interaction and the social dialectic. *Social Forces*, 60(2), 304–322.

Kirkup, N. & Sutherland, M. (2015). Exploring the relationships between motivation, attachment and loyalty within sport event tourism. *Current Issues in Tourism*, 20(1), 1–8.

Kyle, G. & Chick, G. (2002). The social nature of leisure involvement. *Journal of Leisure Research*, 34(4), 426–448.

Loureiro, S.M.C. (2014). The role of the rural tourism experience economy in place attachment and behavioural intentions. *International Journal of Hospitality Management*, 40, 1–9.

MacDonald, R. & Jolliffe, L. (2003). Cultural rural tourism: Evidence from Canada. *Annals of Tourism Research*, 30(2), 307–322.

Mason, P. & Beaumont-Kerridge, J. (2004). Attitudes of visitors and residents to the impacts of the 2001 Sidmouth International Festival. In I. Yeoman, M. Robertson, J. Ali-Knight, S. Drummond & U. McMahon-Beattie (Eds.) *Festival and events management*. Oxford: Butterworth-Heinemann (311–328).

McMillan, D.W. & Chavis, D.M. (1986). Sense of community: A definition and theory. *Journal of Community Psychology*, 14(1), 6–23.

Mendoza, C. & Morén-Alegret, R. (2012). Exploring methods and techniques for the analysis of senses of place and migration. *Progress in Human Geography*, 37(6), 762–785.

Minar, D.W. & Greer, S. (1969). *The concept of community: Reading with interpretations.* London: Butterworth & Co Ltd.

Perić, M., Đurkin, J. & Wise, N. (2016). Leveraging small-scale sport events: Challenges of organising, delivering and managing sustainable outcomes in rural communities, the case of Gorski Kotar, Croatia. *Sustainability*, 8(12), 1–17.

Pettersson, R. & Zillinger, M. (2011). Time and space in event behaviour: Tracking visitors by GPS. *Tourism Geographies*, 13(1), 1–20.

Philo, C. (1993). Postmodern rural geography? A reply to Murdoch and Pratt. *Journal of Rural Studies*, 9(4), 429–436.

Picard, D. & Robinson, M. (2006). Remaking worlds: Festivals, tourism and change. In D. Picard & M. Robinson (Eds.) *Festivals, tourism and social change: Remaking worlds.* Clevendon: Channel View Publications (1–31).

Pitchford, S.R. (1995). Ethnic tourism and nationalism in Wales. *Annals of Tourism Research*, 22(1), 35–52.

Pritchard, A. & Morgan, N. (2001). Culture, identity and tourism representation: Marketing Cymru or Wales? *Tourism Management*, 22(2), 167–179.

Proshansky, H.M., Fabian, A.K. & Kaminoff, R. (1983). Place-identity: Physical world socialization of the self. *Journal of Environmental Psychology*, 3(1), 57–83.

Quinn, B. (2005). Changing festival places: Insights from Galway. *Social & Cultural Geography*, 6(2), 237–252.

Raffaetà, R. & Duff, C. (2013). Putting belonging into place: Place experience and sense of belonging among Ecuadorian migrants in an Italian Alpine Region. *City & Society*, 25(3), 328–347.

Shamai, S. (1991). Sense of place: An empirical measurement. *Geoforum*, 22(3), 347–358.

Sharpley, R. & Jepson, D. (2011). Rural tourism: A spiritual experience? *Annals of Tourism Research*, 38(1), 52–71.

Su, B. (2011). Rural tourism in China. *Tourism Management*, 32(6), 1438–1441.

The Telegraph (2012). World Alternative Games. *The Telegraph*, available at: www.telegraph.co.uk/travel/activity-and-adventure/World-Alternative-Games-2012/.

Theodori, G.L. (2005). Community and community development in resource-based areas: Operational definitions rooted in an interactional perspective. *Society & Natural Resources*, 18(7), 661–669.

Tuan, Y. (1977). *Space and place: The perspective of experience.* London: Edward Arnold.

Urry, J. (2002). *The tourist Gaze.* London: Sage Publications.

Welsh Assembly Government (2008). *Event Wales: A major events strategy for Wales 2010–2020.* Cardiff: Welsh Assembly Government.

Williams, R. (1960). *Border country.* London: Chatto & Windus.

Williams, R. (1973). *The country and the city.* London: Chatto & Windus.

Wilson, S., Fesenmaier, D.R., Fesenmaier, J. & Van Es, J.C. (2001). Factors for success in rural tourism development. *Journal of Travel Research*, 40, 132–138.

Wise, N. (2015a). Football on the weekend: Rural events and the Haitian imagined community in the Dominican Republic. In A. Jepson & A. Clarke (Eds.) *Exploring community festivals and events.* London: Routledge (106–117).

Wise, N. (2015b). Placing sense of community. *Journal of Community Psychology*, 43(7), 920–929.

Wise, N. & Harris, J. (Eds.) (2017). *Sport, events, tourism and regeneration*. London: Routledge.

World Alternative Games (2016a). *Llanwrtyd Wells: events & activities*. Llanwrtyd Wells: Welsh Country Magazine.

World Alternative Games (2016b). World Alternative Games 2016, available at: www.worldalternativegames.co.uk/about/.

Yolal, M., Çetinel, F. & Uysal, M. (2009). An examination of festival motivation and perceived benefits relationship: Eskişehir international festival. *Journal of Convention & Event Tourism*, 10, 276–291.

Ziakas, V. & Boukas, N. (2013). Extracting meanings of event tourist experiences: A phenomenological exploration of Limassol carnival. *Journal of Destination Marketing and Management*, 2(2), 94–107.

# 12 Re-creating the clan

## "Brotherhood" and solidarity at the Masters World Championship Highland Games

*James Bowness*

### The Highland Games

This chapter is based on data collected at the 2014 Masters World Championship (MWC) Highland Games event in Inverness. The broader aim of the study was to understand the experiences of Masters athletes participating in a sport that challenges common narratives of ageing men and women. In-depth semi-structured interviews were used with 19 Highland Games Masters athletes in the eight months following the championships. Interviews involved the eclectic combination of life history, ethnographic and phenomenological approaches. An ethnographic approach was used to comprehend the processes of meaning making and ritual within the Masters Highland Games community (Hammersley, 2006).

Participants in the study came from a variety of nations, with many claiming an ancestral attachment to the homeland of the Highland Games, Scotland. The migration of people from Scotland has been well documented, with emigration within the former British empire well known (Devine, 2011, 2012; Fry, 2014). From the 18th century, Scottish related associations germinated in Canada, the United States, New Zealand and Australia (Sullivan, 2014). These groups give individuals the space to learn about their heritage (Leith & Sim, 2016) and perform an ethno-national culture (Edensor, 2002). Such spaces host an array of Scottish or Highland activities that aim to protect and reproduce a cultural identity. Sport plays an important role in these associations. Whilst a variety of sports have been used to maintain an affiliation to Scotland (Bairner & Whigham, 2014), the Highland Games is at the forefront of diasporic sporting celebrations.

The Highland Games are a series of popular community events that take place in multiple nations around the world, whilst remaining synonymous with the northern Highland region of Scotland. The Games involve multiple sporting events including Highland dancing, track and field and heavy athletics – the latter of which includes the iconic discipline of caber tossing. The history of the games is contested, but the accounts of Jarvie (1989) and Webster (2011) both point to the 11th century as the birthplace of the event. Fast forward almost a millennium and in 2018 there are 64 scheduled events to be held between May and September in Scotland (Scottish Highland Games Association, 2018).

Across the Atlantic, a North American Highland Games scene contrasts substantially with the games held in Scotland (Jarvie, 2005). Further afield the Highland Games also take place in both Australia and New Zealand. A few non-English speaking nations also hold contemporary Highland Games (see for example the Zederik Games held in the Netherlands). However, the nations most often associated with the migration of Scottish people (Canada, USA, Australia and New Zealand) all developed Highland Games during the 18th to 20th centuries (Brewster et al., 2009).

Many nations have adapted the rules of heavy athletics at the Highland Games. For example, in Germany the sport is played as a team event consisting of teams that represent corporations or public houses (Hesse, 2014). Furthermore, the US Games sees athletes compete over multiple events to achieve an overall standing. In Scotland athletes often compete in standalone individuals events. As such, a fragmented culture exists around the games, with each nation having their own context. Jarvie (2005) suggests that the North American Games retain a romanticized notion of Scotland, whilst Hesse (2014) notes the games' corporate collegiality. As many of these events are often planned by organizations devoted to maintaining Scottish/Highland identity, it would not be illogical to assume that those taking part in such activities have some personal link to Scotland. Sullivan (2014) found that the majority of those involved with Scottish associations in Canada, New Zealand and Australia knew their exact genealogical link to Scotland. Sullivan (2014) also notes that these Scottish cultural organizations were often exclusionary of those without Scottish heritage. The contemporary formation of these associations is now more inclusive and allows membership for those who wish to advance Scottish culture regardless of actual blood links (Sullivan, 2014). The transnational participation in Highland Games has developed alongside a new inclusivity within the Caledonian societies that wish to retain Scottish culture. Scottish cultural celebrations and sport are therefore consumed by more than simply the Scottish diaspora. Joining those without genealogical links to Scotland, are Masters athletes. This 21st century phenomenon involves the continuation or beginning of a career in the Games for those over 40 years of age.

## Masters sport and the games

Aside from the influx of a range of nationalities, the Games have also seen a demographic shift in those who participate. Traditionally young men have taken part in the heavy athletics and young women in Highland dancing. However, the last two decades have seen men and women continue their participation beyond the age of 40 and, in the process, form a new competition space for Masters athletes. The first Masters World Championship event was held in Arkansas, USA (2001) and a championship has been held every year since. As of 2017, 12 editions had been held in the US, 3 in Scotland and 1 each in Canada and Iceland (Scottish Masters, 2018). In 2018 the competition is to be held in Stuttgart, Germany (Scottish Masters, 2018). The competition is open to men and women over the age of 40 and the competition format follows a North American figuration which includes eight heavy athletic events and an overall standing. MWC competition takes place across different age groups and, for the men, weight categories are also used to provide more equitable competition for those athletes under 200lbs (90kg). The MWCs bring together people from a variety of countries, many of which are not associated with a Scottish diaspora. There are no criteria for participation other than age.

The experience of study participants varied, with the most experienced having competed for over a decade whilst the least experienced had only joined two years prior to interviewing. Many of the athletes had only been involved with the sport as Masters athletes. This is unique for Masters athletes, who tend to be what Dionigi (2015, p. 54) refers to as "continuers" – those who have played a sport continuously throughout their lives. The socio-economic status of participants was, in general, high. Most participants had college educations and skilled secure work. These participants had the financial capital to partake in transatlantic travel for themselves and often their families. There were a few notable exceptions, with one participant having her trip sponsored by various parties in her local community.

Not all members of the community claim Scottish identities. This chapter will therefore consider how solidarity as Masters athletes undermines a serious concern with legitimate claims to national identity and in many ways contests the notion of place when looking at events. Whilst many athletes do feel a strong attachment to place and nation, there was a strong rejection of an exclusionary nationalism that would outcast those with no Scottish heritage. Instead a national identity more associated with civic nationalism underpins a group solidarity often verbalized through the idea of a "brotherhood". This chapter will first describe the national identities of these Highland Gamers before detailing the importance of community and solidarity. Running throughout this chapter is an inherent link to space, place and events, for this transnational community exists in places of diasporic importance and in virtual space.

## Feelings of Scottishness

Despite no participants being born in Scotland, and only one participant residing in the nation, most identified themselves with Scotland. A range of associations existed, with some taking great pride in having some genetic link to Scotland and others giving it very little importance. To find out about their pasts, many had undertaken genealogical research to discover previous generations who had been a part of Scottish society before emigration. Basu (2007, p. 37) refers to this phenomenon as "heritage tourism", a process that has become more accessible with the expansion of the internet and the increased mobility associated with globalization generally (Blain, 2014). The age of many Masters athletes aligns with research that has examined the age groups most disposed to completing genealogical research (Basu, 2007). In the life histories of many participants it was clear that their genealogical research had either led them to the Games or at least changed the meaning of their participation:

> It's made it more fun because it's actually been able to. It's got me more interested in the genealogy cause when I first started throwing I wanted to make sure I would wear the proper tartan and represent the right clan so I started digging back with the help of my sister to see what we could find and that's it.
>
> (Hazel, 56, F)

> Honestly, I had never been "proud" of being Scottish until I got to researching behind the scenes knowledge of kilts and things. I became proud, almost like a rebel. I look the part, also. My dad even did DNA to determine if we were indeed MacGregors instead of MacFarlanes. Due to the family tree, it was thought that we were what's called "Hidden MacGregors". As it turns out, we are not. We are MacFarlanes (my maiden name is McFarland). I love history now and when I was younger I did not. Now, I care and want to pass that knowledge to my children.
>
> (Jane 45, F)

The discovery of "roots" was more than just new information. For some their validated Scottish identity lead to the occasional performance of "symbolic ethnicity" (Gans, 1979), an ethnicity that Leith and Sim (2016, p. 2654) define as "a nostalgic allegiance to an ancestral homeland". The results of genealogical research led to the increasing value of places in Scotland. This allegiance was often directed towards a nation that many athletes were visiting for the first time. The Highlands were sometimes framed as a lost homeland, a concept present amongst many diasporas (Anwar, 1979; Safran, 1991). Whilst these were individual ideas, their content refers to a collective group of people. Genealogical research is therefore more than an individual practice as it brings along a host of familial links and significant others that construct a more legitimate sense of self based around a variety of places. This "collective memory" draws upon "the aid of material traces, rites, texts and traditions left behind" (Halbwachs, 1992, p. 175). Using the emigration of previous generations, Scotland was understood to transcend simply existing in a space, instead taking the form of an emotion, a character or an idea. Two examples of the mythical reconstruction of Scotland, and being Scottish, are highlighted in the following quotes:

> Yes Yes. And like I say, I tell everybody err Scotland is not a place it's a feeling of the heart, you know you might be 5000 miles away from it but the feeling is still there, and like I say to people who wanted to come to Inverness to walk down the river Ness and you know hopefully see Nessy you know it's a dream they've had all their lives since they were little.
>
> (Edward, 75, M)

> Any time that my wife and I come back here, we goes places that I've never been before and I feel – it's that whole Deja-vu that you feel, you've been there before- just coming here where we were staying, I went down to help some people who were bogged down, and they ended up getting taken down by the tow truck- my phone died, I had no directions how to get there, just my internal senses said nope you're going the right way and ended up getting there just a short time after the people who had a map and knew how to get there. It's just one of those things, it's an innate sense to me.
>
> (Glen, 47, M)

Whilst both athletes were born and resided in the US, their Scottishness of was great importance to them. It was also interesting to note a stratification of places as more important in the re-imagining of Scotland. Most of the Scottish population lives in the central belt, consisting of the two major cities of Edinburgh and Glasgow. Yet these places were only referred to as airport destinations that were spaces passed through on route to the Highlands and islands. Scotland, in the consciousness of many, was imagined specifically as the Highlands. The romanticism of these areas has been covered elsewhere (see Basu, 2007; Gold & Gold, 1995; Hughes, 1992; MacDonald, 1998), but it is nevertheless interesting to note how certain locations were given heightened importance. Inverness, as the place in which the MWCs took place, was associated with a mythical past. The idea of this had been passed down generations within the diasporic community:

> We really care about Scottish culture and being removed from it. I guess when you are born and it's all around you and you tend to take it for granted, where we are over there like for all the people who come over except for a few of us, *Inverness was just a story book place they had read about and it was on the to do list, something we got go to some-day.* This event caused them to move it up to the front of the list, they started raising money to come and we got a bus load of them.
>
> (Edward, 75, M; emphasis added)

The ideas presented above are complemented by a specific tourist strategy aimed to exploit and reproduce meanings of Scottishness. The MWCs have been held in Inverness three times, with two occurring within a "homecoming" year. The year of "homecoming" is a Scottish government-backed tourist strategy that aims to entice members of the diasporic population back to their "homeland" (Leith & Sim, 2014). The Scottish government's (2010) *Disasporic Engagement Plan* details homecoming years as a celebration of Scotland's people, descendants and culture. The 2014 MWCs sat alongside the Ryder Cup and Commonwealth Games as sporting events incorporated into the homecoming strategy (Harris & Skillen, 2016). The tourist strategy that is used to encourage transnational tourism relies upon kitsch imagery of Scotland that highlights the invented traditions of the Highlands

(Trevor-Roper, 1983). The 2014 MWCs were themselves situated in a weekend of traditional celebrations based in and around Inverness. This included a "parade of the Clans", a shinty cup final and a Highland Clan exhibition. The MWCs therefore make up a wide range of activities that reproduce a particular notion of what Scotland and its culture is.

So far I have explored some of the examples of those Highland athletes who strongly identify as being Scottish via heritage. Yet many were aware of their lack of heritage. Within those who had no heritage claim to Scottishness, two relations to the Highlands and its culture existed. First there were individuals who had a strong cultural attachment to the nation and exhibited what Kiely et al. (2005) refer to as a claim to Scottishness based on "belonging". The second includes those individuals who do not claim any link to Scottishness and have subjective meanings about their participation that have no link to Scottish national identity. Being born outside of Scotland and having no familial link to the nation meant that claims to Scottishness were based on an individual's chosen attachment to a national culture and space. This sense of cultural attachment led Brad to move to Scotland to maintain the culture he had come to love:

> I was a master film technician for 18 years. Film industry dried up my partner said what do you want to be when you grow up. I said I want to do Highland Games full time. That's what I wanna do I want to run organise and get things moving forward for the Highland Games if it be it on a junior level an open level a Masters level I want to do every aspect of it because I think it's important to maintain this cultural icon which came from the Highlands of Scotland it's a very very small unique area in a small country on a big globe and why is it that all of a sudden we have this tiny little section of Scotland has become very popular worldwide literally worldwide has maintained this idea of tossing weights cabers hammers and things like that, so my theory was it feeds a niche there is a niche for everything, this was feeding the niche for people like myself that needed something.
>
> (Brad, 45, M)

Others also undermined the importance that blood claims to Scottishness had amongst the community. Some participants engaged in the sport as it provided competitive opportunities that Masters track and field was seen to be lacking. Others had transferred from other sports and had no heritage link. However, if desired, athletes could still engage in the Highland rituals. The inclusive nature of some clan societies was one way in which those without heritage could still perform Scottishness, as the following comments show:

> No, I don't think heritage is important in my life. Certainly, those of Celtic heritage take another level of pride when competing, especially if they wear their clan tartan. I was "adopted" by Clan Claus, and wear their badge on

my kilt. When competing in Canada, the issue of being a Canadian or American comes up frequently (jokingly) during Games. There was a large regional Games where the AD added a "clan" award to the athlete that most represented their clan. Athletes without a clan could ask a clan to "adopt" them, and then you would be that clan's champion. A female HG athlete and I approached the tent of Clan Claus, mostly because they seem super nice and everybody dresses like Santa and Mrs Claus. They jumped at the chance, and have invited us to their Burns Dinner, they ask about our competitions and they always cheer for us if they see us at a Games. They are very nice. It's a very sweet way to add another dimension on to the Games, and I wear my clan badge patch proudly on my kilt.

(Barry, 47, M)

As far as heritage goes, I've been asked that question several times by newspaper and television reporters. My answer to that question is always, "on game day, we are all Scottish no matter what your authentic background may be whether Irish, Scottish, Dutch, African American, etc., etc., etc."

(Jacob, M, 49)

Both accounts demonstrate that these individuals feel welcomed into their sporting community, relegating the need for claims to Scottishness. This community was therefore more inclusive than some of the Scottish cultural associations that Sullivan (2014) identified as historically being strict with regards to membership.

## The "brotherhood"

The Highland Games Masters community was always represented in a positive way. The amalgamation of athletes from across the world brought together people from 14 nations and four continents at the 2014 MWC's. Most athletes came from North America, but individuals also came from Australia and Japan. Many Highland athletes kept in contact via social media, but the MWC event was the only occasion when athletes from across North America and Europe could meet in person and compete alongside each other. The new and old friendships that had blossomed and developed within the Games community aided continued participation, especially for those who had accepted the realities of ageing and were less interested in the performance aspect of their sporting involvement. The community feel was important. This group solidarity was presented by participants as a "brotherhood", with one example coming from Sam:

Oh I mean I hope to still be doing it at 80 years old like some of these, you know those two guys who are throwing today, I really hope I'll still be able to do it and all that other stuff even if I don't throw I can see myself coming and hanging out, you know a lot of times it's not the competition you know with these other guys, we will come and hang out and it's like a brotherhood …

(Sam 40, M)

"Hanging out" often involved jokes and humor, which were a key component of the social experience of the Games. One term that was frequently used to describe this social pull of the Games was "comradery", a term used by many to emphasize the jovial relations between competitors. Attending the Games was as much about having fun socially as performing well physically. Athletes would often make jokes about their own injuries and the ongoing physical problems of others, but always within accepted parameters. Making fun of each other's ageing bodies was a way of being ironic in the face of stereotypes around ageing. This idea is best explained by the following participants:

As I previously stated, I started as a Master in the games. The running joke when we, masters, get together it is like, "what do you have going on?" Me: "I got a knee and wrist." The other guy: "I have an ankle and shoulder." Different guy: "Pinched nerve in my neck and turf toe." It doesn't always go like that, but we're pretty much hurting somewhere most of the time. Guys never have a problem telling you what hurts especially if they have a bad toss.

(Trevor, 49, M)

Just this past weekend, there were three of us sharing my tent for a little break from the sunshine and we referred to it as the wall for the supple hippos (kind of joke based off of the currently popular Supple Leopard mobility book). There are very few of us that could pose on a bodybuilding magazine and we all know it. So we poke fun at one another in jest and we laugh. Laughter is what keeps us going through the long day of throwing.

(Jacob, 49, M)

Whilst the use of humor was a tool to downplay the pain and injuries of Masters athletes, there was still a more serious side to the comradery of athletes. If athletes were seriously injured then it was suggested that everyone would chip in to help. During the 2014 MWCs an athlete was involved with a minor car crash on route to the competition. Fellow athletes drove out to the stranded athlete, returned her to the Games field and aided her in any way possible between attempts at the caber toss. Help came from fellow competitors who provided medication, strapping and a seat between attempts. This attitude of communal solidarity is exemplified by Glen, who describes how Masters athletes prioritise the wellbeing of competitors above the competition itself:

We have a thrower, he was inducted into the Hall of Fame last year, he has leukaemia most people with leukaemia kind of give up, he is still here competing and has actually gotten bigger and stronger and because that's our nature, we don't let, we power through injuries and every-thing and other things like that we tend to look at it like it's just another challenge, it's not an obstacle it's not a problem it's just another challenge that keeps us going mentally and physically and then because of *that comradery even if someone is even almost your nemesis of you competing at times, like I said you never want to win because of that so you're still there cheering for that person.*

(Glen, 47, M; emphasis added)

Another key aspect of the group's solidarity was the way in which children were incorporated into the space. The family-inclusive nature of the sport aided these Masters athletes in continuing (or starting) their sporting careers. Caring respon-sibilities were taken care of by other non-competing members of the community and the event was generally seen as family friendly. This removed a significant barrier for those athletes with young children. Jacob, a father of two, highlights the role of family inclusivity in his perception of the community:

Besides the competition with one another there is the personal comple-tion to constantly progress and get a new PR (personal record). *The comradery the competition, the joking and laughing coupled with being outdoors is in my opinion the perfect combination for a family-friendly weekend activity.* I have friends who bring their kids to play with other athletes' children and it's a great way for the kids to socialize and met other children from all over the world.

(Jacob, 49, M; emphasis added)

The Games playing field is therefore more than simply a competition space. It is an area for international social relations, comradery, family days out and a shared subjectivity of being a Masters athlete. This chapter has so far explored the varying attachments to a Scottish identity and the group solidarity displayed amongst the Games community. This final section will examine the ways in which different ethnicities and nationalities fit into the group and explore how the Highland Games of the 21st century is more inclusive than the Scottish dia-sporic events and associations of previous centuries (Sullivan, 2014).

## A civic nationalist community

The previous section has detailed some of the positive aspects of the Highland Games Masters community. The "brotherhood" and group solidarity in general was also inclusive of both women and ethnic minorities. This liberal approach to the participation of a Scottish tradition is something that Hazel remarks upon:

Oh, I think a lot of it is the, for me the comradery on the field. It's not a kind of a cut-throat type of competition everybody helps everybody get better and I think that draws quite a lot of athletes in regardless of the nationality or culture, they enjoy the actual sport of it.

(Hazel, 56, F)

For Hazel, the Games community was about group inclusivity and everyone helping each other regardless of national/cultural background. There is also the suggestion that Masters sport is less competitive and therefore more inclusive and attractive. Getting involved in the Games was therefore repositioned as having a separate logic than that of those wanting to use the Games as a performance of national identity (Edensor, 2002). Nevertheless, perceived differences of nationality were still present, and the groups comradery was necessary to overcome apparently obvious differences. National stereotypes (outside of Scotland's) were also used to find a shared interest that would cut across geographical boundaries. For example, Glen discusses how US and German competitors share specific personality traits:

It's that kind of thing, but the Americans a) the Americans and the Germans love competitions and even though we can be you know ultra-competitive at the end of the day I think a lot of them strive and really long for the comradery and this is one of the few sports like I said where you have that really intense competition yet just as strong comradery and it's one of those sports that you can get back, and because of that, so I think that's why you have such a strong US contingent.

(Glen, 47, M)

As with Hazel, Glen appears to identify essential differences based on nationality, whilst also suggesting that shared traits induce a sense of comradery that brings the group together. Aside from the belief in shared personality traits, the ways in which athletes present themselves also sideline ethnic or national differences. The verbalization of a "brotherhood" was therefore recast as a transnational community of people who shared interests and dispositions. The careful negotiation of accepting others, whilst acknowledging seemingly objective differences, is present in Patrick's conceptualization of the community:

this is our Celtic, *even if these people have no Celtic blood at all, like Kengo, he has no Celtic blood, he is Japanese, but he is part of our Highland athletic family,* and I will always respect him for that as a friend and as a competitor so if anything were to ever happen to him, and speak of the devil here goes, you know we always would remember the good times we've had with that person.

(Patrick, 46, M; emphasis added)

This somewhat contradictory process of both identifying difference and promoting inclusivity can be explained through the idea of nationalism being Janus-faced (Nairn, 1990, 1997). With regards to the modern formations of nationalism, the modern Janus represents the ways in which nationalistic thinking incorporates both a backward looking ethnic nationalism and a forward-orientated civic multiculturalism. The relegation of birth and blood ties to Scotland means that the Masters community instead rewards participation in a way that can be thought of as an act of belonging (Kiely et al., 2005). This can be understood through the term "civic nationalism". The Scottish national identity described in this chapter is shared amongst people who share a place (the Games field), rather than people who are from the same tribe or clan (McCrone, 2017). This constitutes what I see as a re-creation of the clan, a group of people brought together by a shared interest and a shared place.

## Conclusion

This chapter has explored the different attachments to Scottish identity and its relevance to the communities of people who take part in the MWC Games. Place and space has importance but in different ways. The Highlands of Scotland and Inverness have unique meanings for those who place great importance on Scottish identity. For others the event space itself is an area for an inclusive community that is verbalized through the concepts of comradery and brotherhood. Whilst this intersubjective experience of comradeship was positioned as unique to the Games, other research has also found such feelings within older players of basketball (McNelly, 2001). It could be assumed that this drive towards sociability over performance was a specific trait within Masters sport, yet the same process of shifting focus away from performance has also been found amongst elite athletes (Carless & Douglas, 2013). Nevertheless, this chapter has highlighted the vagaries of the Highland Games Masters community and its relation to place, space and national identities.

## References

Anwar, M. (1979). *The Myth of Return*. London: Heinemann.
Bairner, A. & Whigham, S. (2014). Sport and the Scottish diaspora. In Leith, M. & Sim, D. (eds.) *The Modern Scottish Diaspora: Contemporary Debates and Perspectives*. Edinburgh: Edinburgh University Press (206–221).
Basu, P. (2007). *Highland Homecomings: Genealogy and Heritage Tourism in the Scottish Diaspora*. London: Routledge.
Blain, J. (2014). Ancestral 'Scottishness' and heritage tourism. In Leith, M. & Sim, D. (eds.) *The Modern Scottish Diaspora: Contemporary Debates and Perspectives*. Edinburgh: Edinburgh University Press (153–170).
Brewster, M., Connell, J. & Page, S. J. (2009). The Scottish Highland Games: Evolution, development and role as a community event. *Current Issues in Tourism, 12(3)*, 271–293.

Carless, D. & Douglas, K. (2013). Living, resisting, and playing the part of athlete: Narrative tensions in elite sport. *Psychology of Sport and Exercise, 14(5)*, 701–708.

Devine, T. M. (2011). *To the Ends of the Earth: Scotland's Diaspora, 1750–2010.* London: Penguin.

Devine, T. M. (2012). *Scotland's Empire: The Origins of the Global Diaspora.* London: Penguin.

Dionigi, R. A. (2015). Pathways to masters sport: Sharing stories from sport 'Continuers','Rekindlers' and 'Late Bloomers'. In Pheonix, C. & Tulle, E. (eds.) *Physical Activity and Sport in Later Life.* Basingstoke: Palgrave Macmillan UK (54–68).

Edensor, T. (2002). *National Identity, Popular Culture and Everyday Life.* Oxford: Berg.

Fry, M. (2014). The Scottish diaspora and the empire. In Leith, M. & Sim, D. (eds.) *The Modern Scottish Diaspora: Contemporary Debates and Perspectives.* Edinburgh: Edinburgh University Press (32–46).

Gans, H. J. (1979). Symbolic ethnicity: The future of ethnic groups and cultures in America. *Ethnic and Racial Studies, 2(1)*, 1–20.

Gold, J. R. & Gold, M. M. (1995). *Imagining Scotland: Tradition, Representation and Promotion in Scottish Tourism since 1750.* Aldershot: Scholar Press.

Halbwachs, M. (1992). *On Collective Memory.* Chicago: University of Chicago Press.

Hammersley, M. (2006). Ethnography: Problems and prospects. *Ethnography and Education, 1(1)*, 3–14.

Harris, J. & Skillen, F. (2016). Sport, gender and national identities. In Blain, N., Hutchison, D. & Hassan, G. (eds.) *Scotland's Referendum and the Media: National and International Perspectives.* Edinburgh: Edinburgh University Press (83–96).

Hesse, D. (2014). *Warrior Dreams: Playing Scotsmen in Mainland Europe.* Oxford: Oxford University Press.

Hughes, G. (1992). Tourism and the geographical imagination. *Leisure Studies, 11(1)*, 31–42.

Jarvie, G. (1989). *Culture, Social Development, and the Scottish Highland Gatherings. The Making of Scotland: Nation, Culture, and Social Change.* Edinburgh: Edinburgh University Press.

Jarvie, G. (2005). The North American Émigré, Highland Games, and social capital in international communities. In Ray, C. (ed.) *Transatlantic Scots.* Tuscaloosa: University of Alabama Press (198–214).

Kiely, R., Bechhofer, F. & McCrone, D. (2005). Birth, blood and belonging: Identity claims in post-devolution Scotland. *The Sociological Review, 53(1)*, 150–171.

Leith, M. S. & Sim, D. (2014). *The Modern Scottish Diaspora: Contemporary Debates and Perspectives.* Edinburgh: Edinburgh University Press.

Leith, M. S. & Sim, D. (2016). Scotland's diaspora strategy: The view from the current American diaspora. *Scottish Affairs, 25(2)*, 186–208.

MacDonald, F. (1998). Viewing Highland Scotland: Ideology, representation and the 'natural heritage'. *Area, 30(3)*, 237–244.

McCrone, D. (2017). *The New Sociology of Scotland.* London: Sage.

McNelly, D. (2001). How the road to fitness led me to a "fountain of youth". *Journal of Gerontological Nursing, 27(5)*, 50–52.

Nairn, T. (1990). *The Modern Janus: Nationalism in the Modern World.* London: Hutchinson Radius.

Nairn, T. (1997). *Faces of Nationalism: Janus Revisited.* London: Verso.

Safran, W. (1991). Diasporas in modern societies: Myths of homeland and return. *Diaspora: A Journal of Transnational Studies, 1(1)*, 83–99.

Scottish Highland Games Association. (2018, May 2). Events. Retrieved from www. shga.co.uk/events.php.

Scottish Masters. (2018, May 2). Results. Retrieved from www.scottishmasters.org/Results Main.html.

Sullivan, K. (2014). Scots by association: Clubs and societies in the Scottish diaspora. In Leith, M. & Sim, D. (eds.) *The Modern Scottish Diaspora: Contemporary Debates and Perspectives*. Edinburgh: Edinburgh University Press (47–63).

Trevor-Roper, H. (1983). The invention of tradition: The highland tradition of Scotland. In Hobsbawm, E. & Ranger, T. (eds.) *The Invention of Tradition*. Cambridge: Cambridge University Press (15–41) (Original work published 2013).

Webster, D. P. (2011). *The World History of Highland Games*. Edinburgh: Luath Press.

# 13 La Monoestrellada and the display of identity politics in Puerto Rico

## Cultural activism and placemaking in *78 pueblos y 1 bandera*

*Brenda L. Ortiz-Loyola & José R. Díaz-Garayúa*

### Introduction

Art is a powerful form of communication. Public art can be used as means of motivating social and political change through the encouragement of shared notions of identity (Buser et al., 2013, p. 606). It also can foster resistance, providing spaces for the (re)definition of social, economic, and political relations. Public art and other forms of creative practices have become increasingly pertinent to the field of geography because they have the potential of contributing to placemaking. If, as Cresswell (2004) notes, a place develops when humans invest meaning in it, events that rely on cultural activism can forge alternative imaginaries. This chapter focuses on the relationship between events, cultural activism, identity politics, and the process of placemaking in Puerto Rico by assessing the movement *78 pueblos y 1 bandera*. Here, the word "movement" is used to describe a series of events organized by the artist Héctor Collazo Hernández, who signs his art as Héctor PR. The goal is painting a mural of the Puerto Rican flag in each of Puerto Rico's 78 towns. Initially conceived as a one-time event, the activity has developed into national event gatherings attracting people from all over the island as well as tourists.

Puerto Rico is still relevant for the study of identity politics due to its relationship with the United States (hereafter U.S.). Puerto Rico, a former Spanish colony, was ceded to the U.S. after the end of the Cuban-Spanish-American War in 1898. Since then, this Caribbean island has been an unincorporated territory of the U.S. In other words, Puerto Rico is neither a state of the United States of America nor an independent country. Scholars define Puerto Rico's current political situation as a modern colony or a postcolonial colony (see Duany, 2002; Grosfoguel, 2009). This means that the island lacks political sovereignty, but Puerto Ricans enjoy U.S. citizenship as well as metropolitan democratic and civil rights (Grosfoguel, 2009). They also share the responsibilities that come with the citizenship, such as serving in the armed forces and paying a series of federal taxes (with exemption from federal income tax for those not working for the federal government), despite the fact that they have no representation in the U.S. Congress.

Despite the absence of a nation-state, Puerto Ricans have developed a strong and distinctive national identity. This particular form of identity-building process, known as cultural nationalism, recognizes that Puerto Ricans constitute a community with a shared history, language, and culture. In other words, Puerto Ricans are a national group without a state (see Duany, 2002). Consequently, the Puerto Rican flag has been a contested symbol in the battle for constructing and consolidating a national identity. Originally designed in the nineteenth century as the flag of the future republic, the banner was declared illegal in the 1940s for its association with the independence movement, and was later adopted as the official flag of the Commonwealth of Puerto Rico. Nevertheless, the dispute over the Puerto Rican flag is far from over. In times of political and economic crisis, the "monoestrellada" emerges as symbol of non-conformity. Currently, Puerto Rico is experiencing one of these moments. The local government has admitted its inability to pay the country's debt and the U.S. Congress has responded by imposing a non-elected Financial Oversight and Management Board to precede the island's government. The decision has faced opposition from those who see the imposition of the board as evidence of Puerto Rico's unequal relationship with the U.S.

The popularity of the movement *78 pueblos y 1 bandera* coincided with Puerto Rico's economic crisis. The current political and economic climate should be considered when analyzing the reasons for the overwhelming support of the event. Our aim is to explain how painting murals of the Puerto Rican flag has helped promote a sense of place while creating a discourse of hope and national pride amid the economic crisis of the island. The notions of sense of place and placemaking are explored in this chapter. Sense of place refers to the meanings people give to a particular space, site, or location (see Wise, 2015) while placemaking is when people get together to (re)think/(re)create/(re)work a particular space, site, or location (see de Brito & Richards, 2017). Both conceptual notions are used in this chapter. We also explore how this optimism has been channelled through the promotion of tourism. In order to do so, we first explore the ways in which events use and depend on cultural activism to help develop a sense of place and reinforce placemaking. Because *78 pueblos y 1 bandera* privileges the Puerto Rican flag as an artistic expression with political undertones, we then explain the meanings ascribed to the flag and the origins of the economic crisis in which the event developed. In the last section we present an analysis of the movement and its impact on the local community.

## Events, cultural activism, and placemaking

Events are multifaceted; on the one hand, they are the result of a desire to create and promote shared understandings and identities (Feighery, 2016), whereas on the other hand, events have an effect on the places where they are organized, performed, and consumed. But events can also be significant in the way they challenge the present order. The study of events requires an examination of the plural nature of their causes as well as the connections, forces, and strategies at play (see MacKenzie & Porter, 2016).

Political events are probably the best example of events that challenge the established order, as they provide a space for the disruption of official discourses of power and have the potential to empower communities (see Shobe, 2008). As this chapter will show, cultural events can also become political through cultural activism. Buser et al. (2013) define cultural activism as that which calls upon art to disrupt commonly held assumptions and expectations, often by forging alternative spatial meanings. For them, the political nature of art resides in its transforming capacity. It allows dissidents or marginalized groups to create spaces through which they can represent themselves (McCann, 1999, p. 168). Public art displays, thus, turn spaces into a contested terrain.

Regardless of the intention of planners and government officers, public spaces are always in a process of being shaped, reshaped, and challenged by spatial practices (McCann, 1999). The possibility of making and remaking a space through everyday practices or lived experiences suggest that events can provide physical spaces with new meanings. Meaning and experience are key aspects of the transformation of a space into a place. As Cresswell (2004, p. 12) explains, "place is how we make the world meaningful and the way we experience the world". At the same time, he adds, "place is the raw material for the creative production of identity" (Cresswell, 2004, p. 39). Art as a creative tool and the creative use of art are essential to cultural activism. Art projects developed by cultural activists can, therefore, help further a sense of place through the reconnection of a community with its surroundings.

The relationship between identity and cultural activism as event is manifest in the way certain places become referent for collective visions. In the case of *78 pueblos y 1 bandera*, as we will show, the appropriation and resignification of national imagery has been instrumental in fostering identity and collective action. Not only have a wide range of spaces been transformed but community involvement has resulted in new relations. Crucial to understanding the transformation is considering the reasons for its organization and the ways in which it has been perceived. In the next two sections we provide the information needed to contextualize the movement, the significance of the symbol chosen, and the economic situation that heightens its political undertones.

## Identity politics and La Monoestrellada

Flags are a pillar of nationhood (Eriksen, 2007), seen as vessels through which identities can be forged or contested, and their usage is susceptible to political or economic changes. In the case of Puerto Rico, the intensity in flag use has varied with the degree to which the identity represented through it has been threatened by the U.S. Examples of the interrelationship between identity politics and national symbols date back to the beginning of the twentieth century, when the U.S. undertook a sustained and pervasive Americanization campaign designed to assimilate Puerto Ricans (Morris, 1995). The goal of the campaign was bringing the island up to U.S. standards by rearranging the legal and educational system and replacing Spanish institutions (Morris, 1995). Spanish language and other emblems of Puerto Rico's Hispanic heritage were targeted. While teaching the Spanish language was relegated to a special subject and the display of the flag was deemed unacceptable, saluting the U.S. flag and teaching English language and U.S. history became the norm.

Independence supporters reacted to the aforementioned impositions by adopting the flag designed in 1895 as symbol of their opposition to U.S. rule and by the 1920s the controversy over the Puerto Rican flag was well established. In 1922, for instance, Governor Emmet Montgomery Reily made "public reference to the single-star Puerto Rican flag as a 'dirty rag'" (Morris, 1995, p. 34). His comments generated a complaint from the Puerto Rican Senate. Asking the U.S. president to remove Reily from office, the Senate authored a resolution recognizing the Puerto Rican flag as "a symbol of local sentiment," and asserting that as such it "is consecrated and respected by the entire Puerto Rican community" (Morris, 1995, p. 35). Confrontations over the flag escalated when police intervention was required in order to enforce an order of the Department of Education barring students from hanging the flag during commencements (Morris, 1995). That same year, 1922, the pro-independence Nationalist Party adopted the single-star flag as its emblem.

The increasing correlation between flag display and political opposition during the 1930s and 1940s culminated in the passing of the Gag Law in 1948. The law made it illegal to own or display Puerto Rico's flag, and to fight for the independence. It was not until 1952 that the single-star banner was legalized and adopted as the official Puerto Rican flag. The change was possible due to Puerto Rico's new political status. In 1947, the U.S. granted Puerto Ricans the right to democratically elect their own governor and in 1951 Puerto Ricans voted in a referendum supporting the establishment of a commonwealth. Under the commonwealth, Puerto Ricans were allowed to draft their first constitution. The 1952 constitution provided a degree of internal autonomy as well as the possibility of adopting national symbols without challenging the U.S. control over Puerto Rico.

Despite its officialization, the association between flag and resistance has not disappeared completely. On the one hand, Puerto Ricans consider the flag a unifying national symbol. At this emotional level the flag represents all Puerto Ricans. On the other hand, there have been instances in which flying the single-star flag alone has exposed the uneasy relationship between Puerto Rico and the U.S. Two cases reveal the continual tension: the battle over the flags led by Carlos Pesquera, and Alberto de Jesús's (also known as Tito Kayak) occupation of the Statue of Liberty. In 2002 Carlos Pesquera, president of the New Progressive Party (pro-statehood party), burst into the Women's

Advocate Office to place the U.S. flag alongside the Puerto Rican flag. The incident unfolded after María Dolores Fernós, head of the Woman's Advocate Office, neglected to put both flags inside the building's lobby (Puerto Rico Herald, 2002, online). Because governmental regulations stipulate the displaying of both flags, pro-statehood politicians saw Fernós's actions as a challenge to the ties between Puerto Rico and the U.S. In a more defiant fashion, Puerto Rican environmental activist Alberto de Jesús hung a Puerto Rican flag and the Vieques flag from the crown of the Statue of Liberty in 2000 (Noticel, 2017). With his action, De Jesús wanted to call attention to Puerto Rico's colonial situation and the fight against the U.S. Navy. Two years before, a security guard named David Sanes Rodríguez was killed by a bomb fired during training exercises. His death sparked massive mobilizations demanding the U.S. Navy to withdraw from Vieques. De Jesus's action was, thus, surrounded by political controversy. It must be noted that in 1977, thirty Puerto Rican nationalists occupied the Statue of Liberty demanding freedom for four Puerto Rican political prisoners (Breasted, 1977).

The different feelings Puerto Ricans exhibit toward the single-star banner mirror Thomas Eriksen conclusions surrounding the role of national flags in modern states. According to Eriksen,

> flags representing modern nation-states have an emotional and an instrumental pole in their range of signification. The emotional pole attaches the individual to an abstract collective entity, a metaphoric kin group. The instrumental pole may be political or commercial, intended to mobilise for conflict or to integrate peacefully.
>
> (Eriksen, 2007, p. 10)

The movement and associated events aligned with *78 pueblos y 1 bandera* also fit Eriksen's description. As we will show, the murals have multiple meanings for Puerto Ricans. They are at the same time a vehicle to instil national pride, a tourist destination, a place of enjoyment, and an instrument of mobilization. The last aspect is inextricably related to the economic crisis Puerto Rico is currently facing. The points of interpretation outlined here have been observed in related event studies research (e.g. George, 2015; Hannam et al., 2016; Richards et al., 2013; Shobe, 2008; Smith, 2012; Wise & Harris, 2016).

## Chronicles of an economic crisis foretold

On June 2015 the governor of Puerto Rico announced that the island's debt was unpayable. His announcement was the foreseeable outcome of an economic recession that began in 2006. The origin of the crisis is, however, complex as it is partly rooted in the country's lack of sovereignty and partly in the inefficiency of the local government. From the beginning of the twentieth century the U.S. Congress developed an economic plan based on federal corporate tax exemptions: "no export duties shall be levied or collected on exports from Porto Rico [sic]" (*Jones Act* § 3; 1917). The strategy was adopted by the government of Puerto Rico in 1947 through legislation that granted U.S. industries zero taxes on income and property. The program, known as Operation Bootstrap, aimed to attract U.S. industries. However, by the end of the 1970s it was clear that the model of development created under Operation Bootstrap had been exhausted. Instead of helping to diversify Puerto Rico's economy, Operation Bootstrap made the country more dependent on U.S. investment. Operation Bootstrap had formulated no strategy to incentivize the local industry. In turn, U.S. corporations chose to operate in Puerto Rico to take advantage of "the exceptional profit-enhancing opportunities offered by a potentially zero-tax milieu" (Dietz, 2003, p. 15), but contributed little to island's economy. Consequently, in 1978, the Operation Bootstrap regime of full local tax exemption came to an end (Dietz, 2003). Despite the changes, tax exemptions continued under the U.S. Internal Revenue Code. In 1976, the U.S. Congress approved Section 936 of the Internal Revenue Code, which converted federal tax exemptions in Puerto Rico to a foreign tax credit.

By the 1990s, there was again a general concern that the supposed benefits of the tax exemptions, namely more jobs and better income, could no longer be justified (Dietz, 2003). The belief resulted in the discontinuation of Section 936 in 1996. The legislation that abrogated section 936 established a ten-year transition period for companies operating under this section of the tax code. The period expired in 2006, coinciding with the beginning of the economic crisis. Ever since 2006, unemployment and poverty levels have increased. Emigration has also been constant. It is estimated that 300,000 Puerto Ricans left the island over the past decade, shrinking the government's tax base (González, 2017a; Morales, 2015). In order to face the decline in revenues the local government relied on policies that accelerated borrowing for public works and health care, a practice that started after the failure of Operation Bootstrap but escalated in 1990s (García Colón & Franqui-Rivera, 2015; Morales, 2015). The consequence was a staggering debt of $72 billion.

Addressing the debt has proven difficult under Puerto Rico's political status. As a commonwealth, Puerto Rico does not have the option of bankruptcy. Originally Puerto Rico was included under Chapter 9 of the U.S. Bankruptcy Code, which provides for the adjustment of debts of a municipality. However, an amendment passed on 1984 left the island without protection (González, 2017b). U.S. Congress responded to the absence of a procedure for sorting out Puerto Rico's debt by enacting the Puerto Rico Oversight Management, and Economic Stability Act (PROMESA) in 2016. PROMESA creates a Financial Oversight and Management Board to restructure the debt and oversee the development of fiscal plans for Puerto Rico. The board consists of seven members appointed by the government of the U.S. and one ex-officio member designated by the governor of Puerto Rico. The establishment of a federal financial board has political and economic implications for the island. Politically, as Alyosha Goldstein affirms, the imposition "unequivocally confirms the colonial subordination" of Puerto Rico (2016, p. 9). Financially, the solutions proposed by the board are based on an austerity plan that could further depress Puerto Rico's economy. The suggestions include tax increases, reducing the size of the government, cuts to public services, the closing of public schools, lowering the minimum wage and retirement pensions, and privatization of public corporations. In offering such measures the board ignores the fact that similar policies have been implemented since Governor Luis Fortuño's administration without tangible results. In 2009 Puerto Rico's government passed Law 7, a legislation declaring a fiscal emergency that provided a plan for stabilizing Puerto Rico's economy. The law stipulated reductions in the government's budget, the suspension of increases in salary, and massive layoffs as a way to reduce the size of the government.

Puerto Rico's uncertain future has caused both concern and resistance. According to an article published in the newspaper *Diálogo* most of the economists in Puerto Rico have rejected the idea of the federal fiscal board (Caraballo, 2016). Similarly, various civil groups have organized to oppose the board as well as to educate about the consequences of its decisions. Among the groups are *Campamento Contra La Junta, Unidos Contra La Junta, Coalición Ciudadana Contra La Junta De Control Fiscal*, and *Se Nos Va La Vida*. Similarly, on May 1, 2016, 2017, and 2018, thousands of Puerto Ricans marched against the imposition of a federal fiscal board. Puerto Rico's economic situation must be considered when analyzing the development of *78 Pueblos y 1 Bandera*. Although not directly opposing the board, *78 pueblos y 1 bandera* has effectively managed a politically charged discourse. It has been able to mobilize Puerto Ricans around a symbol that reaffirms their cultural identity and their strength as a nation. Moreover, communities that are trying to revitalize their surroundings have welcomed and supported the event. As a result, new relations between people and space have developed.

## The movement

On 2016, Héctor Collazo Hernández painted the Puerto Rican flag close to his house in the town of Villalba. The mural was the culmination of a healing process that had its origin in the death of Collazo's brother (Santiago Túa, 2017). However, after a while Collazo noticed that people were taking pictures of the mural he painted. He interpreted the reaction as evidence of the positive effect that the flag as symbol has on Puerto Ricans (Santiago Túa, 2017). The favorable reception of his art encouraged him to paint a Puerto Rican flag on each of the 78 towns into which Puerto Rico is divided. The idea gave birth to the movement known as *78 pueblos y 1 bandera*.

Puerto Rico's economic and political crisis provided a fertile ground for Héctor's project. As mentioned in the previous section, in 2016 a board assumed the management of Puerto Rico's finances, stripping the local government of the autonomy it had. Puerto Ricans reacted to the imposition in different ways. While some people felt frustrated or betrayed, others perceived the board as the best solution. Yet, heated discussions and concerning calls for unity in action emerged constantly. The attractiveness of *78 pueblos y 1 bandera* resides precisely in its attempt to foster a sense of national unity and belonging. According to Héctor, his goal is to unite Puerto Ricans and to show that Puerto Ricans can move forward despite all adversities (note, unless otherwise indicated, the comments included in this section have been taken from social media outlets. All translations are those of the chapter authors). Nevertheless, the discourse of solidarity has not been free of controversy. Debates over the colors of the flags have revealed the political undertones of the movement as well as the battle over the use of public spaces.

In July 2016 the colors of an iconic painting of the Puerto Rican flag located in Old San Juan were changed to black and white (Figure 13.1). The alteration was the reaction of a local group of artists known as "Colectivo La Puerta" to the enactment of PROMESA. It was evidence of their discontent. Besides the door where the painting was located, the group posted an open letter "calling for solidarity against the 'Junta' represented by PROMEZA's Fiscal Control Board [...] calling attention to its authoritarian dimensions and the sacrifice of democracy on the altar of colonial capitalist accumulation" (Haiven, 2016, online). Shortly after, similar flags started to appear across the island and, eventually, Héctor included the alternative design on his murals. He later clarified on a Facebook post that he agrees with the message represented by the black flag. On the post, Héctor explained that the black flag means that "Puerto Ricans are standing up to fight ["en pie de lucha"] [...] despite the wrongful administration of public funds" (August 9, 2017). Héctor's comment reinforces the traditional association between flag and resistance. It shows that cultural activism matters in a country where it was forbidden to own or display a Puerto Rican flag (Haiven, 2016). The display of the black flag generated, however, a mixed reaction. For some of Héctor's followers, the adoption of the black design was a contradiction: "My friend, if you say 78 towns and 1 flag, why don't you paint all the flags the same color [...] our flag is not black or gold [...] [with this action] you are not conveying the [unity] message" (January 29, 2018). For others, it was an accurate representation of public sentiment.

In a conciliatory effort, Héctor included a golden version of the single-star banner as another alternative design for his murals across the island (Figure 13.2). He defines the meaning of the golden version as "victory." Héctor has asserted on social media that the golden flag: "represents our victories inside and outside of the country. For us, it is a victory when you wake up every day at 6:00 AM to begin your working day" (January 29, 2017). His comments emphasize the pride Puerto Ricans take in the contributions they make to the country. He is, in a sense, encouraging people to work every day to overcome the crisis. The golden flag has helped in

*Figure 13.1* An iconic painting of the Puerto Rican flag in black and white in Old San Juan.

*Figure 13.2* A golden version of the single-star banner, an alternative mural design in Puerto Rico.

transmitting a message of national pride and hope among Puerto Ricans living on the island and abroad. Puerto Ricans in Buffalo, for example, have shown their support by reproducing the golden flag in a local cultural centre: "You have been an inspiration! Greetings from Buffalo! This is my center of *Bomba* and *Plena*, in honor of my island!" (August 9, 2017).

Nevertheless, Héctor's murals have brought back to the fore other issues about the colors of the national flag. In Puerto Rico, the hue of the blue portion of the banner has political nuances. In an ideologically divided country, light or sky blue has been associated with pro-independence movements.

Conversely, royal blue has been linked to supporters of the *status quo* and navy blue (similar to the U.S. flag) to pro-statehood advocates. When Héctor announced his plans for a mural in the town of Moca, the mayor publicly rejected the project. The mayor denied the permission requested because he disagreed with the type of blue Héctor uses to paint. In an interview with the newspaper *El Nuevo Día*, Moca's mayor José Avilés declared that the flag must have "the official colors." It must be painted with the hue of blue that "Luis Muñoz Marín hoisted on the 25th of July, 1952" under the creation of the commonwealth (Delgado Rivera, 2018, online). The mayor's reaction revived old ideological disputes over the use of the Puerto Rican flag and its political meaning. From his perspective, Héctor's murals were promoting a nationalism that verged on an independence sentiment. Although Héctor acknowledged a desire to stimulate national pride, he discarded the mayor's claims arguing that "the Puerto Rican flag is the Puerto Rican flag regardless of the hue of blue" (Delgado Rivera, 2018, online). For Héctor, "it is unfortunate that a simple color has so much power to divide the people" (Delgado Rivera, 2018, online). The issue about the colors exposed the contradictory nature of national symbols. As we mentioned before, the meaning of symbols is susceptible to politic and economic changes. They can be used to nourish solidary feelings or to create division. In order to avoid further polarization and to prove the absence of a specific political stance he eventually painted the mural with all three shades of blue (Figure 13.3). Yet, it is important to note that Héctor's decision was restricted to the town of Moca. Later murals have incorporated the light blue flag and the black flag maintaining, to some extent, a politically charged discourse.

The attitude of Moca's mayor also underscores the importance of spatial practices in the resignification of public spaces. Murals and graffiti are usually linked to marginal practices. They are a way of usurping and redefining a space and its inhabitants. This appropriation, however, is considered an unlawful act. Héctor, in fact, was detained and fined for painting the flag in an area near the lighthouse in the town of Guánica. At that time, he thought about ending the project but the support he received from the people was overwhelming (Jiménez, 2017). Interestingly, the incident changed the way every event is organized. Originally, Héctor chose the locations without seeking governmental authorization. His intention was to revitalize or beautify urban voids, leftovers, and abandoned places (Jiménez, 2017). But the incident in Guánica forced him to rethink the organizational process and start requesting permission and to seek for people's suggestions. With the participation of Puerto Ricans in the planning process, the event began to resemble what Ings (2016) describes as rhizomatic growth. People not only recommend locations but also cooperate in disseminating the event, supplying materials or food for the participants, and providing entertainment. Now, even the murals are part of a collective effort, as Héctor invites everyone to paint with him: "the lines are perfect because [they] are painted in team, encouraging people's unity" (Santiago Túa, 2017, online).

*Figure 13.3* A mural of the Puerto Rican flag painted with three shades of blue.

The movement's organizational structure helps overcome political divisions in favor of a message of unity. Furthermore, it has had a significant impact on local communities. As a collaborative effort, each event facilitates reconceiving the space through the empowerment of the community and the establishment of new relations. New relations are both personal and spatial. At a personal level, people attending the event have described it as an opportunity to expand their social network or a way to make new friends. In some instances, the same group of people have met by chance at every event: "Although hard to believe, you will meet new people and you will form friendship bonds" (May 6, 2018). In terms of spatial relations, it is common among the movement's followers to express through social media how proud they are of being from a town where the flag has been painted. If by sense of place we mean the "subjective and emotional attachment people have to a place" (Cresswell, 2004, p. 7), the comments suggest that the murals have strengthened the sense of belonging that characterizes the placemaking process. Here, in this chapter, the notion of placemaking looks at how people are united based on a shared identity. The concept of placemaking is engaged with differently in several chapters—showing how we use and interpret conceptual notions and practical understandings differently. For instance, Chapter 5, by Nicholas Wise, Jelena Đurkin, and Mark Perić, assesses how planners and destinations managers are trying to achieve placemaking as the city of Rijeka plans to host the 2020 European Capital of Culture—in Puerto Rico we see how placemaking has evolved through a collective movement of people as opposed to seeking ways to plan it.

Emotional attachment is not the only reason for the increasing popularity of *78 pueblos y 1 bandera*. Communities around the island have welcomed the event for the economic benefits it brings. The incident in Moca is again an example of the transformative potential locals ascribe to the event. When Moca's mayor stopped the event, Héctor asked for recommendations on his Facebook page. In a short time, he received a message from a resident of Moca offering a location as well as financial support (January 26, 2018). The location was close to a promenade with small businesses known as *Paseo Artesanal*. Entrepreneurs saw the event as an opportunity to promote the local economy and increase tourism: "We wish to develop tourism in our beloved town and we think this [event] will help us, even without the mayor's support" (January 26, 2018). An apparent increase in internal tourism has arguably been a positive result of *78 pueblos y 1 bandera*. Traveling the flags' route (*ruta de las banderas*) is now one of the most popular road trips in Puerto Rico. Travelers visit one location at a time or multiple sites in one day. In any case, the trip usually involves spending, with gatherings resulting in spontaneous "informal" events that help connect people at each site—which emphasizes a sense of identity and placemaking.

Contributing to the economy has been part of the movement's rationale from the very beginning. Héctor has consistently declared that he wishes "to directly support the economy through the promotion of internal tourism" (January 9, 2018). It is important to remember that Puerto Rico's economy relies heavily on foreign investment, and the neoliberal policies proposed by the financial board's call for austerity measures could further affect the economy. Within this context, supporting local commerce has been presented as a necessity. It is not surprising that many murals are near restaurants, commercial districts, and tourist destinations. Puerto Ricans, in fact, are dedicating blogs and web pages to the flags' route and providing pictures, addresses, and remarks about the experience. In some instances, the comments work as reviews, encouraging people to visit the places. For instance, a traveller rating a restaurant located near the flag painted in the town of Orocovis mentioned that: "everything was delicious! A family environment and a beautiful view! Highly recommended!" (January 16, 2018). The growing interest in the flags' route has also extended to the Puerto Rican diaspora. Héctor's Facebook page shows that Puerto Ricans living abroad are visiting the places where the murals are located whenever they are on the island: "From Dallas, Texas, to Puerto Rico. We visited Maunabo, Humacao, Patillas, and La Perla. All were beautiful and we plan visiting more" (January 24, 2018). But tourism and spending do not only happen after the event. Because *78 pueblos y 1 bandera* is a collective enterprise, the event itself generates business transactions. Although distances in Puerto Rico are fairly short, some of Héctor's followers have transformed the event into a weekend vacation: "I made a reservation in a hotel from Saturday to Monday" (January 26, 2018). For Puerto Ricans living on the island and abroad, the revitalization of spaces as tourist places has been a way to compensate for the country's current economic situation, a proof that Puerto Ricans can and will contribute to reducing the negative impact of the crisis.

## Concluding remarks

The exponential development of *78 pueblos y 1 bandera* suggests that "the process of eventification is not necessarily driven and effected by the individual creator [...] alone, but it is also significantly stimulated, enhanced and supported by the nature of the event itself and by its socio-cultural context" (Hauptfleisch, 2016, p. 2). In Héctor's case, what started as a personal form of expression became a collective event; a site where many people gather to participate in an experience believed to contribute to moving Puerto Rico forward. Little did Héctor know that in a period of economic crisis his art was going to instil hope and reshape the public space. This is important because "events that rely on cultural activism can forge alternative imaginaries" (Cresswell, 2004, p. 10). Héctor's artistic choices and the Puerto Rican flag, which arguably may be credited for his success, have given space to all Puerto Ricans to produce an alternative political-economic imaginary. The Puerto Rican flag, as a national symbol, has a unifying potential capable of producing "political mobilization around cultural identity" (Castree et al., 2013). Simultaneously, murals, as well as the processes corresponding to the making of murals, help communities to reclaim and redefine their relationship with surrounding spaces, endowing them with new meanings (Ings, 2016). They also serve to articulate shared understanding, struggles, and to spread the message of a community's most pressing needs.

The *78 pueblos y 1 bandera* movement has positively impacted some abandoned areas across Puerto Rico. Recovered spaces, in turn, provide a platform for short- and long-term community projects. Admittedly, because *78 pueblos y 1 bandera* is an ongoing project it is difficult to assess its long-term effect. So far, 50 murals (by June 2018) have been completed. Yet, the overwhelming support from companies, to clubs, to individuals that Héctor has received, and the apparent increase in internal tourism suggests a positive impact. Despite the political or ideological conflicts that have emerged, *78 pueblos y 1 bandera* has been able to unify Puerto Ricans, underscoring their willingness to work toward the recovery of the local economy.

## References

Breasted, M. (1977). 30 in Puerto Rican Group Held in Liberty I. Protest. *The New York Times*, October 26, 30.

Buser, M., Bonura, C., Fannin, M., & Boyer, K. (2013). Cultural Activism and the Politics of Place-Making. *City* 17(5), 606–627.

Caraballo, J. (2016). ¿Por qué no gusta la PROMESA del Congreso? *Diálogo*. May 28. http://dialogoupr.com/por-que-no-gusta-la-promesa-del-congreso/.

Castree, N., Kitchin, R., & Rogers, A. (Eds.) (2013). *A Dictionary of Human Geography*. Oxford: Oxford University Press.

Cresswell, T. (2004). *Place: A Short Introduction*. Malden, MA: Blackwell Publishing.

de Brito, M.P. & Richards, G. (2017). Guest Editorial: Events and Placemaking. *International Journal of Event and Festival Management* 8(1), 2–7.

Delgado Rivera, J. (2018) Héctor PR asegura que 'la bandera se va a hacer sí o sí' en Moca. *El Nuevo Día*, January 10. www.elnuevodia.com/noticias/locales/nota/hec torprdicequelabanderasevaahacersiosienmoca-2389068/.

Dietz, J. (2003). *Puerto Rico: Negotiating Development and Change*. Boulder, CO: Lynne Rienner Publishers.

Duany, J. (2002). *Puerto Rican Nation on the Move. Identities on the Island and in the United States*. Chapel Hill, NC: University of North Carolina Press.

Eriksen, T. (2007). Some Questions about Flags. In T. Eriksen & R. Jenkins (Eds.). *Flag, Nation, and Symbolism in Europe and America*. London: Routledge (1–13).

Feighery, W. (2016). Critical Discourse Analysis: Towards Critiquing the Language of Events. In T. Pernecky (Ed.). *Approaches and Methods in Event Studies*. London: Routledge (81–95).

García Colón, I. & Franqui-Rivera, H. (2015) Puerto Rico is Not Greece: Notes on the Role of Debt in U.S. Colonialism. *Focaal: Journal of Global and Historical Anthropology*. August 26. www.focaalblog.com/2015/08/26/puerto-rico-is-not-greece-the-role-of-debt-in-us-colonialism/#sthash.wYMjICBv.dpuf.

George, J. (2015). Examining the Cultural Value of Festivals: Considerations of Creative Destruction and Creative Enhancement within the Rural Environment. *International Journal of Event and Festival Management* 6(2), 122–134.

Goldstein, A. (2016). Promises Are Over: Puerto Rico and the Ends of Decolonization. *Theory & Event* 19(4), 1–14.

González, J. (2017a) Puerto Rico's $123 Billion Bankruptcy is the Cost of U.S. Colonialism. *The Intercept*. May 9. https://theintercept.com/2017/05/09/puerto-ricos-123-billion-bankruptcy-is-the-cost-of-u-s-colonialism/?comments=1#comments.

González, J. (2017b). The Crisis of Puerto Rico explained in 5 Graphs. *Global Politics and Law*. April 22. www.globalpoliticsandlaw.com/2017/04/22/crisis-puerto-rico-explained-5-graphs/.

Grosfoguel, R. (2009). The Divorce of Nationalist Discourses from the Puerto Rican People. In F. Vázquez (Ed.). *Latino/a Thought: Culture, Politics, and Society.* Lanham, MD: Rowman & Littlefield (417–437).

Haiven, M. (2016). Black Flags and Debt Resistance in America's Oldest Colony. *Roar.* https://roarmag.org/essays/black-flags-debt-resistance-americas-oldest-colony/.

Hannam, K., Mostafanezhad, M., & Rickly, J. (Eds.) (2016). *Event Mobilities: Politics, Place and Performance.* London: Routledge.

Hauptfleisch, T. (2016). Eventification: Framing the Ordinary as the Extraordinary. In T. Pernecky (Ed.). *Approaches and Methods in Event Studies.* London: Routledge (36–52).

Ings, W. (2016). The Creative Guerilla: Makers, Organisation, and Belonging. In T. Pernecky (Ed.). *Approaches and Methods in Event Studies.* London: Routledge (53–66).

Jiménez, L. (2017). ¡Sigue la bandera! *Primera Hora.* January 26. www.primerahora.com/suroeste/noticias/puerto-rico/nota/siguelabandera-1202327/.

MacKenzie, I. & Porter, R. (2016). Evental Approaches to the Study of Events. In T. Pernecky (Ed.). *Approaches and Methods in Event Studies.* London: Routledge (25–35).

McCann, E. (1999). Race, Protest, and Public Space: Contextualizing Lefebvre in the U.S. City. *Antipode* 31(2), 63–184.

Morales, E. (2015). The Roots of Puerto Rico's Debt Crisis—And Why Austerity Will Not Solve It. *The Nation.* July 8. www.thenation.com/article/the-roots-of-puerto-ricos-debt-crisis-and-why-austerity-will-not-solve-it/.

Morris, N. (1995). *Puerto Rico: Culture, Politics, and Identity.* Westport, CT: Praeger.

Noticel. (2017). Los arrestos de Tito Kayak. September 3. www.noticel.com/ahora/los-arrestos-de-tito-kayak/621128968.

Puerto Rico Herald. (2002). Pesquera, 3 Others Charged With Inciting a Riot. June 29. www.puertorico-herald.org/issues/2002/vol6n26/Pesq3Charged-en.html.

Richards, G., de Brito, M.P., & Wilks, L. (Eds.) (2013). *Exploring the Social Impacts of Events.* London: Routledge.

Santiago Túa, L. (2017). ¿Cómo surgió el movimiento 78 Pueblos y 1 Bandera? *Metro.* August 28. www.metro.pr/pr/dimealgobueno/2017/08/28/bandera-fomenta-amor-patrio.html.

Shobe, H. (2008). Football and the Politics of Place: Football Club Barcelona and Catalonia, 1975–2005. *Journal of Cultural Geography* 25(1), 87–105.

Smith, A. (2012). *Events and Urban Regeneration.* London: Routledge.

Wise, N. (2015). Placing Sense of Community. *Journal of Community Psychology* 43(7), 920–929.

Wise, N. & Harris, J. (2016). Community, Identity and Contested Notions of Place: A Study of Haitian Recreational Soccer Players in the Dominican Republic. *Soccer & Society* 17(4), 610–627.

# 14 Follow the leather brick road

## Place, community and the Folsom Street Fair in San Francisco and beyond

*Lindsey Gaston*

## Introduction

Every September, San Francisco California plays host to 'Leather Pride Week' and the annual Folsom Street Fair, which welcomes members of the leather and Bondage, Discipline, Sadism and Masochism (BDSM) communities from around the globe. Folsom Street Fair has turned into the world's largest leather and BDSM event (AXS, 2017) and the state of California's third largest outdoor event, with an estimated attendance of 400,000 people occupying 13 city blocks within San Francisco's South of Market District (SOMA). Along with providing an environment that is inclusive of sexual freedom, the Folsom Street Fair raises financial resources for various community-supported organizations.

To understand the role of Folsom Street Fair in contemporary society it is critical to understand how San Francisco, and more specifically the SOMA district, became an epicentre for the leather and BDSM communities. This will be done by first establishing a brief description, as well as the possible origins, of the 'leather community'. This will be followed with a possible explanation of how cities like San Francisco became hubs for gay communities. The chapter will identify how the 'gay place' of San Francisco came under attack by city developers and the emergence of the mystery Gay Related Immune Disease (GRID), now known as HIV/AIDS. This resulted in the gay community having to fight to retain their place in the city's SOMA district, converting a defined place into a significant place. The Folsom Street Fair was a critical element in the community's defense strategy, thus making Folsom Street an identifiable place that represents both a physical and a symbolic place for the gay and leather community, which now trades globally as a sign of authenticity within the leather community (Goh, 2018; Heath, 2018; Vorobjovas-Pinta, 2018).

## The possible origins of the leather community

While the actual origins of the leather community are not confirmed, it is popularly believed that much of the credit for its creation is due to the post-World War II biker culture (Rubin, 1998; Van Doorn, 2016). It has been suggested that the 'biker' was a symbol of social freedom that publicly rejected cultural norms. This rejection of conventional social norms resonated well with gay men, who felt that they also existed outside the boundaries of conventional society. The emotional connection to the 'biker' matched well with the visual representation of Marlon Brando's role from the 1953 production of *The Wild One*. Brando's hyper-masculine image in a leather jacket and Muir cap spoke to a segment of the gay community (Edwards, 2006). This new outlaw figure rejected the camp/effeminate image of being a gay man. As a result, the 'Leatherman' became an image of both the celebration and rejection of conventional society and the effeminate gay.

The leather community centres itself on the wearing of leather clothing and accessories in relation to sexual activities (or for a particular sexual fetish). Items can include, but are not limited to: boots, chaps, body harnesses and jackets. As a result, those in the leather community have developed the nickname 'Leatherman'. Mosher et al. (2006, p. 93) define a 'Leatherman' in similar tone as a 'gay male subculture that eroticises leather dress and symbols'. Mosher et al. (2006), along with Rubin (1998), identify the wearing of leather as a way to demonstrate a level of 'heightened masculinity' and to express 'sexual power'. Moreover, Ridinger (2002) suggests that the leather community is a small segment of the gay population, but it is mostly visible among gay men. However, leather should not be associated exclusively with gay men. The participation of women in the leather fetish community has been explored in the literature as well (e.g. Califia & Sweeney, 1996; Hale, 1997; Kennedy & Davis, 2014; Moskowitz et al., 2011).

Because of the style of dress, it is not uncommon for the leather community to be linked to the BDSM community. While BDSM is practised within the leather community, and evidence exists that the two communities are strongly linked, they are not mutually exclusive (see Hopcke, 1991; Mosher et al., 2006). It was the publication of the *Leatherman's Handbook* that directly linked BDSM to the leather community (see Townsend, 1972). As a result, the role of BDSM has become a defining element within the Folsom Street Fair. Public performance of BDSM activities are encouraged, adding to the sex-positive environment as well as incorporating the sexual fetishes of exhibitionism and voyeurism.

BDSM has seen an increase in social acceptance, which could be due to the increasing inclusion of BDSM in the mainstream entertainment industry. The publication of E. L. James' *50 Shades of Grey* (in 2011), *50 Shades Darker* (in 2012) and *50 Shades Freed* (in 2012), which also led to a movie series under the same names, presented BDSM to a wider audience. This resulted in increased interest among women (Barker, 2013; Pillai-Friedman et al., 2015; Rye et al., 2015) and led to a discussion of how fetish is consumed by women (Parry & Light, 2014). Socio-gender issues regarding BDSM approaches to feminist thought, regarding the presentation of BDSM in books and film adaptations, has added further conceptual insight (Musser, 2015; Stevens, 2014; Van Reenen, 2014). BDSM has entered a greater level of public awareness and public consumption. As a result, greater academic insight into and interpretation of BDSM is needed. This chapter attempts to add to this body of literature by focusing on the leather and BDSM communities from the perspective of event studies, considering how the notion of place can add insight to this widening sociological literature base.

## How did San Francisco become the centre of the global leather community?

The San Francisco LGBT community fully formed in the 1920s and 1930s (Sibalis, 2004). A significant contributor to the establishment and growth of the San Francisco gay community was the United States Navy's growing practice of issuing 'blue discharges', also known as 'blue notices', originally used to remove service men who enlisted and were later discovered to be too young to serve in the military (Bérubé, 2010). The 'blue notice' then became a popular tool to remove gay men and African Americans from military service (Miller, 1995). The notice would be fully executed once a ship arrived in a navy port. As a result, port cities, like San Francisco, became drop off points for gay men (The Bold Italic, 2018). While the 'blue notice' was not classified as dishonourable, they were issued based on 'habits and traits of the individual that make his contributions in service undesirable' (*New York Times*, 1949). Miller (1995) argues that because of the shame and stigma of receiving a 'blue notice' many gay men felt they could not return to their home, especially for those that originated from small or rural communities. Those that received a 'blue notice' quickly became stigmatized and discriminated against, resulting in difficulties of acquiring employment because of their discharge status (Meyer, 1998). In addition, those who received 'blue notices' were also denied veteran benefits including access to medical care and the G.I. Bill to fund their education (Bérubé, 2010; Mettler, 2005). As a result, they sought out a life within a growing gay culture in neighborhoods like those emerging in San Francisco.

San Francisco became directly linked to the LGBT community following a June 1964 *Life Magazine* article entitled, 'Gay San Francisco.' The *Life Magazine* article would be the first time a national US publication had ever reported about homosexuality in an exposé format, and thus San Francisco was branded the 'gay capital of America' (Ormsbee, 2012). Shortly after the *Life Magazine* publication, SOMA's leather community started to grow. Leather venues, Febe's and Stud, were established and called Folsom Street home. Soon thereafter, the Ritch Street Bathhouse and Ramrods established a home in SOMA, which was a signal for much more to come. By the end of the 1970s, 30 different leather bars, including The Arena, The Ambush, The Black and Blue, The Boot Camp, The Eagle, The Folsom Barracks,

Folsom Prison and Powerhouse had opened along with clubs, merchants and bathhouses that catered specifically to a gay cliental. The proliferation of SOMA's gay centred entertainment became known as the 'Miracle Mile', as it was the most concentrated and densely populated leather neighborhood in the world (Rubin, 1998). Not only was there an increase in gay and leather venues, but the city swelled in numbers of gay people. The city's gay male population reportedly rose from 30,000 at the beginning of the 1970s, to 100,000 by the end of the 1970s (Cochrane, 2004). This is significant as by the end of the 1970s, San Francisco's overall population was 660,000 (Cochrane, 2004), making gay men almost one-sixth of the city's population.

## Origins of Folsom Street Fair

Today, the Folsom Street Fair is a celebration of sexual self-expression and operates as a fundraiser for local and national charities. However, the origins of the fair are rooted in political defiance during a time of great fear and uncertainty. Much of this played out in the early 1980s, when SOMA was being attacked on two fronts: one attacker was the unknown disease affecting the gay community who heavily occupied the SOMA district; and the second was land developers who wanted to convert the industrial warehoused area into modern high rises.

As the GRID epidemic took hold in San Francisco, the city responded by placing greater restrictions and regulations on bar activity as well as shutting down venues, which were believed to be possible environments that could spread the exposure to what would eventually become known as HIV/AIDS (Rubin, 1997). As a result, many of the venues that catered to the gay community were being systematically closed. As established gay and leather bars were being closed in SOMA, San Francisco looked to redevelop the once industrial warehouse district to residential and commercial high rises. Rincon Hill, one of the sub-neighborhoods of the SOMA district was rezoned to become a high-density residential area providing additional housing for the city's financial district (Rincon Hill Plan, 2005). The successful economic redevelopment of Rincon Hill, along with the increase in regulation of gay entertainment venues due to the emergence of an unknown virus, heavily affected the gay community. The freedom and relative autonomy once enjoyed by the SOMA district as a gay place was in danger of being reduced or eliminated (Rubin, 1997).

Because of the perceived impending attack on the neighborhood, SOMA community activists mounted a public relations campaign to develop a more secure place amongst the wider San Francisco community. A coalition of interested parties, which consisted of housing activists and community organizers, decided that a street fair would be an effect way of opening their community to the wider San Francisco community and to increase the visibility of the SOMA community. Along with opening their community, there was a goal to fundraise for community development projects as well as to provide a vehicle to share information and educate the gay and leather community about HIV/AIDS and safer sex (Rubin, 1998). Because of their efforts, community organizers successfully defended the district from the two-pronged attack, and the fair would eventually become the weeklong festival that exists today.

## Community of interest

As originally defined by Anderson (1983), an imagined community is a socially defined and constructed group of people who perceive themselves as a part of a collective based on a set of shared beliefs or ideals. The imagined community can also be constructed based on a similar dress or outward look. The visual image of the leather community, as well the use of a shared language, is key to its identification, both for those within and those who stand outside of the community. The visual image and shared vernacular are particularly helpful in the leather community as they help in establishing a relatable relationship.

The Folsom Street Fair, which started as a political demonstration to defend one of the first established gay spaces, became an important symbolic space for the imagined leather community. Thus, the place name 'Folsom Street' came to define the event and its impact on society in San Francisco and elsewhere around the world. The need to defend the physical space of SOMA from land developers, as well as the need to defend the community from a mysterious disease, added to the chaos and created a genuine struggle that help bond the community. This shared struggle helped in the transition from space without meaning (topa) to a place (chora) rich with substance and value because of community activism. This perspective is supported by Berger and Luckmann's (1966, p. 96) position that, 'all societies are constructions in the face of chaos'.

Out of the chaos, the leather/BDSM community was forged ever closer, creating a community based on interest. These communities of interest are typically not spatial, but for the leather community there is a direct connection to SOMA and specifically to Folsom Street. It is this connection to Folsom Street, which provides a symbolic spatial location to bridge and bond the imaged community. In addition, the name 'Folsom' provides a level of authenticity to events that use the name across the globe. By using the name 'Folsom', the imagined community of interest (leather/BDSM) can create a space (chora) symbolic of a location that grants authenticity. This is particularly important for members of the imagined community that cannot physically occupy the topa of SOMA/Folsom Street. By attending an event that is 'Folsom' in title, the attendees are a part of the Folsom experience. Regardless of whether they are in SOMA, New York, Toronto or Berlin, attendees are actors in the promotion and recreation of the history and future of the leather community.

## Extending the Folsom brand beyond San Francisco

The Folsom Street Fair name represents the history and heritage of leather and BDSM pride, providing a setting to celebrate and experiment without judgement. The importance of place, and name, is not lost on the Folsom Street Events organizers, as they have had to act to protect their interests by registering their ownership of the name 'Folsom Street Fair' in forty (of the fifty) states. The organization is also a registered trademark in Canada, the European Union and in Australia. By licensing the Folsom Street Fair name, the event is automatically given a level of credibility and authority within the global leather and BDSM communities. In exchange, the satellite Folsom events must follow certain rules in order to use the Folsom Street Fair name. Demetri Moshoyannis, executive director of Folsom Street Events, described the licensing scheme as follows:

> Part of our agreement with groups has always been that we will license you the name; however, we are going to hold you to certain standards for the Folsom name.
>
> (Miksche, 2016, p. 1)

The main reason Folsom Street Events can monetize the name of a street in San Francisco's SOMA district is the authenticity that the street in question represents. A key factor in the branding and consumption of cultural experience is the issue of authenticity (Chhabra, 2010). Napoli et al. (2014) further argue that the authenticity of a brand has become a critical factor in establishing a positive relationship between a product and a customer.

The legitimacy of San Francisco as a gay place comes from being a physical location that represents critical moments in gay history, as well as a location that is active in the development and cultivation of the gay heritage-making process (Su, 2018). This notion of authenticity is key to the exportation of the Folsom name in the creation of leather events outside of San Francisco. This is based on San Francisco's authentic, tangible heritage, through physical locations such as the Castro neighborhood and Folsom Street itself (Cameron, 2008; Jerome, 2008). San Francisco also possesses an intangible heritage, represented by the current concentration of gay people who are active in the day-to-day construction and participation of gay life, which is helping to evolve gay heritage (Harrison, 2013; Harvey, 2001; Smith & Haider-Markel, 2002). In addition to the historical insight presented in this chapter, San Francisco was a key player in the gay liberation movement that started in the 1970s. A crucial factor that mobilized the gay community to act was the 1969 Stonewall Riots in New York City, which were a chain of protests by members of the gay community in response to a police raid that took place at the Stonewall Inn (a well-known gay bar). The Stonewall Riots became a pivotal event in the Gay Liberation

Movement (Frizzell, 2013), and inwhat would become the modern campaign for LGBTQ equality.

Shortly after the riots in New York, San Francisco activists became vigorous in promoting the rights of gay people. News publications emerged printing politically motivated materials regarding the rights of gays and identifying gay persecution. San Francisco along with New York City, Los Angeles and Chicago took part in public marches on the weekend of 27–28 June 1970. These marches would evolve into what is now the modern-day pride marches. What would be considered small acts today were significant steps in the path of the gay liberation movement. San Francisco's gay bars, which once painted over their windows to protect the identities of their customers, replaced their windows with clear glass signifying that gay men and lesbians will no longer hide behind darkened glass.

## Folsom North, East and Europe

The Folsom Street Fair has emerged as an international commercial brand for the leather and BDSM communities around the world since the 1980s. Because of the legitimacy of San Francisco as a creator of gay culture, several leather events have adopted the name 'Folsom' in the attempt establish authenticity through the event experience. This can be seen in the examples of Folsom North (in Toronto, Canada), Folsom East (in New York City) and Folsom Europe (in Berlin, Germany). The name of 'Folsom' has created a 'brand' of sort, which reflects a common identity that provides a level of legitimacy and authenticity within the imagined community. Folsom North, Folsom East and Folsom Europe could all still operate without Folsom being in the title, but the use of 'Folsom' becomes a moniker to the leather community. The history of the place of Folsom, as outlined above, allows the leather community attending one of the events to automatically recognize a unique semblance of place authenticity.

It could be argued that because of the recognition of the Folsom name by the imagined community of leather, events that share the name have become the largest of their type in their respective regions. For example, Folsom East is the largest LGBTQ+ and fetish festival east of the Mississippi River (AXS, 2017) and Folsom Europe is the largest fetish event in Europe (AXS, 2017). Such satellite Folsom Street Fairs illustrate the power of the Folsom name in the reproduction of place for the imagined leather and BDSM community. Like the original Folsom Street Fair, the goals of the satellite festivals mirror the goals of creating safe spaces,raise funds for charity and the advancement of gay culture and heritage.

Folsom Street San Francisco describes itself as a force for change, which allows the celebration of the past whilst also enabling the face of Folsom to ever evolve. Folsom Street Fair organizers stated about the festival:

As a neighborhood or place of work, South of Market magnetically attracts the pioneers, the changelings, the cutting edge of industry, arts, entertainment, human and social relationships. Not too far behind the concrete facades, a pulsating, living mosaic-like community is alive and well. On September 23, Folsom will close to traffic and open its heart to the world.

(Connell & Gabriel, 2018)

The essence of the above quote is about establishing a community of difference, based on the celebration of that difference. That tone of language can be seen in the mission statement of the organizers of Folsom Street East about community, safe space and philanthropy:

The mission of Folsom East: Folsom Street East, Inc. celebrates and inspires participation and pride in fetish, kink, and LGBTQ communities through the creation of safe spaces for public expression of our sexual identities. Folsom Street East promotes and provides grants to other non-profit organizations serving these communities.

(Folsom Street East, Inc., 2018)

This is furthered by the organizers stating a three-point vision of a world they would like to create which, according to Folsom Street East, Inc (2018), includes:

1. A place where sexual self-discovery and fulfilment is supported by an environment that is safe, sane and affirming.
2. A place where access to a diversity of fetish/kink community spaces is expanded and fear of stigma and negative repercussions are diminished.
3. A place where all people are empowered to challenge sexual norms and embrace and add to a broad spectrum of sexual identities and expressions.

Folsom Europe wants the create an environment in which event guests can 'chill out' and 'relax', which insinuates an open and judgement free environment. The goal of Folsom is not just about creating an inclusive and safe environment, but also to generate resources for organizations that promote social change. Like the original Folsom fair, the satellite events place emphasis on raising money for local and national charities that help members of the community. In 2017 the San Francisco Folsom Street Fair donated over $322,000 to San Francisco-based local and national charities. (Folsom Street Events, 2018). In a press release issued by Folsom Street East, they announced they have 'granted more than $250,000 to local community organizations since our first street festival in 1997' (Folsom

Festival, 2017). Folsom Europe explicitly recognizes the goal of philanthropy, stating:

> The establishment of Folsom Europe was done with the specific purpose to reproduce the 'non-profit leather festival concept pioneered by the Folsom Street Fair in San Francisco'.
>
> (Berlin Pride, 2017)

Former Berlin mayor, Klaus Wowereit summed up the purpose of Folsom when he spoke about Folsom Europe:

> An event such as Folsom Europe is just right for the people of Berlin: as a meeting point for people from across the world, who visit a tolerant and cosmopolitan city to party and meet with likeminded folks and to raise funds for charitable causes and hence help to overcome prejudices.
>
> (Berlin Pride, 2017)

The creation, as well the as the examination, of these spaces, is extremely important to investigate as there is still a high level of homophobia and heteronormativity (see Johnston, 2018). To develop a better understanding of the leather community it is imperative to look at environments and events in places where communities meet and interact (Binnie & Valentine, 1999; Castells & Murphy, 1982; Valentine, 2007). However, before an exploration of that space can occur it is important to understand how that space was created.

## Concluding remarks

The important take away message in this chapter is that San Francisco has been at the forefront of the gay liberation movement since even before there was a gay liberation movement. Folsom Street is not just about one street, in one district, within one city, but its symbolism as a place name signifies meaning that unites an imagined community (Anderson, 1983; Henri & Pudelko, 2003). San Francisco has provided a haven for gay men and women for generations. San Francisco was the place that became a beacon for those who felt excluded because of their sexuality. As a result, gay men and women moved to San Francisco and populated areas within the city such as Castro and SOMA. They quickly developed communities, neighborhoods and businesses, creating the densest concentration of gay people in America. Castro and SOMA became districts within the city with greater levels of acceptance and tolerance. A mass migration to the west coast of the United States occurred for those seeking acceptance once the city was given the unofficial title of America's gay capital. Those that did not move to the Castro and

SOMA became gay pilgrims who journeyed to the city to celebrate a place with their history, heritage and culture.

At the heart of all of it, was one street. One street that served as the epicentre that allowed San Francisco to become the 'Gay Capital of America'. One street that was used to start an event that would protect the community location from the threat of commercial redevelopment. One street that would be used to help inform the gay community about the HIV/AIDs crisis. One street that would become the title for one of the largest outdoor festivals in the state of California. Folsom Street became a part of both the tangible heritage of gay San Francisco and the intangible development of gay culture, thus giving Folsom Street a unique and unquestionable authenticity in the gay, leather and BDSM communities. It is the unquestionable authenticity of Folsom Street that has allowed the name of Folsom to become more than just a street. The name 'Folsom' has become an important signifier for the gay, leather and BDSM communities, to the extent that satellite events have been established with the name Folsom to create authenticity and replicate a Folsom-like community.

These events are used to unite people and celebrate community and bring together worlds that have traditionally been shunned and classified as deviant. The attempt to reproduce 'Folsom Street' is aimed at creating an inclusive/exclusive, safe and judgement free environment allowing participants to publicly explore and celebrate their sexual fetishes. This is clearly seen in the examples of Folsom East, Folsom North and Folsom Europe. It was the goal of this chapter to illustrate how the shared symbolic name of Folsom creates a psychological sense of shared global place. Recognizing the place name and event as a safe space helps show how Folsom establishes boundedness and rootedness for the global fetish community.

## References

Anderson, B. (1983). *Imagined communities*. London: Verso.
AXS. (2017). Folsom Street Fair, world's largest leather event, may attract 400,000. www.axs.com/folsom-street-fair-world-s-largest-leather-event-may-attract-400-000-65306.
Barker, M. (2013). Consent is a grey area? A comparison of understandings of consent in Fifty Shades of Grey and on the BDSM blogosphere. *Sexualities*, 16(8), 896–914.
Berger, P. L. & Luckmann, T. (1966). *The social construction of reality: A treatise in the sociology of knowledge*. New York: Doubleday.
Berlin Pride. (2017). Folsom Europe Berlin. www.berlin-pride-guide.de/en/events/folsom-2/.
Bérubé, A. (2010). *Coming out under fire: The history of gay men and women in World War II*. Chapel Hill: University of North Carolina Press.
Binnie, J. & Valentine, G. (1999). Geographies of sexuality – a review of progress. *Progress in Human Geography*, 23(2), 175–187.

The Bold Italic. (2018). Gay (and not so gay) movements in San Francisco history. https://thebolditalic.com/gay-and-not-so-gay-moments-in-san-francisco-history-the-bold-italic-san-francisco-f92c3a7bfb92#.lw0c3sum8.

Califia, P. & Sweeney, R. (Eds.). (1996). *The second coming: A leatherdyke reader.* New York: Alyson Books.

Cameron, C. (2008). From Warsaw to Mostar: The world heritage committee and authenticity. *APT Bulletin,* 39(2–3), 19–24.

Castells, M. & Murphy, K. (1982). Cultural identity and urban structure: The spatial organization of San Francisco's gay community. In N.I. Fainstein & S.S. Fainstein (Eds.). *Urban policy under capitalism.* Beverly Hills, CA: SAGE (237–259).

Chhabra, D. (2010). Branding authenticity. *Tourism Analysis,* 15(6), 735–740.

Cochrane, M. (2004). *When AIDS began: San Francisco and the making of an epidemic.* London: Routledge.

Connell, K. & Gabriel, P. (2018). The power of broken hearts: The origins of evolution of the Folsom Street Fair. www.folsomstreetevnts.org/heritage/.

Edwards, S.J. (2006). Motorcycle leathers and the construction of masculine identities among homosexual men. Annual National Conference of Popular Culture Association and American Culture Association. April 2006, Atlanta, Georgia.

Ferguson, M. (2018). Book review: Erotic city: Sexual revolutions and the making of modern San Francisco. *Journal of Homosexuality,* 65(8), 1114–1117.

Folsom Festival. (2017). The festival. www.folsomstreeteast.com/the-festival/.

Folsom Street. (2018). Fair at Folsom Street in San Francisco Tickets – September 30, 2018. www.sfstation.com/folsom-street-fair-e1408992.

Folsom Street East, Inc. (2018). About Folsom Street East. www.folsomstreeteast.com/about.

Folsom Street Events. (2018). Leather events for good causes: Beneficiaries. www.folsomstreetevents.org/beneficiaries/.

Frizzell, N. (2013). Feature: How the Stonewall riots started the LGBT rights movement. www.pinknews.co.uk/2013/06/28/feature-how-the-stonewall-riots-started-the-gay-rights-movement/.

Goh, K. (2018). Safe cities and queer spaces: The urban politics of radical LGBT activism. *Annals of the American Association of Geographers,* 108(2), 463–477.

Hale, C.J. (1997). Leatherdyke boys and their daddies: How to have sex without women or men. *Social Text,* 52/53, 223–236.

Harrison, K. (2013). *Sexual deceit: The ethics of passing.* Lanham, MD: Lexington Books.

Harvey, D.C. (2001). Heritage pasts and heritage presents: Temporality, meaning and the scope of heritage studies. *International Journal of Heritage Studies,* 7(4), 319–338.

Heath, T. (2018). Saving space: Strategies of space reclamation at early women's film festivals and queer film festivals today. *Studies in European Cinema,* 15(1), 41–54.

Henri, F. & Pudelko, B. (2003). Understanding and analysing activity and learning in virtual communities (PDF). *Journal of Computer Assisted Learning,* 19(4), 474–487.

Hopcke, R.H. (1991). S/M and the psychology of gay male initiation: An archetypal perspective. In M. Thompson (Ed.). *Leatherfolk: Radical sex, people, politics, and practice.* Los Angeles, CA: Alyson Books (65–76).

Jerome, P. (2008). An introduction to authenticity in preservation. *APT Bulletin,* 39(2/3), 3–7.

Johnston, L. (2018). Intersectional feminist and queer geographies: A view from 'down-under'. *Gender, Place & Culture,* 25(4), 554–564.

Kennedy, E.L. & Davis, M.D. (2014). *Boots of leather, slippers of gold: The history of a lesbian community.* London: Routledge.

Mettler, S. (2005). *Soldiers to citizens: The GI Bill and the making of the greatest generation.* Oxford: Oxford University Press.

Meyer, L. D. (1998). *Creating G. I. Jane: Sexuality and power in the Women's Army Corps during World War II.* New York, NY: Columbia University Press.

Miksche, M. (2016). The Folsom Franchise. www.dailyxtra.com/the-folsom-franchise-71967.

Miller, N. (1995). *Out of the past: Gay and lesbian history from 1869 to the present.* New York, NY: Vintage Books.

Mosher, C.M., Levitt, H.M. & Manley, E. (2006). Layers of leather: The identity formation of leathermen as a process of transforming meanings of masculinity. *Journal of Homosexuality*, 51(3), 93–123.

Moskowitz, D.A., Seal, D.W., Rintamaki, L. & Rieger, G. (2011). HIV in the leather community: Rates and risk-related behaviors. *AIDS and Behavior*, 15(3), 557–564.

Musser, A.J. (2015). BDSM and the boundaries of criticism: Feminism and neoliberalism in Fifty Shades of Grey and The Story of O. *Feminist Theory*, 16(2), 121–136.

Napoli, J., Dickinson, S.J., Beverland, M. B. & Farrelly, F. (2014). Measuring consumer-based brand authenticity. *Journal of Business Research*, 67(6), 1090–1098.

New York Times. (1949). Army expands plans to rush discharge. https://timesmachine.nytimes.com/timesmachine/1944/05/12/87446854.html.

Ormsbee, T.J. (2012). *The meaning of gay: Interaction, publicity, and community among homosexual men in 1960s San Francisco.* New York, NY: Lexington Books.

Parry, D.C. & Light, T.P. (2014). Fifty shades of complexity: Exploring technologically mediated leisure and women's sexuality. *Journal of Leisure Research*, 46(1), 38–57.

Pillai-Friedman, S., Pollitt, J.L. & Castaldo, A. (2015). Becoming kink-aware – A necessity for sexuality professionals. *Sexual and Relationship Therapy*, 30(2), 196–210.

Ridinger, R.B.M. (2002). Things visible and invisible: The leather archives and museum. *Journal of Homosexuality*, 43(1), 1–9.

Rincon Hill Plan. (2005). City and county of San Francisco. commissions.sfplanning.org/cpcpackets/2010.1044X.pdf.

Rubin, G. (1997). Elegy for the Valley of Kings: AIDS and the leather community in San Francisco, 1981–1996. In M.P. Levine, P.M. Nardi & J.H. Gagnon (Eds.). *Changing times: Gay men and lesbians encounter HIV/AIDS.* Chicago, IL: University of Chicago Press (101–144).

Rubin, G. (1998). The miracle mile: South of Market and gay male leather, 1962–1997. In J. Brook, C. Carlsson & N.J. Peters (Eds.). *Reclaiming San Francisco: History, politics, culture.* San Francisco, CA: City Lights Books (247–272).

Rye, B.J., Serafini, T. & Bramberger, T. (2015). Erotophobic or erotophilic: What are young women's attitudes towards BDSM? *Psychology & Sexuality*, 6(4), 340–356.

Sibalis, M. (2004). Urban space and homosexuality: The example of the Marais, Paris' 'Gay Ghetto'. *Urban Studies*, 41(9), 1739–1758.

Smith, R. & Haider-Markel, D. (Eds.). (2002). *Gay and lesbian Americans and political participation.* Santa Barbara, CA: ABC-CLIO.

Stevens, S. (2014). Rope sluts, and bottoms, and subs, oh my: 50 Shades of Grey and the shifting discourse on female submission in feminist kink porn. *The Communication Review*, 17(3), 256–268.

Su, J. (2018). Conceptualising the subjective authenticity of intangible cultural heritage. *International Journal of Heritage Studies*, 24(9), 919–937.

Townsend, L. (1972). *The Leatherman's handbook*. Paris: Olympia Press.

Valentine, G. (2007). Theorizing and researching intersectionality: A challenge for feminist geography. *The Professional Geographer*, 59(1), 10–21.

Van Doorn, N. (2016). The fabric of our memories: Leather, kinship, and queer material history. *Memory Studies*, 9(1), 85–98.

Van Reenen, D. (2014). Is this really what women want? An analysis of Fifty Shades of Grey and modern feminist thought. *South African Journal of Philosophy*, 33(2), 223–233.

Vorobjovas-Pinta, O. (2018). Gay neo-tribes: Exploration of travel behaviour and space. *Annals of Tourism Research*, 72(1), 1–10.

# 15 Whose Europe?

## Representing place in the Ryder Cup

*Don Colley & John Harris*

## Introduction

The Ryder Cup is a biennial golf match between Europe and the United States of America. Despite suggestions that it is the third biggest sporting event in the world (although this is a contested title to claim), it has received relatively little attention from academics in event management and related areas of study. Bale (2003) suggests that "sports are struggles over *space* [...] and sports teams almost always represent a *place*" (p.172, original emphasis). Bale's (2003) notion of sports as struggles over space can be read as multi-dimensional in that sport and sporting events are struggles on and in a space but are also struggles for the control of (a) space (see also, Vertinsky & Bale, 2004). Both involve a complex set of power relationships in the domination and definition of sports spaces. Issues involving the control and production of space can be understood within geography by a structural (or Marxist/critical) perspective (Harvey, 1985; Smith & Dennis, 1987).

However, the economic, political and social structures which organize around struggles over space only address one side of the equation when dealing with the relationship between sporting events and geography. Representations of place, that is the discursive definitions of spaces and places, are important for understanding an event such as the Ryder Cup because "people identify with a place through sport, arguably more so than through any form of culture" (Bale, 2003 p. 172). Place, and place-identity, as explained through cultural identification, was introduced primarily by humanist geographers as a reaction to the structural perspectives of positivist and Marxist philosophies. It can also be expressed in cross-disciplinary terms as an agency-based perspective. A critical-humanist approach is one which:

> rejects a dependence on standards of either "objective" geographic knowledge or radical anti-foundationalism. It examines the various contexts – whether marked by difference in class, race, gender, sexuality, or nationality – within which individual meanings and social practices are produced, understood, and negotiated.
>
> (Adams et al., 2001, p. xvii)

How then does this address Bale's (2003) conceptualizations of struggles over space and representations of place? A critical humanist perspective is about "an interest in the everyday, a privileging of individuals' understandings of their physical, social, and symbolic contexts, and, most significantly, the theoretical and empirical study of place" (Adams et al., 2001, p. xvii), but is also "equally concerned with how human creativity is hemmed in by large-scale social, political and economic structures" (p. xix). Furthermore, critical humanism establishes communication as fundamental to the process of exploring the struggles over space and the representations of place. This perspective does not claim to be all-encompassing and draws on work from many major strands of social thought rather than narrowly defining each as intrinsically distinct from one discipline to the next. However, as a geographically focused analysis of media reporting on the 2008 Ryder Cup, it will be explained through a discussion centred on geographical concepts related to the particular understanding of space and place highlighted when looking at the biggest team competition in the sport of golf.

In an era of accelerated globalization, the social construction of scale creates a need for the re-conceptualization of the region. We try to explain how the creation of economic, political and social regions (like the European Union) relates to the development and perception of sports regions and new representations of place, and further explore how changing representations of place are conveyed through mediated images of place and media personalities. Mediated images and personalities are formed through the pervasiveness of national discourses and the relationship of the region to the nation and the individual to both. We also acknowledge the way in which these nationalistic discourses are aged, raced, sexed, gendered and classed. Finally, the chapter will conclude with a discussion of how scaled identities are conveyed through mediated (re) presentations of place within a mega-event.

## (Re)assessing scale and (re)imagining place: The Ryder Cup and Team Europe

Some may confine the discussion of scale to the false dichotomy of the global against the local, but many geographers and sociologists of sport alike have challenged this conceptualization and position the nation as something constructed by both global and local forces at an intermediary level (e.g. Andrews & Ritzer, 2007; Cox, 2005). This positioning of the nation between local cultures and global flows draws on the idea that while there are real political units (the state) which are in some ways tied to nations, many "nationalist" sentiments are conjured up through mediated discourses, power relations and grass-roots movements, which attempt to define one group as different from another in order to formulate identity. Bairner (2001) demonstrates how the nation, whether real or imagined, is the product of local representations in global contexts and exists as a buffer between the two forces. Yet as Cox (2005, p. 185) observes, "spatial imaginaries, like the local/global, are always constructed from the standpoint of particular social positions". This issue in the social construction of scale has become more prominent as "contemporary conditions of advanced globalization have seriously undermined the economic and political autonomy that helped constitute the modern nation" (Silk et al., 2005, p. 2).

When the Ryder Cup was first staged in 1927, it was a match between the United States of America and Great Britain. Golfers from England and Scotland made up the earliest Great Britain teams with players from Wales (1937) and Northern Ireland (1947) making their debuts decades later. In 1953, the team included a player from the Republic of Ireland, although the name of the team would not change to Great Britain and Ireland until 1973. Beyond this, further expansion was argued for as early as 1959 because of the American dominance of the event. As Feherty notes,

> [a]mong the suggestions was to let the rest of Europe join the British. Or let them recruit members of the Commonwealth (after all, South Africans Gary Player and Bobby Locke, and Australian Peter Thomson, had won nine of the previous eleven Open Championships).
>
> (Feherty, 2004, p. 112)

Despite these efforts, Great Britain (and Ireland) remained until after the fiftieth anniversary of the Ryder Cup in 1977. Finally, in 1979 the first match between Europe and the USA took place. However, the European team still consisted of nine players from Great Britain (Scotland and England), one from Ireland and two from Spain. In 1981, Team Europe expanded slightly to include the first player from Germany. Throughout the 1980s the team included a steady influx of Spanish players before incorporating individuals from Italy (1993), Sweden (1995), France (1999), Denmark (2008) and Belgium (2012). Since expanding to Team Europe in 1979, only twelve different nations have been represented.

Whose Europe then does this team represent? The spatial imaginaries of the European Union and the European Ryder Cup team do not meet the representations of place constructed through media and political discourse. Drawing on the influential work of Benedict Anderson (1991), Levermore and Millward (2007, p. 146) note that "collective identities are 'imagined' through symbolic and discursive practices [...] [and] in the contemporary era, the imagined boundaries may be less clear as societies open up to more (real and virtual) economic and cultural interactions through global processes". It is often assumed that nationalist identities are tied to specific territories, yet if we imagine Europe in the case of the Ryder Cup we can very clearly see that the territory its nationalist image is drawing on is not the territory, in general, that it represents. In fact, widening the context to include other sports, attempting to construct a representative "pan-European" sporting identity may be impossible from internal institutional policies. It would seem that a pan-European sports identity faces additional difficulties in being accepted externally through the conflicting spatial imaginary presented through American media discourse.

## Context and thematic analysis

Whannel (2002) argues that methodological choices in general, and media analyses specifically, have become intensely personal topics that frequently cause debate. Qualitative analyses offer deep insights into the production processes, which construct particular perceptions of people and places rather than a quantified notation of importance explicit in content analyses (e.g. Kian et al., 2008). The narratives derived from internet newspaper articles, news articles, blog articles and the commentary by different fans on these sites from 15 to 29 September 2008 (approximately the week during and after the 2008 Ryder Cup) form the basis of the themes discussed in this chapter.

The first step in choosing the appropriate sites to monitor for Ryder Cup coverage was to eliminate those sites that were explicitly covering only the United States team. Secondly, attempts were made to find those sites that were ubiquitous in their access and popularity to the general population of the United States. Therefore, the internet newspaper choices included *The New York Times* and *Los Angeles Times*, from which articles were identified as being relevant to the study. Additionally, the *International Herald Tribune* conducted a "global sports forum" prior to the event, which was especially useful. Furthermore, internet coverage of *Yahoo! Sports* provided useful articles, while *Golf.com* was also used alongside the websites of *NBC Sports* and *ESPN*. Some of the articles identified were produced by the Associated Press (AP) and appeared in several of the sources, so they are only counted towards the total articles for the sites in which they were first inspected. A final step was to explore the perception of the Ryder Cup from prominent sports blogs on the British Broadcasting Corporation (BBC) website for indications of similarities and differences in their reporting to that outlined above. Perhaps because of the cross coverage of the AP sources and the generally low coverage of the event, there was a lower number of source materials identified for this project than one might expect to be found for an international sporting event. The relatively low total of media-generated coverage further challenges the often-stated assertion that the Ryder Cup is now the third biggest sporting event in the world (see Harris et al., 2017). Before moving on to explore some of the dominant themes emerging from the study, the following section further outlines the context and thematic analysis used to underpin the work and the findings presented herein.

Several themes were identified, which were either explicitly noted in the bylines of the articles or were dominant discourses present within the text. These themes displayed a temporal quality that either strengthened or waned throughout the course of the event. For example, one of the dominant themes prior to the event was how the absence of Tiger Woods would affect the outcome for the US. While this was heavily debated, what remained constant was that as the US team began to lead on the first day of the match, all talk of Tiger Woods was absent from the journalists' discourse. Furthermore, the impact of the absence of Woods is reflected by the journalists' portrayal of a more unified image of "Team USA versus Team Europe" rather than as a match of individuals.

The perceived impact of a "Tiger-less" US team on the image of Europe's motivation and status in the contest against the US, and Woods' absence intensified the focus on the two captains and therefore on each of the places they were representing. The representation of Europe is continually (re)constructed and (re)presented throughout the Ryder Cup and transforms from being a discussion of a successful team to a group of failed individuals led by an overly individualist captain. Whannel (2002, p. 227) reflects that "the validity of semiological, textual and discursive readings in the end rest, it seems to me, in their plausibility and explanatory value to the reader". Therefore, this discussion does not claim to offer any ultimate "truths" as to how Europe is (re) presented but offers some insights and interpretations that problematize the positioning of Europe in a range of discourse. Such a discussion is arguably even more important today as the subject of Brexit dominates news stories about Europe in a range of spheres. To understand and explain the positioning of Europe in Ryder Cup coverage we must also look at representations of Team USA. The spaces and places conceived as Europe and/or European within media accounts are created in ways that often identify how these are different from the USA, and it is to this subject that we now turn.

## Exotic Europe: Not like America

Wexler (2008) suggests that the Ryder Cup "offers a singular opportunity for meaningful team play [...] in a sport otherwise organized solely around individuals". Busbee (2008) argues that while "[t]here's plenty of national pride here at stake [...] national pride isn't enough". The Ryder Cup is more than an individual desire for achievement and fighting for national pride, it is a chance for the individual to unite behind a team and for a team to represent a nation; it is "for your teammates, for your country, for the deepest part of your competitive soul" (McCabe, 2008). Even fans know that "there's a sense of nationalistic pride on the line [...] because the Ryder Cup is different" (McCabe, 2008). Europe, however the term is employed, is generally imagined through both American and British media discourse as a more unified whole than the United States. As Hodgetts (2008) notes "Europe have for many years now added up to far more than the sum of their parts. And the theory generally trotted out is because of greater team spirit and collective desire". Pennington (2008) of the *New York Times* suggests that this collective desire comes from their diversity rather than because they are a group of homogenous nations. He explains that "[t]hey are diverse not just in their nationalities, but in their backgrounds and interests" (Pennington, 2008). Though they represent a diversity of nations and personalities, it is believed that their common participation on the European Tour has allowed them to bond more easily than the individuals who excel on the American PGA Tour (Hodgetts, 2008; Pennington, 2008). Indeed, during the 2006 event the heavy defeat of Team USA was attributed in part to the perceived individualist nature of US society (see Harris & Lyberger, 2008).

Yet if these individuals and the nations they represent are seen as a unified whole, why is there so much confusion as to "whose Europe" is being defined? Van Sickle (2008) caricatures the European fans and therefore Europe as "fully-dressed matadors and would-be leprechauns". Commenting during the course of play, Tosches (2008) expresses that "you can't blame these folks for sticking together – people from exotic and strange lands such as Ireland, England, Sweden, Spain, Denmark and Utah. (Just kidding. England is not very exotic)". In this comment, just like in Van Sickle's observation, Tosches identifies the individual nationalities being represented (except for Northern Ireland, which is probably being included in the whole of Ireland) but draws them away as separate from England. In one sense he identifies their unity by suggesting they are places people are unfamiliar with but then reverts back to the dichotomous relationship between the United States and England. Reflecting on this relationship prior to the start of the event, Wexler (2008) cautions that "this might be a good time to remind all concerned that Europeans in general, and the British in particular, are not our enemies". Although this is taken in the larger context of societal relations between the two regions, it clearly represents how any discussion of Europe ultimately relies on a familiarity with Great Britain (see also, Steen, 2015; Vamplew & Kay, 2007). What becomes clear is how the Ryder Cup might just as easily be representative of three separate entities: the United States, Great Britain and the rest of Europe. As an added layer of complexity, the frequent use of England and Britain interchangeably demonstrates how little consideration is given to the differences between the two.

A result of these representations of place is that Team USA's similarity is contrasted to the imagined diversity of Team Europe. Pennington's (2008) descriptor of Team USA notes that "they are 12 polite and persevering men, many with similar American country club backgrounds". This similarity is perhaps a result of the recent series of losses the American team has suffered. Hodgetts (2008) explains that "as with Europe in the past, so with the US now – the expectation of failure can be an equally potent galvanizing force". The fear of losing a fourth straight match may or may not have been a palpable experience for the players on Team USA, but the American media certainly used the sentiment to cast America as underdogs to the dominant European team. Mogg (2008) suggests that "the Europeans […] will have more pressure on them this time" and "[m]aybe the pressure of being the favorite will rattle them on the greens". While much of this is simply pre-game media rhetoric to inspire unity amongst the American crowd, some of it reflects the absence of a widely recognized media personality on the American team.

For example, during the match, the idea of the American "underdogs" is positioned against Team Europe, which has taken Team USA to the "slaughterhouse in the last four years" (Van Sickle, 2008). Yet, "[t]he Americans, playing without Tiger Woods, hopelessly outmanned, with their worst on-paper team since Europe was added to the mix, will pull the Cupset of the Century" (Reilly, 2008). The absence of Tiger Woods serves the media's purpose of (re)constructing and (re)presenting the competing "nations" in two ways. First, it allows them to imagine how Team USA was a group of individuals in the recent past during its defeats to the more unified Europe (Harris & Lyberger, 2008), and second, it positions Team Europe as a favorite to the now team-oriented Americans who "[w]ithout Woods to count on, [...] may play with more fire and passion" (Mogg, 2008).

## Team USA ... not Tiger's team

Tiger Woods, the number one golfer in the world at the time of the 2008 Ryder Cup, came to embody golf in the United States and on the PGA Tour (see for example, Houck, 2006). Yet since he began playing in the Ryder Cup in 1997 the USA has won only once with Woods in the team. Thus, despite a 10-13-2 record at the time of the 2008 event, Woods' absence from the 2008 Ryder Cup following a knee injury was heralded as both a blessing and a curse for the US team and Team Europe. His absence was considered a detriment to the success of Team Europe by some American news columnists. Weinman (2008) points out that Woods has "been more successful in galvanizing the scrappy Europeans than the guys on his own side". Not only is he positioning the Europeans as gutsy fighters, he signifies how they are a unified whole while describing the US team with the loosely phrased "guys on his own side". In fact, by presenting Woods as the face of Team USA in the previous Ryder Cups won by Europe, Weinman develops the idea that Europe is fundamentally the opposite of Tiger Woods and the opposite of the United States. Weinman (2008) continues to elaborate that Europe as a team has "embraced the Ryder Cup's unpredictability" while Team USA is a "disparate collection of multimillionaires", of which Tiger Woods is the worst.

In constructing this narrative, Weinman explains that Team USA may be more successful without Tiger Woods by becoming more like Team Europe. He draws Woods further away from the US team by noting his almost god-like presence, referring to him as "Zeus in soft spikes". Weinman goes on to say that like the Europeans "the mere ordinariness of the American roster stands to be one of its greatest assets". Similarly, Reilly (2008) of ESPN thinks that "without Tiger, [Team USA is] The Little Team That Could" and "the Euros [...] have no Goliath to slay". Forde (2008) sees things quite differently and believes that the "ordinariness" of Team USA stands to be its greatest failure. Forde (2008), addressing an American audience, challenges those who "want us to believe the Americans will rise up and defeat their European oppressors with a team whose whole is greater than the modest sum of its Tiger-less parts". Positioning the argument towards American doubters, he reinforces the image that the United States and Team USA need Tiger Woods if they are to overcome the "oppression" of a dominating European team. The use of such a strong word as oppression invokes nationalist discourses that cast the European Ryder Cup team's success as unnatural and unacceptable by drawing on the historical relationship between the US and Europe (or more specifically Great Britain). Not only does Forde establish a deep divide between the US team and the European team, he further portrays Woods' effect on golf for both sides as comparable to the Lehman Brothers and Merrill Lynch brokerage firms' effect on the New York stock market (Forde, 2008). Without Woods the US is doomed, and Europe will no longer have to try in the Ryder Cup.

Tiger Woods' absence was heavily debated by a panel for the *International Herald Tribune* leading up to the match. While John Huggan of *Scotland on Sunday* expresses Woods' impact as a loss for the Americans because he has been their leading scorer since joining the team, the general tenor is that his absence will help the Americans "because they will try harder". Huggan recants his previous argument and suggests that "[m]ajors are all that matter to the special ones". Mair of the *Daily Telegraph* (England) agrees, reflecting that "perhaps because Woods was not brought up to think Ryder Cup first, like so many of our players", he has been less helpful to the American team. This comment is interesting because we can see how Europe, not the individual countries of which it consists, is imagined as a place that fosters camaraderie and working as a team. The forum does this by noting that European players sport a team-first attitude which Woods cannot understand. What wasn't public knowledge at this time was Woods' personal troubles, which would culminate in a much-publicized car crash outside of his house in 2009 and subsequent treatment for sex addiction.

Developing the argument introduced earlier above, Philip Reid of *The Irish Times* suggests that the Europeans' team mentality is primarily a result of playing soccer. Goran Zachrisson relates the opposite expressions of American and European team identity, noting that during the opening ceremonies of the 2006 Ryder Cup, "[t]he Americans walked in the Order of Merit order. The Europeans walked in alphabetical order" (Clarey, 2008). Subjecting Tiger Woods to the scrutiny of international columnists reveals the underlying nationalist sentiments, which fall back to a (falsely) dichotomous relationship between the team and the individual; because Europe is so much better as a team, the US can be more like Europe and will be better off without their best individual. Forde (2008) disagreed with this idea and consoled himself on the loss of Tiger Woods by drawing attention to the new "American hope", US team captain Paul Azinger, who is "approaching this with a bit more spit-in-your-eye defiance" than those in the past.

## Contrasting captaincy roles and place

The respective roles of the two captains also became important in the (re) presentations of place. Prior to the start of the 2008 event the captains appeared more frequently in the media than is usually the case in the build-up to this biennial event. Part of this relates to the theme noted above whereby the absence of the world's number one player, and the game's prominent sporting celebrity at the time, meant that a new focus was needed. Another possible reason was that both captains enjoyed successful post-playing careers as media commentators and worked on many tournaments together for ABC television in the USA. This then would give the audience a recognition and understanding of the two men and their relationship with each other. As representatives of their particular teams (and nations/regions), Azinger and Faldo were often the focus of media stories on (re)imagining sameness and difference in the framing of Europe.

Morfit (2008) suggests that Paul Azinger and Nick Faldo "are the same [...] [b]ut they're also different". This fits nicely into a critical humanist perspective that draws on postmodern and poststructural understandings of binaries. In that regard, one can never be essentially the same nor different than something else in a truly dichotomous fashion, but rather one becomes the same or different through the process of categorization. The media narratives dominant within the various (re)presentations of Team USA suggest that in order to succeed it is becoming more like Europe and Team Europe's recent success has them becoming more like the USA teams of the past. If we apply this understanding to the captains then we can similarly see how Paul Azinger is fashioned by the media as similar to those European captains who have led Europe to recent victories and how Nick Faldo is described as being too individualistic and, in a way, "too American". Indeed, Faldo's perceived aloofness and (re)presentations of him as a "loner" on the tour link clearly to much of the previous tournaments media observations of the supposed individualistic nature of US society. Before engaging in this discussion, however, it is first important to briefly explore how the captains are imagined in comparison to one another prior to the start of the cup. In observing these descriptions, it is possible to further acknowledge how in comparison to Azinger's Team USA, Faldo's Team Europe represents another version of European identity.

The captain's personality and the style employed in constructing the individual teams has played an important role in how the media represents the United States and Europe. For the United States, Azinger embodies the fighting spirit of the young American team and the need to refresh the perception of the USA as a sporting nation. On the other hand, Faldo personifies a move away from the supposed diversity associated with the inclusion of the various nations of Europe within the Ryder Cup and places the focus on the personal efforts of European veterans, such as Padraig Harrington, whom he chastised prior to the match "for being too chummy, claiming it was holding them back in the individual pursuit of majors" (Hodgetts, 2008). These individuals come to stand for a new representation of place, and through the course of the Ryder Cup their perceived successes and failures allow the media to further (re)construct the spatial imaginaries of Europe.

## Concluding comments: The place of Europe

Prior to the beginning of the 2008 Ryder Cup, the American media focused on constructing an image of Team Europe that the American team could imitate. Through the course of the coverage, this discourse became focused on how the absence of Tiger Woods allowed the United States to be like the successful European teams in the past. Furthermore, to do this they needed the help of an American captain who could fashion the US in Europe's image (Carter, 2008) and who would be different from the European captain Faldo. Simultaneously, the American media depicted Europe as splitting in half without the ability to focus on the dominating presence of Woods. One side was focused on the prominence of England and the individual and the "other" was dedicated to the diversity that had made Europe a winner in the past. Throughout this process, it seems that a European spirit is represented more by the 2008 American Ryder Cup team than by the European team. Therefore, Europe as a place is imagined to exist contemporaneously in the United States, in the economic and political organization of the European Union, in the European Ryder Cup Team, but not in England where Europe and a pan-European sports identity are often an afterthought. The decision of the UK public to vote for leaving the European Union is of importance to note here, for the Ryder Cup has been one of the only places where a visible European identity is prominent. The wider political discussion of Brexit does not usually incorporate any focus on sport, but the Ryder Cup represents a fascinating site to consider the imagined community of Europe.

Various members of the American media constantly shifted the discourse about Europe in order to promote their individual desire to see Team USA succeed and to see the Ryder Cup rejuvenated. The limited spatial imaginaries presented by the media in discussions of Europe are focused on (re)producing the geographies of mostly white, upper-class men both in the media and in the sport. While the analysis presented here considers how Europe is being imagined by the American media and others associated with professional golf, it is as equally limited (and limiting) as those whose work it draws on. Bale (2003, pp. 161–162) expresses that "sports geography has tended to neglect the importance of [...] the sporting worlds inside our heads, our cognitive geographies of sports and the imaginative worlds of sport that are actually written and reproduced". Therefore, an area of study that would extend this discussion of place-making through events is to consider how Europe is imagined from a local, fan-based perspective. It would be interesting to gain insights into wider golf event consumption because "[w]hat people *think* places, regions and countries are like is what is important in the way they form judgments of such places" (Bale, 2003, p. 165). Future research may also critically engage with (re)presentations of Europe across different parts of that region to assess the many different discourses at play in the (re) imagining of Europe and European identity as it relates to the Ryder Cup. Steen's (2015) recent work highlights the ways in which a continental collectivity is visible within British press coverage of the event.

This chapter has critically assessed the importance of place through focusing on an event that has received relatively little attention from scholars to date. The analysis of these narratives, through a framework influenced by the geography of sport, has highlighted the importance of space and place within an international sporting event. This work shows that Europe was created and conceived within US media narratives by continued reference to its perceived difference from the USA. Whilst characteristics associated with recent European successes in the Ryder Cup were omnipresent in many media narratives, this work also clearly shows the ways in which national and regional identities are constantly in a state of flux and can be presented and perceived in numerous ways.

# References

Adams, P., Hoelsher, S. & Till, K. (2001). Place in context: Rethinking humanist geographies. In P. Adams, S. Hoelscher & K. Till (Eds.), *Textures of place: Exploring humanist geographies*. Minneapolis, MN: University of Minnesota Press (xiii–xxxiii).

Anderson, B. (1991). *Imagined communities*, 2nd ed. London: Verso.

Andrews, D. & Ritzer, G. (2007). The grobal in the sporting glocal. *Global Networks*, 7, 135–153.

Bairner, A. (2001). *Sport, nationalism, and globalization: European and North American perspectives*. Albany, NY. State University of New York Press.

Bale, J. (2003). *Sports geography*. London: Routledge.

Busbee, J. (2008, September 15). U.S. preps for its most important Ryder Cup ever. Retrieved from http://sports.yahoo.com/golf/blog/devil_ball_golf?author=Jay+Busbee&pg=11.

Carter, I. (2008, September 22). Azinger fashions US in Europe's image. *Iain Carter Blog*. Retrieved from www.bbc.co.uk/blogs/iaincarter/2008/09/azinger_fasions_us_in_euros_i.html.

Clarey, C. (2008, September 15). Ryder Cup, part one: Impact of Tiger Woods and Colin Montgomerie. *International Herald Tribune*. Retrieved from www.iht.com/articles/2008/09/15/sports/clareyryderone.php.

Cox, K. (2005). Local: Global. In P. Cloke & R. Johnston (Eds.), *Spaces of geographical thought*. London: Sage (175–198).

Feherty, D. (2004). *David Feherty's totally subjective history of the Ryder Cup*. New York: Rugged Land.

Forde, P. (2008, September 17). There's no way Americans are better without their best. *ESPN Conversation*. Retrieved from http://sports.espn.go.com/espn/columns/story?columnist=forde_pat&id=3590967&sportCat=golf.

Harris, J., Lee, S. & Lyberger, M. (2017). The Ryder Cup, national identities and Team USA. *Sport in Society*, 20, 413–427.

Harris, J. & Lyberger, M. (2008). Mediated (re)presentations of golf and national identity in the US: Some observations on the Ryder Cup. *International Journal of Sport Communication*, 1, 143–154.

Harvey, D. (1985). The geopolitics of capitalism. In D. Gregory & J. Urry (Eds.), *Social relations and spatial structures*. New York: St. Martin's Press (312–344).

Hodgetts, R. (2008, September 11). Team spirit key to Cup. *BBC Sport*. Retrieved from www.bbc.co.uk/blogs/robhodgetts/2008/09/team_spirit_key_to_cup.html.

Houck, D. (2006). Crouching Tiger, hidden blackness. Tiger Woods and the disappearance of race. In A. Raney & J. Bryant (Eds.) *Handbook of sports and media*. Mahwah, NJ: Lawrence Erlbaum Associates (469–484).

Kian, E., Vincent, J. & Mondello, M. (2008). Masculine hegemonic hoops: An analysis of media coverage of March Madness. *Sociology of Sport Journal*, 25, 223–242.

Levermore, R. & Millward, P. (2007). Official policies and informal transversal networks: Creating 'pan-European identifications' through sport? *Sociological Review*, 55(1), 144–164.

McCabe, J. (2008, September 19). Nothing matches passion of Ryder Cup: Playing for teammates, country brings more passion, excitement. *NBCSports.com*. Retrieved from http://nbcsports.msnbc.com/id/26727242/.

Mogg, B. (2008, September 5). How the U.S. can win the Ryder Cup. Retrieved from http://blogs.golf.com/top100/2008/09/how-the-us-can.html.

Morfit, C. (2008, September 1). Azinger and Faldo: A dynamic duo: Paul Azinger and Nick Faldo are as different as they are the same. *Golf.com*. Retrieved from www.golf.com/golf/tours_news/article/0,28136,1827658,00.html.

Pennington, B. (2008, September 18). Europeans find a common bond in their diversity. *The New York Times*. Retrieved from www.nytimes.com/2008/09/19/sports/golf/19ryder.html?partner=rssnyt.

Reilly, R. (2008, September 17). 14 ½ reasons why the U.S. will win the Ryder Cup. *ESPN: The Magazine*. Retrieved from http://sports.espn.go.com/espnmag/story?section=magazine&id=3593613.

Silk, M., Andrews, D. & Cole, C. (2005). Corporate nationalism(s): The spatial dimensions of sporting capital. In M. Silk, D. Andrews & C. Cole (Eds.), *Sport and corporate nationalisms*. Oxford: Berg (1–12).

Smith, N. & Dennis, W. (1987). The restructuring of geographical scale: Coalescence and fragmentation of the Northern Core Region. *Economic Geography*, 63, 160–182.

Steen, R. (2015). Uneasy Ryder: The Ryder Cup, anti-Americanism and the 'Yoo-Rop' phenomenon. *Sport in Society*, 18, 347–363.

Tosches, R. (2008, September 20). Ninety minutes of Miller time. Retrieved from http://sports.yahoo.com/golf/blog/devil_ball_golf/post/Ninety-minutes-of-Miller-Time?urn=golf,109262.

Vamplew, W. & Kay, J. (2007). The rough and the fairway: Processes and problems in Ryder Cup team selections 1927–2006. *Studies in Physical Culture and Tourism*, 14, 27–35.

Van Sickle, G. (2008, September 20). After years of poor play by the U.S., the magic is back at the Ryder Cup. *Golf.com*. Retrieved from www.golf.com/golf/tours_news/article/0,28136,1843150,00.html.

Vertinsky, P. & Bale, J. (Eds.) (2004) *Sites of sport: Space, place, experience*. London: Routledge.

Weinman, S. (2008, September 15). Opinion: U.S. team better off without Tiger: Superstar's absence might be just what Americans need to pull off "upset". *NBCSports.com*. Retrieved from http://nbcsports.msnbc.com/id/26723994/.

Wexler, D. (2008, September 16). When it comes to the Ryder Cup, can't we all just get along? *Los Angeles Times*. Retrieved from http://articles.latimes.com/2008/sep/16/sports/spw-ryder16.

Whannel, G. (2002). *Media sports stars: Masculinities and moralities.* London: Routledge.

# 16 Linking geographical and sociological interpretations

## Place, society and Diwali around the world

*Nicholas Wise*

### Introduction

This chapter looks at a festival held around the globe. The Diwali (also called Deepavali) Festival is "the annual festival of light celebrated every autumn around the world" (Independent, 2017). This event is internationally import-ant and culturally significant, linking people around the world—suggesting how events reinforce imagined communities. Diwali offers much insight on places and societies because the shared festival tradition unites people around the world, with much research conducted on the festival (see Booth, 2012, 2015, 2016; Johnson, 2007; Johnson & Figgins, 2006; Kelly, 1988; MacMillan, 2008). This chapter offers a different perspective of events, using geographical and sociological conceptualizations to link events, places and societies. All of the previous chapters have focused on either a specific case, cases or offered regional context. This chapter widens the scope by focus on conceptual con-siderations used by geographers and sociologists, and how these explain Diwali around the world. It does not follow a traditional research paper format or a methodological approach, but the chapter does bring in examples to provide insight and evidence from online/media content on different places around the world to relate conceptual discussions.

Diasporas can showcase how we live in an increasingly fluid and mobile world, and it is significant events such as Diwali that may link and connect people around the world. Diwali also creates an aesthetic, a unique experience for those who participate in or witness the event. Each of these concepts is explored in this chapter in the subsequent sections. Content is blended to link conceptual under-standings with points of evidence blended in to relate to pertinent geographical and sociological understandings. The final section then attempts to show the links across each of the complementing conceptual areas, to illustrate how such a global festival can unite an imagined diasporic community.

Diwali has its traditions and origins in South Asia (MacMillan, 2008), and Kishore and Sehrawat (2017) discuss the festival's meaning, explaining that: "Diwali or Deepawali means long rows of oil lamps, which are mainly put out-side the house to welcome the Hindu goddess of wealth Lakshmi and the lord Ganesha—the god of prosperity and the remover of obstacles". As the festival has expanded around the world from South Asia, through the diaspora, its meaning has taken on global significance:

> Deepavali, or also known as Diwali, is a festival of lights celebrated by those of Hindu faith. It is one of the most important festivals of the year for the Hindus who celebrate by performing traditional customs at homes. Just like most major celebrations by other communities, Deepavali is a time for family reunions. Deepavali is an official holiday in Malaysia as well as in some Asian countries like India, Myanmar, Mauritius and in non-Asian countries like Guyana, Trinidad and Tobago, Suriname as well as Fiji.
>
> (Wonderful Malaysia, 2018)

The above quote highlights the significance of the event in various places around the world as a result of migration and the staging and performing of the festival around the world. To a discussion of diaspora and imagined communities is where this chapter now turns.

## Diasporas and imagined communities: To Australia, Mauritius and the United States

Diasporas refer to the mass migration of people from a place of origin (a country or region of the world). There are various pull factors associated with why diasporas occur, be it due to war or genocide, or to seek better economic opportunities (Cohen, 2008). Diasporas are important to study in disciplines such as human geography or sociology because when people become mobile, they take with them their culture and sense of identity and may attempt to create or (re)create that in a new place (see Booth, 2016; Johnson, 2007). When we consider this from an event studies perspective, people locating and attempting to express their culture and sense of identity not only becomes (re)created, but also staged and performed in a new place (Booth, 2015; Cresswell, 2004; Edensor, 2002; Langellier, 2010). Furthermore, and as will be discussed below, representations in the landscape act to stage or display symbolisms to further connect imagined communities (Edensor, 2002). In this sense, cultural events and rituals become a performance of identity to connect people with their home, as "public Diwali celebrations dot local communities around the world" (Rohit, 2015). When identities are staged and performed, it symbolizes a connection with the place of origin, creating a sense of meaning or reference to "home"—thus connecting those in a (new) place with their place of origin (see Wise, 2011).

Scholars have adopted Anderson's (1991) notion of nations as imagined communities (e.g. Harris, 2008; Shobe, 2008; Wise, 2011), where he suggests people are bound together vis-à-vis "horizontal comradeship". This comradeship now expands beyond national borders (Carter, 2007; Wise, 2011), with the staging and performing of events such as Diwali in various locations (almost simultaneously). Smith (1991) suggested that nations are bounded entities, but in a nascent era of transnational movement, the nation is no longer bounded geographically, per se, but is fluid. In today's world, as people have become increasingly fluid, and thus so have their identities, culture and rituals, social and/or cultural phenomena have become mediators through which people are connected based on their (different) identity—bounded exclusively through the shared association of living in the same place. The culture of a place is a social construction of everyday life and, at times, this becomes contested when people from different cultural background attempt to make their presence felt (see Gruffudd, 1999; Wise, 2015b).

Scholars have referred to imagined communities as the interconnectedness of national societies across borders (see Langellier, 2010), and such an understanding is present during the hosting of events where people from different backgrounds often unite to celebrate or consume what is on offer. For instance, people who have departed South Asia and settled in Australia, Mauritius and the United States bring unique elements of their culture. Each October or November (depending on the moon cycle) Diwali is celebrated, giving those in the new country a chance to experience and understand the relocated culture, to participate and consume this culture. It is, however, important to look beyond the consumption of events, to assess new local productions of events where cultural differences are also important, to recognise how migrants not only shape the current demographics of a place, but also to consider the future construction, production and staging of culture in that new place (see Edensor, 2002). In relation to transnational migrations and their contribution to a new local identity, coinciding with the rapid advances of 'globalization, it is impressions and imaginations of their home, or an ancestral home that they have a significant personal or ancestral connection with (Wise, 2015a). Building on this point, Sarwal (2016) describes how families continue the ritual in Australia, as many are "continuing the tradition of celebrating Diwali along with major festivals of other communities." Other authors add further personal insight. In the United States, Rohit (2015) writes:

> in the Little India district of Artesia, Calif., the streets become illuminated ahead of Diwali. For millions of Indians who live away from India, celebrating Diwali is a way for them to stay connected to their roots. As the second most populous nation on earth celebrates one of the world's brightest and most festive holidays, Indians on the subcontinent and around the world are gathering for a time of family, gifts, and reflection.
>
> (Rohit 2015)

While there is a strong connection to South Asia, particularly India as described here, Rohit (2015), speaking with one member of the community about the festival, describes how Diwali builds connections in communities across the United States:

"We now live in San Francisco and get to participate in the same traditions as I did growing up in New York," Sejal Patel Daswani told NBC News. Daswani grew up in New Jersey and now lives in the San Francisco Bay Area with her family. [She adds] "Our children also participate in the grand Diwali celebrations and there are also special guidance annually with the timings, audio, and step-by-step instructions on how to do the Diwali puja [prayer]". Dawani adds that Diwali helps her stay in touch with her Indian heritage.

(Rohit 2015)

A similar emphasis on connection is addressed in Australia as well:

Wish you all a very Happy Festival of Lights, Diwali, which is celebrated in India with a lot of enthusiasm and bonhomie, is now being celebrated all around Australia by the Indian diaspora. Many cultural and traditional celebration marks the festival in all of the metro cities, of course Melbourne and Sydney with its growing Indian population takes the lead.

(Kishore & Sehrawat, 2017)

In Mauritius, for instance, "the Indian influence can be felt in religion, cuisine, arts and music" and "is sometimes also referred as Chota Bharat (mini India)" (NewsGram, 2016). Such semblance of culture is expressed through influence, and years of Hindu presence in Mauritius led to a public holiday to allow those (Hindus and non-Hindus) who actively celebrate Diwali to partake in festivities. As a group of people settle, they begin to build influence, creating a rootedness in place (Godkin, 1980). This helps reinforce links between people from different backgrounds in such a geographically small, but multi-cultural, country. Kishore and Sehrawat (2017) articulate, "celebrating Diwali in Australia has its own charm as it's now a multicultural festival here where not only Indians but people from all different communities join in the celebration with a lot of enthusiasm".

Personal links help individuals and families connect with an imagined community. Makhijani (2017) offers some personal insight, speaking with a local resident:

The rituals of Diwali gave me a strong sense of self; the traditions helped to reinforce both cultural and family values, and provided continuity and connection with my community [...] Now, as the America-born parent of a third-generation American child, I have an even deeper appreciation for the ways in which my parents continued the traditions of Diwali in the United States. This sort of cultural torch-passing is hard work, but I know how crucial these rituals were to my well-being and self-identity. I want to provide my daughter with the same security as well.

(Makhijani 2017)

This above narrative reinforces that sense of imagined community when faced with difference in a new place, as well as preserving a strong sense of identity (to both self and community). It is also that strong connection with "home" that becomes apparent when addressing the notion of imagined communities, as further detailed in the following quote linking connections between the United States and India:

> The then President of the United States, George W Bush, started Diwali celebrations in the White House in 2003. Later, Barack Obama too followed the path of his predecessor when it came to Diwali celebrations. In 2009, Obama lit a traditional lamp in the East Room of the White House on the festive occasion. A year later, his wife Michelle Obama delivered a warm speech on the night of Diwali. "This holiday is celebrated by members of some of the world's oldest religions not just here in America but across the globe. Diwali is a time for celebration. As Barack and I learned during our visit to India, it's a time to come together with friends and family, often with dancing and good food," she said.
>
> (Little India, 2017)

This section has shown how the Diwali Festival is interpreted through notions of imagined communities and links between the original and new places where culture is performed. The next section builds on the community focus, by looking at how this relates to a sense of place and a sense of community.

## Sense of place and sense of community: Life in Malaysia and Singapore

The geographical notion of sense of place has been widely discussed among geographers and has been explored in earlier chapters. Agnew (1987) describes place as location, locale and sense of place. Location refers to a geographical position, impacted by settlement, history and the surrounding environment. Locale refers to the setting or sociological space where interactions (at events) occur. Sense of place is sought and understood vis-à-vis lived experiences—where unique bonds between people and place are experienced (see Rose, 1995). This point is relevant to the understandings discussed by McMillan and Chavis (1986) on sense of community (discussed later in this section). It is important to consider both collective representations, reflective of community, and interpersonal feelings that express insightful meaning. Basso (1996, p. 57) states that "places and their meanings are continually woven into the fabric of social life." Dunham (1986) adds insight here on the notion of community, in relation to place, and processes that help make and define place. Sense of place thus complements understandings surrounding personal perceptions of being in, or one's commitment to, a group (Coulton et al., 2011; Larsen & Johnson, 2012).

A sense of place refers to a sense of belonging, socially and emotionally, through collective attachment. Bringing this insight together, Rose offers a concise statement, noting that sense of place:

> is the phrase used by many geographers when they want to emphasize that places are significant because they are the focus of personal feelings [...[ to refer to the significance of particular places for people. These feelings for "place" are not seen as trivial; geographers argue that senses of place develop from every aspect of individuals' life experience and the senses of place pervade everyday life and experience.
>
> (Rose, 1995, p. 88)

To reinforce the notion of sense of place and Diwali:

> Before the day of the festival, Hindu families throng Little India to gear up at the district's many bazaars and snap photos of the stunning street light-up. The monumental installations, Instagram-worthy decorations and bright festive lights will stand in the neighborhood for about a month after Deepavali, so there's plenty of time to celebrate with the locals [...] To enmesh yourself with the Hindu community, follow the Silver Chariot procession, held twice in the lead-up to Deepavali. Devotees tow a silver chariot that houses an effigy of the goddess Sri Drowpathai Amman all the way from the Sri Mariamman Temple in Chinatown—it's the oldest of its kind in Singapore—to Little India.
>
> (Visit Singapore, 2018)

Perhaps, adding to this understanding, it is useful to consider Tuan's (1974, p. 4) notion of topophilia, referring, for instance, to the "effective bond between people and place." We have seen in several studies from the literature that events can help create such an effective bond when common cultural events are staged and performed (see Johnson, 2007; Johnson & Figgins, 2006; Kelly, 1988; Wise, 2015a). Tuan's (1974) underlying conceptualizations have been acknowledged by many social and cultural geographers seeking to unveil human experiences to forge an understanding of spaces deemed meaningful to individuals. Therefore, places where social congregations occur allow insight into a community's sense of place (Basso, 1996; Wise & Harris, 2016). A general thought among humanist geographers, or more contemporary neohumanist geographers, is that "place" is created though personal meanings and social interactions (Adams et al., 2001; Simonsen, 2012).

Representation and meaning are also important to acknowledge because social and cultural geographers have focused on case-specific studies (Cresswell, 2004). Each study attempts to make sense of the everyday experiences of a particular group of people and meanings embedded in particular places (Larsen & Johnson, 2012). This is a point to suggest for such research on Diwali going forward, and while it is beyond the scope of this chapter to focus on a case study, a comparative analysis of community case studies focusing on a festival such as Diwali needs to be considered. Building on the work of Tuan (1974) and insights from the collection by Adams et al. (2001), nascent humanist thought is concerned with social and material constructions, adding validity to the multiplicity of contexts and representations involved to better our understanding sense of place. With this perception, evolving complexities, heterogeneity and juxtapositions of community are increasingly apparent when considering a contemporary notion of sense of place (see Larsen & Johnson, 2012; Wise, 2015c).

In acknowledging critical perspectives pertaining to alternative notions of place, such as in place/out of place, Cresswell (2004, p. 47) notes that "the 'outside' plays a crucial role in the definition of the 'inside'". In this regard, Diwali can help create, or (re)create, a sense of belonging, or togetherness, and striving to be "in place" is reinforced through relative social and cultural practices. Nonetheless, in this era of transnational movement, staging and performing identities in another place allows groups of people to create a sense of place and connect with their home, by creating spaces, performing rituals or attending events they identify with, which originate from their original or ancestral homeland. Events and festivals are central to this ideology, and participating in or celebrating them remains a vital component of people's identity when settling and residing in a new place. Decorating a home to symbolize festivities or gathering to celebrate Diwali helps people connect with place, and build a sense of community.

According to McMillan and Chavis (1986, p. 19), "a clear and empirically validated understanding of sense of community can provide the foundation for lawmakers and planners to develop programs that meet stated goals by strengthening and preserving community." McMillan and Chavis (1986) presented a definition and theory of sense of community based on four conditions: membership, influence, integration or fulfillment of needs and shared emotional connections. The first condition, membership, is essential, given that communities are often defined or recognized by geographical boundaries (Agnew, 1987; Suttles, 1972). For instance, both Kuala Lumpur, Malaysia and Singapore have specific areas of each city known as "Little India" (The Asian, 2017; Wonderful Malaysia, 2018). However, this directly contradicts some of the arguments made above, where the notion of imagined communities does not place boundaries on membership, as associations are shared around the world. Dunham (1986) framed social processes of place relevant to the attempt to be part of a wider collective group, without forgetting the very places where people forge a sense of community (see also Wise, 2015d). This is apparent in the case of Diwali, where

> the Indian Cultural Fiesta has forged a strong bond within the various ethnic Indian Communities in Singapore. This celebration has created a platform to showcase the multitude of Indian traditions, customs, heritage and practices. This rare display of unity is not found anywhere else in the world and is only unique to Singapore's heritage as

a respected multi-cultural society. This level of integration has encouraged many cultural festivities.

(Little India Singapore, 2018)

The second condition, influence, involves individual and collective contribution (or social capital). Influence can also be based on political, socio-economic or cultural bias—as these contributing variables provide the overarching structures of influence. García et al. (1999) mention that politics (especially), has a profound (and powerful) influence on communities. Integration and fulfillment of needs come into context in numerous community case studies, to position how influential factors/variables reinforce individual and group networks (see Jenkins, 2008). Furthermore, reinforcement acts as a motivator of social behavior and "it is obvious that for any group to maintain a (positive) sense of togetherness the individual-group association must be rewarding for its members" (McMillan & Chavis, 1986, p. 12). García et al. (1999) support this conceptualization because integration and fulfillment can promote and sustain a greater sense of community, so "collective needs can also be fulfilled" (García et al., 1999, p. 731). Event spaces (such as schools, churches, community halls, and pavilions) represent places of integration (where people gather to celebrate and perform Diwali rituals). To bring out this point on uniting, an article in The Asian (2017) notes that Diwali "is a day for people to come together and celebrate with open houses, fireworks, and delicious Indian delicacies". Each of these examples allows members of the community to organize and structure their needs to fulfill community goals—to create a sense of community.

Uniting the first three mentioned conditions is shared emotional connections, the final condition of sense of community outlined by McMillan and Chavis (1986). Building on Sarason's (1974) focus on interrelationships, participation and well-being, these variables are especially important to consider the making of and sense of place. García et al. (1999, p. 731) build upon previously addressed conceptualizations of shared emotional connections, noting that people often discuss their history, celebrate achievements or unite, whereas Clark and Wise (2018) argue it is participation that is a critical driver in increasing well-being and community connections. Collective emotions are supported thought contact, interactions, bonds, investments, culture or beliefs—thus shared emotional connections that reinforce belonging (Brittan, 1973). In Singapore, people have the option to

> chase the scents of floral garlands and incense while browsing through stalls hawking gold jewellery, traditional snacks, embroidered sari (traditional Indian womenswear) and ornamental decorations. Enjoy a musical performance under the stars while getting an intricate henna tattoo done. Or simply park yourself at any of the neighbourhood's many coffee shops with a mug of teh tarik (pulled milk tea) to watch one of the most beautiful festivals in Singapore blossom to life.

(Visit Singapore, 2018)

In Malaysia, Hindus "usually open their houses to guests, friends, and neighbors to feast", and while the event is celebrated in particular communities, many of the major shopping malls are "decorated with an array of colorful lights and Deepavali decorations" (Kuala Lumpur, 2018). This helps reinforce a sense of place and wider associations with the event across the country to strengthen the experience.

Poplin (1979, p. 5) states that "community has been used to refer to a condition in which human beings find themselves enmeshed in a tight-knit web of meaningful relationships with their fellow human beings." Warren (2004, p. 54) notes that "the systematic study of community has developed around the general focus of shared living based on common locality. In a sense the community is the meeting place of the individual and the larger society and culture", and their performances help connect them more holistically with performances taking place elsewhere and afar, expanding the geographical focus and spectacle each October or November. In Singapore, and Malaysia, reinforcing sense of place and community happens by detailing current opportunities to unite locals. At the time of writing, points of emphasis to create a sense of togetherness and sense of place were promoted through: Deepavali street light-up; photo-taking points; Tusker's Kingdom (baby elephant statues majestically rooted to the grounds of Little India); UTSAV Street Parade; Deepavali Festival Village; Deepavali Art Exhibition; and "let's light up Little India" (Little India Singapore, 2018). The information presented on the Little India Singapore (2018) website aims to create a sense of unity and promote activities for families to connect, celebrate and consume culture. Additional activities including learning about art at the Indian Heritage Centre, tying flowers, Rangoli (a form of art where patters are made on floors, living rooms or courtyards with colored rice, dry flour, sand or flower petals) and music (Little India Singapore, 2018). Each of these add elements in the form of festival aesthetics and the formation of unique cultural landscapes.

## Festival aesthetics and luminating landscapes: From Britain to Guyana, Oman to South Africa

Holt (2017) describes Diwali as "a bright and beautiful celebration–and one of the most important celebrations in India and its diaspora", where communities get together and light up the night landscape, creating a festival aesthetic and a spectacle. Perhaps Cosgrove (1984, p. 13) phrased it best when he suggested that the study of landscape represents "not just the world we see, it is a construction, a composition of that world—landscape is a way of seeing the world". Although the event only lasts five days, Diwali is a way of celebrating places by lighting up the night landscape with lights to create aesthetic displays of culture and performance, to help exemplify the experience. Edensor (2002) would add the notions of staging and performing culture to this, to connect the traditional and commercial displays of an event such as Diwali for those who actively practice the event, to those at the destination who can consume this imported cultural tradition.

Place images, settings and landscape features are significant areas of research in tourism and geography (e.g. Kirillova et al., 2014; Maitland & Smith, 2009; Williams & Lew, 2015), but there is also a need to consider the transformation of urban landscapes for the purpose of events and festivals as well (see Wise & Mulec, 2015). Gammon and Elkington's (2015) collection on landscapes of leisure offered nascent insight into how spaces transform and spectacles emerge. Because meanings embedded in landscapes are complex, they are shaped to define a place's identity and heritage (see Daniels et al., 2011; Wylie, 2007). Aesthetics, and the presentation of aesthetics, are vital towards forging (new) images of places; moreover, cultural and natural landscape features greatly assist how we understand aspects of aesthetic design and/or representation (Kirillova et al., 2014; Weaver, 2009). It has been acknowledged that aesthetics enhance experience (Gabrielsson & Juslin, 1996), and during Diwali the displays at night stimulate the senses by lighting the landscape, through the sounds of music and taste of food, all to symbolize culture and identity and to reinforce heritage and tradition. Senses are important, as described thus: "such a lovely sight, the Belgrave Road area of Leicester is bathed in twinkling lights every autumn for Navratri and Diwali celebrations. It's a visual spectacle not to be missed" (VisitEngland, 2018). Furthermore, the Manchester Diwali event is:

> a spectacle of drumming, lanterns, music and dance [...] It's a first for Manchester and indeed any Diwali Mela event-Spark! the amazing LED drummers from Worldbeaters led a vibrant procession of music and dance with hundreds of participants carrying lanterns around Albert Square. Illuminated figurines held by members of the Manchester Indian Association, coupled with an eclectic mix of costumed paraders created an intimate early evening spectacle.
>
> (Walk the Plank, 2016)

Knudsen et al. (2015) suggest that not only is there a need to construct an understanding of aesthetic concepts based around place and landscape, but it is important to explore how aesthetic meanings are communicated, and during Diwali it is through lights, sounds and tastes, with similar displays performed from Britain to Guyana.

Schein (1997, p. 660) mentions that landscape interpretation is a "specific exercise that requires interrogating the role of landscape in social and cultural reproduction, as well as understanding the landscape within wider social and cultural contexts," a notion that is emphasized through some of the content in the above section on sense of community. Likewise, landscapes are consumed and experienced based on what the scene is conveying to the interpreter, oftentimes based on how it engages the senses (Wylie,

2007). In this sense, the cultural phenomena associated with Diwali unite those later generations born in a new place with those who have recently migrated (with the ancestral homeland and all cultural performances in between). As for meanings produced through events and festivities, the identity being celebrated—or consumed—is a cultural texture, or a layer of the landscape, now embedded and performed to locate understandings of place, identity and community (Adams et al., 2001; Wise, 2014). According to Tuan (1976, p. 4) "the landscape is largely a product of human effort." In addition, Clouser (2009, p. 7) suggests that, "the power of a landscape can be seen in its ability to mould thoughts, evoke memories and emotions reinforce and create ideologies, and to relay to the world the values and priorities of place." Diwali as a celebration does just this.

A focus on aesthetics is largely missing from the events and festivals literature, but much context can be borrowed from tourism to build a conceptual understanding. According to Postrel (2003), the age of aesthetics has arrived—and the focus is becoming increasingly important. According to Creighton (2011) on Diwali: "spectacle is employed in the display of lighted diyas, which are at the same time symbols and a ritual of religious faith." Persaud (2018) notes that:

> Diwali, which literally means a row of lights, is celebrated on the 15th day of the Hindu month of Kartik. It is the darkest night of that month and is conducive to the twinkling lights that illuminate every nook and cranny. Worship of the goddess Maha Lakshmi is the main focus of Diwali. The aspirant performs Lakshmi puja and seeks her blessing for material and spiritual fulfillment. The festival encourages the participation of the entire family and it has long been the custom in Guyana for everyone in the home to gather in front of their Lakshmi murti at dusk chanting prayers and mantras before emerging to light their first diya.
>
> (Persaud, 2018)

In this description, the lighting of the place helps illuminate the landscape, which in turn creates a unique event aesthetic. Persaud (2018) adds, "thousands of Guyanese of every stratum of society and cultural belief throng the roads to witness the processions of beautifully decorated and illuminated vehicles depicting the theme of Diwali", which reinforces the event as a spectacle.

Kirillova et al. (2014) focus on aesthetic attributes as elements of beauty, specifically how aesthetics are embodied to create perceived images. (Schofield, 2014) describe how Diwali is "observed by Hindus, Sikhs, Jains and Buddhists all over the world, celebrations are known for being vibrant and colorful, often featuring elaborate firework displays and the lighting of candles and lamps". To Ely (2003), terrain, and what covers the terrain, constitutes the aesthetics of a place, now more often than not a product of modern times. Scenery itself is reminiscent, and for tourists or outside onlookers, stimulations, captured visually or imagined through transcribed narratives, are associations of picturesque beauty. Such beauty, found in narratives of natural or cultural landscapes, defines romanticized images of places or aesthetic pleasures and experiences, which are now embedded in places like Oman with a large population of South Asians. Wang et al. (2008) focus on aesthetic values, or feelings, people have about certain landscapes, and the creation of symbolic landscapes in South Africa during Diwali contribute to the value of rituals and culture—linking imagined experiences through displays of light. Aesthetic notions become omnipresent, seen in promotional materials to enhance the event spectacle (Maitland & Smith, 2009; Weaver, 2009). When we consider the landscape and aesthetic displays, the lighting of the night sky is symbolic of the event, taking on the same meaning and creating a visual spectacle in each place, from Britain to Guyana, Oman to South Africa, as well as across South Asia and into Singapore and Malaysia, or Australia, Mauritius and the United States.

### Discussion: Linking conceptualizations

While Diwali is celebrated around the world, the narrative in each of the articles above address similarities across the different regions. The conceptual diagram presented in Figure 16.1 shows the connections across the points addressed in this chapter. A key consideration here is the practical overlaps. When we consider sense of place and the community, landscapes in this case are created and (re)created, and these are the spaces where interactions occur. The point of using different examples supported by online/media excerpts was to show how Diwali is truly a global event. This helps offer insight into imagined communities, sense of place and the staging of events to illuminate the cultural landscape for the duration of the festival. Thus, each of the abstract areas discussed above are dependent upon interactions, and this is where the notions of staging and performing identities are golden threads linking the geographical and sociological conceptualizations.

In Figure 16.1, the new place in the conceptual diagram could be any of the countries discussed above. If we consider the United Kingdom as a new place, and the other new places being Singapore, Oman, Guyana and Australia, there are links that connect people in these places, to show how events and festivals help reinforce imagined communities. The event is developed in the place of origin, where it is traditionally staged and performed. When diaspora occurs, people move along with their culture and ideas to the new place and (re)created. As outlined in this chapter, there are both geographical and sociological considerations at play. The staging, in a new location, leads to the culture or ritual being performed. Both staging and performing the festival help create and support a sense of place. Performing helps reinforce a sense of community, and a newly found sense of place links to a greater sense of community (Wise, 2015c). The performing of the event or festival results in the event or festival aesthetic, and a sense of

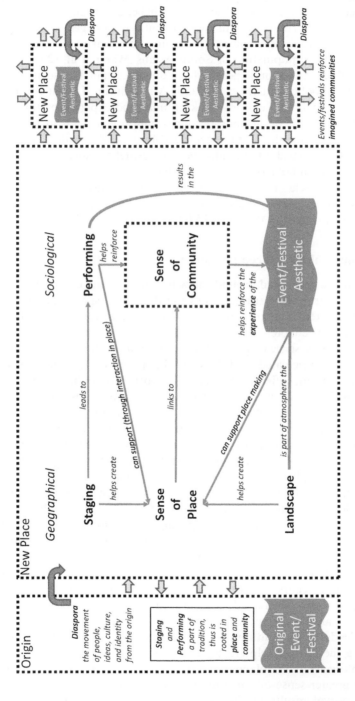

*Figure 16.1* Conceptual connections to reinforce imagined communities and diaspora between places staging and performing, sense of place and sense of community, and the landscape and event/festival aesthetic.

community helps reinforce this because it can enhance the experiences for those participating. The landscape is part of the atmosphere that also helps create the aesthetic, and both of these, based on their geographical presence, help support place making, which in turn helps reinforce a sense of place, because the event or festival is being staged in an actual new place.

## Concluding remarks

Agnew and Duncan (1989) debated locality, or locale, in their collection to integrate sociological and geographical imaginations of place and society. Poplin's (1979, p. 10) approach made this apparent. People interact and therefore have to "adjust and adapt to their territorial milieu." Other geographers have noted that, as individuals and members of a society, we conform to and shape our understanding of space and place by establishing ourselves, along with finding comfort and familiarity in our physical and perceived surroundings (see Sack, 1997; Tuan, 1974). Relationships among people are often rooted in a place and forged through common practices, values, exercises or actions, each an attempt to establish a mutual sense of belonging (Suttles, 1972). Territorial bases and/or locations refer to the geographical implications that serve as the physical setting (Poplin, 1979). To address the international linking of the festival, Rohit (2015) suggested in an interview that:

> Medha Jaishankar, the daughter of an Indian diplomat, told NBC News she grew up experiencing Diwali around the world. She was born in Delhi, but has celebrated Diwali in East Asia, Eastern Europe, the United States, as well as in India. Jaishankar now works as a film executive in Hollywood, but the Indian holiday stays with her and is a welcomed celebration.
>
> (Rohit, 2015)

Whilst (geographically) relevant, boundaries are used to define or signify membership (McMillan & Chavis, 1986); focusing on a place encourages us to spatially identify points among the (often) exclusive boundaries, defining membership and where social cohesion is deemed most significant. However, imagined communities transcend this. Behavioral geographers will argue that people identify with certain points through cognitive references (Barkowsky, 2002; Downs & Stea, 2005; Larsen & Johnson, 2012; Sack, 1997; Wise, 2014), linked to social spaces and the performances they are involved with to connect them with others—especially in the very space(s) where an event takes place and by those celebrating elsewhere. When needs are fulfilled and shared emotional connections are spatially referenced, and when identity and culture is staged and performed, this signifies why both geographical and sociological approaches help lead to multidisciplinary understanding of place and community. This chapter relates to similar understandings addressed in previous chapters, where an event is founded in one place, then staged and performed elsewhere—in this case around the world. As people with a shared sense of identity migrate around the world, festivals such as Diwali hold deep religious and spiritual connotations for Hindu, Sikhs and Jains.

This conceptual chapter shows how Diwali is a truly global event that is celebrated in numerous places to unite people under a shared festival tradition. In future research it may be worth further exploring on a more case-by-case basis or comparative analysis the role and interactions of different places and the festival tradition. Moreover, each conceptual point can be further explored and elaborated on through fieldwork at Diwali events around the world. Each area outlined in this chapter offers a relevant framework to consider when researching cultural events in general, especially events celebrated by diasporic communities in multiple locations around the world.

# References

Adams, P.C., Hoelscher, S. & Till, K. (Eds) (2001). *Textures of place: Exploring humanist geographies.* Minneapolis, MN: University of Minnesota Press.

Agnew, J.A. (1987). *Place and politics.* Boston, MA: Allen and Unwin.

Agnew, J.A. & Duncan, J.S. (Eds) (1989). *The power of place: Bringing together geographical and sociological imaginations.* Boston, MA: Unwin Hyman.

Anderson, B. (1991). *Imagined communities.* London: Verso.

The Asian (2017). Malaysians celebrate Deepavali. *The Asian,* 18 October, available at: www.asianage.com/photo/life/181017/malaysians-celebrate-deepavali.html.

Barkowsky, T. (2002). *Mental representation and processing of geographic knowledge.* Berlin: Springer.

Basso, K.H. (1996). Wisdom sits in places: Notes on a western Apache landscape. In S. Feld & K.H. Basso (Eds). *Senses of place.* Santa Fe, NM: School of American Research Press (53–90).

Booth, A. (2012). Sustain ability and community networks: The case of the Indian diaspora. In T. Pernecky & M. Lück (Eds). *Events, society and sustainability: Critical and contemporary approaches.* London: Routledge (115–129).

Booth, A. (2015). Whose Diwali is it? Diaspora, identity, and festivalization. *Tourism Culture & Communication,* 3, 215–226.

Booth, A. (2016). Negotiating diasporic culture: Festival collaborations and production networks. *International Journal of Event and Festival Management,* 7(2), 100–116.

Brittan, A. (1973). *Meanings and situations.* London: Routledge & Kegan Paul.

Carter, T.F. (2007). Family networks, state interventions and the experience of Cuban transnational sport migration. *International Review for the Sociology of Sport,* 42(4), 371–389.

Clark, J. & Wise, N. (Eds) (2018). *Urban renewal, community and participation – Theory, policy and practice.* Berlin: Springer.

Clouser, R. (2009). Remnants of terror: Landscapes of fear in post-conflict Guatemala. *Journal of Latin American Geography,* 8(2), 7–22.

Cohen, R. (2008). *Global diasporas: An introduction.* London: Routledge.

Cosgrove, D. (1984). Prospect, perspective and the evolution of the landscape idea. *Transactions of the Institute of British Geographers NS,* 10, 45–62.

Coulton, C., Chan, T. & Mikelbank, K. (2011). Finding place in community change initiatives: Using GIS to uncover resident perceptions of their neighborhoods. *Journal of Community Practice,* 19, 10–28.

Creighton, A. (2011). Ramlila and Diwali: Ritual, spectacle and cultural impact. *Starbroek News,* 23 October, available at: www.stabroeknews.com/2011/sunday/arts-on-sunday/10/23/ramlila-and-diwali-ritual-spectacle-and-cultural-impact/.

Cresswell, T. (2004). *Place: A short introduction.* Oxford: Blackwell.

Daniels, S., DeLyser, D., Entrikin, N. & Richardson, D. (Eds) (2011). *Envisioning landscapes, making worlds.* London: Routledge.

Downs, R. & Stea, D. (Eds) (2005). *Image & environment: Cognitive mapping and spatial behaviour.* London: AldineTransaction.

Dunham, H.W. (1986). The community today: Place or process. *Journal of Community Psychology,* 14(4), 399–404.

Edensor, T. (2002). *National identity, popular culture and everyday life.* Oxford: Berg.

Ely, C. (2003). The origins of Russian scenery: Volga River tourism and Russian landscape aesthetics. *Slavic Review,* 62(4), 666–682.

Gabrielsson, A. & Juslin, P.N. (1996). Emotional expression in music performance: Between performers intention and the listener's experience. *Psychology of Music,* 24, 68–91.

Gammon, S. & Elkington, S. (Eds) (2015). *Landscapes of leisure: Space, place and identities.* Basingstoke: Palgrave Macmillan.

García, I., Guiliani, F. & Wiesenfeld, E. (1999). Community and sense of community: The case of an urban barrio in Caracas. *Journal of Community Psychology,* 27(6), 727–740.

Godkin, M.A. (1980). Identity and place: Clinical applications based on notions of rootedness and uprootedness. In A. Buttimer & D. Seamon (Eds). *The human experience of space and place.* New York, NY: St Martin's Press (73–85).

Gruffudd, P. (1999). Nationalism. In P. Cloke, P. Crang & M. Goodwin (Eds). *Introducing human geographies.* London: Arnold (199–206).

Harris, J. (2008). Match day in Cardiff: (Re)imaging and (re)imagining the nation. *Journal of Sport & Tourism,* 13(4), 297–313.

Holt, M. (2017). Best Diwali events 2017 - Where to celebrate in Britain from fireworks displays to Henna tattoo workshops. *Mirror,* 20 October, available at: www.mirror.co.uk/news/diwali-best-uk-events-fireworks-9143718.

Independent (2017). Diwali 2017: Festival of light celebrations around the world. *Independent,* 19 October, available at: www.independent.co.uk/news/world/diwali-2017-festival-light-world-pictures-hindu-celebrations-india-sri-lanka-a8008481.html.

Jenkins, R. (2008). *Social identity.* London: Routledge.

Johnson, H. (2007). 'Happy Diwali!' performance, multicultural soundscapes and intervention in Aotearoa/New Zealand. *Ethnomusicology Forum,* 16(1), 71–94.

Johnson, H. & Figgins, G. (2006). Diwali downunder: Transforming and performing Indian tradition in Aotearoa/New Zealand. *MEDIANZ,* 9(1), 1–18.

Kelly, J.D. (1988). From Holi to Diwali in Fiji: An essay on ritual and history. *Man,* 23(1), 40–55.

Kirillova, K., Fu, X., Lehto, X. & Cai, L. (2014). What makes a destination beautiful? Dimensions of tourist aesthetic judgement. *Tourism Management,* 42, 282–293.

Kishore, V. & K. Sehrawat (2017). Indians celebrate Diwali with fervour in Australia. *SBS Hindi*, 25 October, available at: www.sbs.com.au/yourlanguage/hindi/en/article/2017/10/18/indians-celebrate-diwali-fervour-australia.

Knudsen, D.C., Metro-Roland, M.M. & Rickly, J.M. (2015). Tourism, aesthetics, and touristic judgment. *Tourism Review International*, 19(4), 179–192.

Kuala Lumpur (2018). Deepavali in Malaysia 2018: Malaysia Events & Festivals. *Asia Web Direct*, available at: www.kuala-lumpur.ws/magazine/deepavali-in-malaysia.htm.

Langellier, K.M. (2010). Performing Somali identity in the diaspora. *Cultural Studies*, 24(1), 66–94.

Larsen, S. & Johnson, J.T. (2012). Toward an open sense of place: Phenomenology, affinity, and the question of being. *Annals of the Association of American Geographers*, 102(3), 623–646.

Little India (2017). Indians seek Diwali holiday in US schools. *Little India*, 18 September, available at: https://littleindia.com/indians-seek-diwali-holiday-us-schools/.

Little India Singapore (2018). Experience the 5 senses with us: Latest happenings in *Little India Singapore*, available at: www.littleindia.com.sg/.

MacMillan, D.M. (2008). *Diwali: Hindu festival of lights*. Berkeley Heights, NJ: Enslow Publishers.

Maitland, R. & Smith, A. (2009). Tourism and the aesthetics of the built environment. In J. Tribe (Ed). *Philosophical issues in tourism*. Bristol, UK: Channel View Publications (171–190).

Makhijani, P. (2017). Making Diwali our own, and passing it on. *Washington Post*, 19 October, available at: www.washingtonpost.com/news/parenting/wp/2017/10/19/making-diwali-our-own-and-passing-it-on/?noredirect=on&utm_term=.bf59502b2874.

McMillan, D.W. & Chavis, D.M. (1986). Sense of community: A definition and theory. *Journal of Community Psychology*, 14(1), 6–23.

NewsGram (2016). Indian diaspora in Mauritius. *NewsGram*, 26 April, available at: www.newsgram.com/indian-diaspora-in-mauritius/.

Persaud, V.V. (2018). Diwali the festival of lights. *Explore Guyana*, available at: http://exploreguyana.org/event/diwali-festival-of-lights/.

Poplin, D.E. (1979). *Communities*. New York: MacMillan Publishing.

Postrel, V. (2003). *The substance of style: How the rise of aesthetic value is remaking commerce, culture and consciousness*. New York: Perennial.

Rohit, P.M. (2015). Diwali, the 'festival of lights,' connects Indians around the world. *NBC News*, 11 November, available at: www.nbcnews.com/news/asian-america/festival-lights-connects-indians-around-world-diwali-celebrated-n460661.

Rose, G. (1995). Place and identity: A sense of place. In D. Massey & P. Jess (Eds). *A place in the world*. Oxford: Oxford University Press (87–132).

Sack, R. (1997). *Homo geographicus*. Baltimore, MD: The Johns Hopkins University Press.

Sarason, S.B. (1974). *The psychological sense of community: Prospects for a community psychology*. San Francisco, CA: Jossey-Bass.

Sarwal, A. (2016). Diwali celebrations in Australia – From assimilationist to multicultural. *SBS Hindi*, 26 October, available at: www.sbs.com.au/yourlanguage/hindi/en/audiotrack/diwali-celebrations-australia-assimilationist-multicultural.

Schein, R. (1997). The place of landscape: A conceptual framework for interpreting the American scene. *Annals of the Association of American Geographers*, 87(4), 660–680.

Schofield, C. (2014). 8 spectacular ways to celebrate Diwali across the UK. *Wow24/7*, 21 October, available at: www.wow247.co.uk/2014/10/21/8-spectacular-ways-to-celebrate-diwali-across-the-uk/.

Shobe, H. (2008). Place, identity and football: Catalonia, Catalanisme and Football Club Barcelona, 1899–1975. *National Identities*, 10(3), 329–343.

Simonsen, K. (2012). In quest of a new humanism: Embodiment, experience and phenomenology as critical geography. *Progress in Human Geography*, 37(1), 10–26.

Smith, A. (1991). *National identity*. London: Penguin.

Suttles, G.D. (1972). *The social construction of communities*. Chicago, IL: The University of Chicago Press.

Tuan, Y-F. (1974). *Topophilia*. Englewood Cliffs, NJ: Prentice Hall.

Tuan, Y-F. (1976). Humanistic geography. *Annals of the Association of American Geographers*, 66(2), 266–276.

VisitEngland (2018). Experience Leicester's festival of light: Leicester, Leicestershire, available at: www.visitengland.com/experience/experience-leicesters-festival-light.

Visit Singapore (2018). Home: Festivals & events: Deepavali, available at: www.visitsingapore.com/festivals-events-singapore/cultural-festivals/deepavali/.

Walk the Plank (2016). A feelgood celebration that brings everyone together. *Arts Council England*, available at: http://walktheplank.co.uk/project/manchester-diwali/.

Wang, Y., Xia, Z. & Chen, W. (2008). Aesthetic values in sustainable tourism development: A case study in Zhangjiajie National Park of Wuling Yuan, China. *Journal of China Tourism Research*, 4(2), 205–218.

Warren, R.L. (2004). Older and newer approaches to the community. In W.A. Martin (Ed). *The urban community*. Upper Saddle River, NJ: Pearson Prentice Hall (54–71).

Weaver, A. (2009). Tourism and aesthetic design: Enchantment, style and commerce. *Journal of Tourism and Cultural Change*, 7(3), 179–189.

Williams, S. & Lew, A.A. (2015). *Tourism geography: Critical understandings of place, space and experience*. London: Routledge.

Wise, N. (2011). Transcending imaginations through football participation and narratives of the other: Haitian national identity in the Dominican Republic. *Journal of Sport & Tourism*, 16(3), 259–275.

Wise, N. (2014). Layers of the landscape: Representation and perceptions of an ordinary (shared) sport landscape in a Haitian and Dominican community. *Geographical Research*, 52(2), 212–222.

Wise, N. (2015a). Football on the weekend: Rural events and the Haitian imagined community in the Dominican Republic. In A. Jepson & A. Clarke (Eds). *Exploring community festivals and events*. London: Routledge (106–117).

Wise, N. (2015b). Maintaining Dominican identity in the Dominican Republic: Forging a baseball landscape in Villa Ascension. *International Review for the Sociology of Sport*, 50(2), 161–178.

Wise, N. (2015c). Placing Sense of Community. *Journal of Community Psychology*, 43(7), 920–929.

Wise, N. (2015d). Spatial experiences: Using Google Earth to locate meanings pertinent to sense of place. *Cityscape*, 17(1), 141–150.

Wise, N. & Harris, J. (2016). Community, identity and contested notions of place: A study of Haitian recreational soccer players in the Dominican Republic. *Soccer & Society*, 17(4), 610–627.

Wise, N. & Mulec, I. (2015). Aesthetic awareness and spectacle: Communicated images of Novi sad, the exit festival and the event venue Petrovaradin Fortress. *Tourism Review International*, 19(4), 193–205.

Wonderful Malaysia (2018). Frequently asked questions: Festivals: Deepavali. *Wonderful Malaysia*, available at: www.wonderfulmalaysia.com/faq/deepavali.htm.

Wylie, J. (2007). *Landscape*. London: Routledge.

# Conclusion

## Expanding (inter)disciplinary perspectives in research on events

*John Harris & Nicholas Wise*

The chapters presented in this collection all highlight the links between events, places and societies. We did not wish to impose a particular theoretical framework or specific approach to this and wanted to allow contributors to identify the issues that they believed were most important to the particular events being looked at. This interpretive and inductive approach has framed both our individual and collaborative research over the years (see for example, Harris, 2006; Harris & Wise, 2011; Wise, 2014; Wise & Harris, 2017). In bringing together contributors from a number of different disciplinary backgrounds to look critically at events 'in the round', and to explore the different ways that people make sense of place, we hoped to introduce some diverse perspectives into the analysis of events.

The focus on place as outlined in the introduction and considered further in Velvet Nelson's chapter evidences the research expertise of some contributors from a geography background. Others draw upon their training in sociology and associated fields to provide the foundation for the study of other events. Despite increasing internal demands and external pressures, both influenced and accelerated by the pace of globalization, it is clear that place matters. Predictions of the decline of the nation-state and the erosion of national identities have proven unfounded as clearly shown (for example) in the continued importance of major international sporting events. In this collection we have brought together studies on a whole host of different events of varying shapes and sizes. Some of the cases clearly highlight the strong sense of identity attached to meanings of a particular place and the ways in which local, regional and national identities are central to the development and sustainability of events.

A number of events have been looked at through a variety of different lenses in this collection. Collectively, these offer illuminating insights into the different ways in which individual and groups engage with events. Some find a strong sense of community through participating or through volunteering. Others clearly believe that events can helps to develop business opportunities through increased tourism development and other avenues. For some people, events provide a way of escaping from the pressures of everyday life. Events mean different things to different people.

The boundaries that signify the borders between places and the boundaries that exist between academic disciplines are important to recognize here. Raymond Williams spent his life working on the borders of different academic disciplines. He grew up in a small Welsh village close to the border of England and wrote eloquently about the similarities and differences between places (see Williams, 1960, 1973). Williams was of the view that borders were meant to be crossed, despite social, cultural, political and economic differences. Ward (1991) noted how borders and boundaries are also necessarily political and that whilst much may be shared there may also be different languages spoken. However, the disciplinary boundaries within academia are not always easy to cross. Research on events has developed in various spheres and there is now a sizeable body of literature on the subject. The direction of research in events not only depends on disciplinary foundations and widely accepted theories, but transcending perspectives across the social sciences, business and management.

The impacts that events can have on people and places is evidenced throughout the various chapters. We see examples of community development highlighted in the chapter by Lucia Aquilino and John Harris on the World Alternative Games, and also observe the ways in which community is created in Lindsey Gaston's contribution on the Folsom Street Fair. Vanja Pavlukovic, Tanja Armenski and Juan Miguel Alcántara-Pilar showed how the EXIT festival laid bare some of the concerns of local residents and the importance of consultation in developing future events.

There are of course always tensions around place, as many of our contributors have shown. Brij Maharaj provided an insightful account of how an event that didn't happen also has very important implications for place. Natalie Koch reflected on the politics of place and the tensions inherent in the privileging of place in Doha, whilst Trine Kvidal-Rovik and Kari Jaeger showed how cultural tensions exist in Alaska. The politics of place was further explored in Brenda L. Ortiz-Loyola and José R. Díaz-Garayúa's chapter on place-making through public art in Puerto Rico and in Maurício Polidoro's work on Carnival in Brazil.

The ways in which events can be used to promote place is also evident, as outlined by Xiaolin Zang, Bouke van Gorp and Hans Renes who looked at the Qingdao International Beer Festival. Events are increasingly recognized as an important part of marketing campaigns relating to destination development and place branding. Alexandra Gillespie and C. Michael Hall showed how food can be used as a powerful expression of place. Dorota Ostrowska's chapter on the Cannes International Film Festival powerfully conveyed how significant an event can be in developing the image of a city. Nicholas Wise, Jelena Đurkin and Marko Perić showed the importance of event-led regeneration in Rijeka towards 2020. All of these chapters critically assessed the place-making strategies of a range of different stakeholders.

Events can also provide a sense of attachment. As Nicholas Wise showed in his overview of Diwali, and James Bowness explored in sharing the experiences of Masters athletes at the Highland Games, there can also be a strong link to diasporic identities through events. At a time when the news channels in the UK are dominated by debates around Brexit it is interesting to reflect on the place of the Ryder Cup. Don Colley and John Harris show how this is one of the only places where a collective European sports identity is visible, but also remind us that Team Europe was created out of pragmatism and was not borne out of any particular attachment to the idea of a European identity.

The study of events has developed exponentially in recent years. Scholars from a range of disciplinary backgrounds have made valuable contributions to the development of this field. Future research may explore interdisciplinary studies into different events and further ethnographic research may begin to unpack the importance of events at the local level. This collection clearly highlights the importance of case studies to explore a variety of different events in some detail. No two events are the same and different events also change and develop over time. As our contributors have shown, there are often struggles over place and events may be contested arenas for the representation and/or reclamation of place. Drakeman (2016) has highlighted how getting a variety of academic disciplines to become more engaged with each other can lead to potentially better policy analysis and work towards better solutions. This highlights the ways in which interdisciplinary work on events can help pave the way for research that has the potential to make a difference.

# References

Drakeman, D. (2016). *Why we need the humanities: Life science, law and the common good*. Basingstoke: Palgrave Macmillan.

Harris, J. (2006). The science of research in sport and tourism: Some reflections on the promise of the sociological imagination. *Journal of Sport & Tourism*, 11(2), 153–172.

Harris, J. & Wise, N. (2011). Geographies of scale in international rugby union. *Geographical Research*, 49(4), 475–483.

Ward, J.P. (1991). Preface. In T. Pinkney (Ed.). *Raymond Williams*. Bridgend: Seren (vii–x).

Williams, R. (1960). *Border country*. London: Chatto & Windus.

Williams, R. (1973). *The country and the city*. London: Chatto & Windus.

Wise, N. (2014). Layers of the landscape: Representation and perceptions of an ordinary (shared) sport landscape in a Haitian and Dominican community. *Geographical Research*, 52(2), 212–222.

Wise, N. & Harris, J. (Eds.) (2017). *Sport, events, tourism and regeneration*. London: Routledge.

# Index